Mohammad R. Salama is Assis
State University and specializes i
and postcolonial thought, intellec
is the co-editor of *German Colon*
Germany (2011).

ISLAM, ORIENTALISM AND INTELLECTUAL HISTORY

MODERNITY AND THE POLITICS OF EXCLUSION SINCE IBN KHALDŪN

MOHAMMAD R. SALAMA

I.B. TAURIS
LONDON · NEW YORK

New paperback edition published in 2013 by I.B.Tauris & Co Ltd
6 Salem Road, London W2 4BU
175 Fifth Avenue, New York NY 10010
www.ibtauris.com

Distributed in the United States and Canada Exclusively by Palgrave Macmillan
175 Fifth Avenue, New York NY 10010

First published in hardback in 2011 by I.B.Tauris & Co Ltd

ISBN: 978 1 78076 450 4

A full CIP record for this book is available from the British Library
A full CIP record is available from the Library of Congress

Library of Congress Catalog Card Number: available

Typeset by Swales & Willis Ltd, Exeter, Devon

Printed and bound by CPI Group (UK) Ltd, Croydon, CR0 4YY
from camera-ready copy edited and supplied by the author

For my parents,
Aziza and Ramadan,
and for my children,
Salma, Malachi, and Aliya

CONTENTS

ILLUSTRATIONS

Maps

Figures

NOTE ON TRANSLATION AND TRANSLITERATION

Unless otherwise noted in the text or endnotes, all translations from Arabic and French are my own. For the purposes of clarity, I use the standard Western spelling of terms that have entered the English language like 'Arab,' 'Islam,' and country names. I use the standard Library of Congress transliteration system for all other Arabic terms.

ACKNOWLEDGMENTS

I wish to express my gratitude to San Francisco State University for granting me a Presidential Award to work uninterruptedly on this study, and to Dr. Paul Sherwin, Dean of the College of Humanities at San Francisco State University, for his generous support. My colleague and friend Edwin Williams has read most of this work and provided me with excellent feedback. My gratitude also extends to my graduate students at SFSU who joined in the discussion of the issues raised in this book during seminars on Islam and modern Arabic literature and culture. Several friends and colleagues have read this manuscript at various stages, either in whole or in part: Muḥammad Azadpur, Shirin Khanmohamadi, and Jillian Sandell of San Francisco State University; Luis Madureira, Dustin Cowell, and Marjorie Rhine of the University of Wisconsin; Gerhard Richter of UC Davis; Jacques Lezra of NYU; Muhsin al-Musawi of Columbia University; Jan Plug of the University of Western Ontario; Steven Salaita of Virginia Tech University; Ghada Osman of San Diego State University. Their criticisms were stimulating and important in helping me formulate my ideas. The defects are of course mine.

Much of the writing of this book was done between San Francisco, Madison-Wisconsin, and Peterborough, Ontario. Colleagues, librarians, and friends of these three cities added much to the enrichment of this work. I am especially grateful to Nezar AlSayyad, Emily Gottreich, Mejgan Massoumi, and the CMES staff and faculty of the University of California, Berkeley, for hosting a presentation on this book. I am equally thankful to the English Department at Trent University for inviting me to give a talk on the topic.

In Egypt, my gratitude goes first to ustāth Fū'ād Ghoneim, my Alexandrian High School teacher of English, who showed me the beauty of the

English language, boosted my very humble beginnings and told me that he could see me at the end of the road. To Salwa Bahgat, of ʻAyn Shams University, who opened her home for many intellectual discussions and whose untold kindness and unceasing support solidified my steps along the way. To Shebl al-Komy, a remarkable Egyptian scholar. To ʻAbd al-Rahmān ʻAbd al-Salām, Wagīh Yaʻqūb, Manāl Ghoneim and ʻĀṭif Bahgāt, outstanding professors of Arabic at ʻAyn Shams University whose friendship and support and the many books they generously sent me from Egypt have been of fundamental value for my research. At various archives and libraries there are a number of helpful people. My special thanks go to the library staff of al-Hay'a al-Miṣriyya al-ʻĀmma lil-Kitāb who helped me during my research in Cairo to find documents I would have never found without their support. I am deeply thankful to the circulation desk staff of the Memorial Library at UW-Madison, especially Mary Weber, Ron Larson, and Jimmy Johnson (J.J.), with whom I worked for five years, and who were as kind to me as my own family. My thanks also go to all my students in Al-Alsun of ʻAyn Shams University, UW-Madison, Beloit College, UW-Whitewater, and San Francisco State University.

My sincere gratitude goes to Hāla Ghoneim who gave me the idea for "Denshawai" and pushed me for it. The daunting task of formatting and copy-editing a convoluted and diacritical manuscript was performed heroically by Rachel Friedman, now a graduate student at UC Berkeley. Her diligence and intelligence made the preparation of the manuscript a teachable process. Likewise, I am grateful to Dustin Cowell for his patient and thorough proofreading. My sincerest thanks are owed to the editors of I.B.Tauris, especially Rasna Dhillon, for her helpful encouragement and instructive directions. I am indebted to Matthew Brown for his work in preparing, typesetting, proofreading and indexing the text.

Finally, this book would have been impossible without the patience, support, and love I received from Kelly McGuire, who followed its composition with all its ebbs and flows. My greatest debt by far is to her.

PROLOGUE

Thinking about Islam and the West

As a literary scholar, I never thought I would venture to write a book on Islam. While Islam was the lived experience of three decades I spent in Egypt and is surely a penetrative force and an inevitable discourse in all the Arabic texts I read and analyze, authoring a work exclusively dedicated to the relationship between Islam, the West, and intellectual history was, at one time, far from imaginable. I began writing this book early in the summer of 2006, after I flew from San Francisco to Canada in order to obtain my new work visa. Immediately upon my arrival at the US Consulate in Toronto, I was singled out from a group of seven similarly circumstanced Europeans applying for the same type of work visa. I was profiled by the visa officer, who, acting on specific orders from the US Department of State, fingerprinted me, put a "cancelled without prejudice" stamp on all my previous US visas since 1993, and took my Egyptian passport. He told me that I could not re-enter the USA until I heard from his office, and that I "should find a place to stay because it is going to be a long wait." I was soon to learn that mine was not an isolated case and that there are thousands of male Muslims with Middle Eastern names going through the same ordeal at various US embassies and consulates. Confused, stranded, indignant, and in limbo for three months until the US State Department decided that I was not a threat to its national security, I began working on this present study.

While in Canada, the two writers that I often read and reread were Theodor Adorno and Walter Benjamin. Perhaps it was because they were both exiled that I felt a strong and renewed affinity for their work. Adorno's *Minima Moralia* restored my faith in the emancipatory power of hope after failure and gave me the strength to cope with the negative effects on my own life affected by the so-called "war on terror." His definition of exile as the sharing of the suffering of humanity and a renunciation of the "administered" world of commodities and consumer culture humbled my short-lived ordeal. "It is even part of my good fortune not to be a house-owner," writes Adorno, echoing Nietzsche's words in *The Gay Science*, "[T]oday we should have to add: it is part of morality not to be at home in one's home."[1] Benjamin's theses on the concept of history were a different source of intellectual forbearance, allowing me to situate myself in a larger context and to observe history with Benjamin's eyes. Benjamin's thesis reassured me that the struggle for justice and humanism is far from over, that "when the fields are still, and the tired men and dogs all gone to rest," we too must "cross and recross the strips of moon-blanch'd green," and like Matthew Arnold's stubborn Scholar Gypsy, must "come, and again renew the quest."[2]

Reflecting on Klee's famous painting "Angelus Novus," Benjamin speaks about "the angel of history" who seems ready "to move away from something he is fixedly contemplating. His eyes are staring, his mouth is open, his wings are spread. This is how one pictures the angel of history. His face is turned toward the past. Where we perceive a chain of events, he sees one single catastrophe which keeps piling wreckage upon wreckage and hurls it in front of his feet."[3] This conflicted angel, whose gaze is endlessly captured like the Laocoön's silent cry,[4] looks back for a lost harmony among nations and epochs past, while more destruction and disharmony is yet to come as the angel of history steps forward towards an unforeseeable future. This magnificent image of the angel of history readily sums up the main idea of this book, in which I seek to reconstruct the recent prehistory of Islam and 'the West' with the intention of analyzing the connections between knowledge and politics.

The chapters in this book examine modern encounters between Islam and the West from the point of view of intellectual history, which broadly touches upon the Enlightenment, European modernity, colonialism, and the postcolonial. I strongly believe that the task of radical historiography in both Islam and the West begins with reading history as a history of "responsibility." This responsibility means that we must resist the reading of history as an act of confirmation or totalization and must always leave room for doubt.

As a critic and cultural theorist, I am not particularly eager to take sides in overdetermined battles of "civilizationisms" or engage in futile clashes of ignorance. Instead, this book poses a set of fundamental questions. To what and to whom does the term 'Islam' refer, and what does this reference imply today? How can 'the West' speak meaningfully about Islam when there are many references on the subject and no absolute concept that channels our knowledge, and how do Muslims in turn understand 'the West'? If there is no absolute code of knowledge or criterion for validity, then certainly struggles or disputes over Islam's religiosity and meaning will continue to emerge. In other words, Islam has fallen into a textual trap, one that often derives its material from world events, but which is mostly rhetorical in its reproduction of such material. If Islam is the world's third Abrahamic religion to appear, why has its appearance and geographical spread over the last one and a half millennia posed a threat to existing religions or beliefs in the West? Has Islam ever really coexisted with Judaism and/or Christianity, and if so, to what extent? Who were Muslims and who are they now? Is there only one Islam or are there indeed multiple Islams? If so, what are the core differences between those varieties of Islam and between Islam and other religions? What are the relationships between Islam and violence, Islam and women, or Islam and freedom? What does this tell us about the differences between Islam and religious beliefs in the West?

Addressing each of these questions from all aspects would certainly require a book-length reply, and most of them have been asked before, but to ask them now – after Islam has been just recently re-subjected to the negative implications of media coverage during the recent US presidential campaigns – is to open an old wound that was closed but never healed. It is unfortunate that then-presidential candidate Barak Obama had to spend millions of dollars on brochures distributed across the USA just to let Americans know that he is not Muslim, while his opponent, Republican John McCain, took every chance to emphasize the Judeo-Christian values of his campaign where there was no tolerance for "fundamentalism" or "radicalism," the two famous descriptors for Islam today.

Announcing in an economically challenged post-Bush America that "the United States is not and will never be at war with Islam," as President Obama said on his first visit to Turkey, is a step of good faith and a sign of hope, as are all Nobel Prize-worthy visits to the Middle East to promote peace through public diplomacy. The fact that Obama felt the need to make this declaration confirms the grim reality that in America today, a ruthless war on Islam has been taking place and that there is no guarantee that this war would stop or would not flare up again at the slightest provocation.

And flare up it did, except this time it erupted on a small scale and against no one but the president himself. In the late summer of 2009 the GOP Tea Party proponents roamed the streets of Washington D.C. to show their disapproval of President Obama's health coverage reform plan, while in the process revealing the naked face of flagrant anti-Islamic racism. In post-September 11 America, it has somehow become unremarkable to "accuse," falsely of course, the first African American President of being "an Indonesian *Muslim* turned welfare thug,"[5] while it is understandably horrendous to utter racist or anti-Semitic remarks about anyone.

More recently, Islam re-surfaced in the political arena when Senator Lindsey Graham of South Carolina, speaking before *The Atlantic*'s First Draft of History Conference on October 2, 2009, said that the right-wing "birthers" who think that President Obama was not born in Hawaii or was a "closet Muslim" are simply "crazy." Coming from a Republican senator reprimanding members of his own base, this would be a promising critique, except that Graham went on to explain to those who question President Obama's religious background and loyalty to the country that "the President is not a Muslim, he is a good man."

How did things get to this point? Although I don't think that "Muslim" was ever automatically seen as "good" in the USA, when did the two become mutually exclusive? These images and statements are painful enough to evoke the unutterable disappointment of the six million Muslims who live in the USA and of the billion Muslims around the world. But the mainstream US media again laughed the matter off and dismissed the associations and accusations as slander and smear propaganda. The problem is multi-sided. On the one hand, there is the ignorant disrespect and desperate attempt to tarnish someone's image for political gain. On the other hand, Islam has become the material for this "tarnishing." While the President has every right to stop having others describe him inaccurately, how did Islam become a sanctioned label for negative accusations in the USA and Europe under the watch of the whole world? One does not need to be a Muslim to feel the offense.

We must not forget that the word George Bush mentioned in his first reaction to the war against terror was "crusade." This is a heavily loaded term only used anachronistically to describe medieval Christian military campaigns against Islam to restore Christian dominion over the Holy Land. Soon after, Bush modified his tone and announced that the USA was not at war with "good Muslims." How are we to understand these contradictions?

Did the Bush administration *really* believe that there was such a person as a "good Muslim"? How can we not think that Orientalism is still alive and metamorphosed in a 'new speak,' *à la* George Orwell, that takes the sin of a man hiding in a cave to besmear the whole of Islam? Maybe there is a teachable formula or a magic recipe that Islam somehow misses.

Why, one might ask again, has Christianity managed to wash its hands of the Ku Klux Klan, Eric Rudolph, Terry Nichols and Timothy McVeigh? How has Germany persevered after the Holocaust, and Judaism survived Baruch Goldstein, while Islam has failed to shake itself of Osama bin Laden? There is naturally a substantial difference in the volume and magnitude of various crimes committed against humanity. The fact that bin Laden is still on the loose aggravates the tension, while the threat of his large-scale criminality is still a viable one. But we should not pick and choose. All such crimes are combined products of sociopolitical abnormalities and the darker side of the human soul and should be treated as such, and not as a symptom or indication of one religion's irreparably violent nature.

Perhaps the most telling sign that there is something dangerous or "something wrong," to play on the title of a polemical book on Islam, is the silence among many of its "experts." In the face of widespread skeptical and disenchanted critiques of Islam, relatively few have come forward to assert that Islam is not to be misunderstood as a religion promoting violence and terrorism, or that Islam should not be confused with the inhumane agenda of bin Laden's al-Qaeda.

To me, such silence suggests either resignation or concurrence, and a sense that many so-called "experts" on Islam have abandoned their responsibility to epistemology and to the world community. Either that, or they simply agree that Islam is a violence-promoting religion, i.e., that it is what the US mass media says it is, without any historical verification or careful investigation. No sense of responsibility remains on behalf of a religion abandoned by its "experts" and misunderstood by millions in the USA and Europe. This lack of action is stunning in comparison with the astounding number of classes and seminars taught, presentations and lectures delivered, conferences convened, books and newspaper columns published, television and radio shows aired, and films produced on a regular basis to raise awareness of issues such as racial profiling, gender equality, and anti-Semitism.

In the face of these phenomena, the desire to prevent the fatal "return of the same," if it hasn't already been here, and the urgent need to interrogate false continuums and prejudiced associations do not require extensive justification. For a better grasp of the present condition of Islam as a perceived threat to Western Europe and America, we need to make sense of the roots of this predicament. In very broad terms, one can distinguish at least five points of exclusion at work between Islam and 'the West': Europe's Greco-Roman heritage, its Judeo-Christian tradition, and the bewildering mingling of the two categories; secular modernity; colonialism; and finally globalization. These points of reference reveal the complexity of research and scholarship on Islam and its relation to 'the West' as well as how pivotal periods in recent history, especially colonialism, which led to the rise of Arab nationalism, could become much more than a minor supplement or background to the economic and political history of the Arab-Muslim world.

Frantz Fanon makes an important observation on the bias of the Western historian of colonialism, arguing that "the history which he writes is not the history of the country which he plunders but the history of his own nation."[6] This tendency to silence or marginalize the colonial experience among some Western scholars is also underlined by Edward Said, who makes a salient argument about the "obstinate assumption that colonial undertakings were marginal and perhaps even eccentric to the cultural activities of the great metropolitan cultures."[7] I am not assuming that colonialism was the only significant factor that shaped the contemporary Arab-Muslim world, but its deepest consequences should not be overlooked. Fanon and Said warn us that this thread of excised colonial historiography will almost inevitably be reproduced in the postcolonial. If this reproduction indeed exists, how can one understand it without a radical interrogation of all postcolonial historiographies on Islam and the Arab world developed in the Western world?

To answer this question, I take a few steps back and investigate the dynamics of historiographical thinking in Western Europe since the rise of modernity. In fact, the term 'modernity,' which has often been seen from a mainstream Western perspective to be at odds with Islam, is a pivotal point of departure for this study. One of the arguments I explore in this book is that European modernity has misunderstood its responsibility towards history. This misunderstanding did not occur because history did not exist or was fabricated, but because in a moment of colonial triumph, Western Europe reconstructed its past to suit its present interests. While a critique of European modernity has been the material for many books and critical essays, I do not argue that the current animosity towards Muslims in Europe and North America is simply a residual effect of this historicized colonial imagination; but neither do I say that the tension between Islam and the West today is something new or marks a break with all pasts. I do assert, however, that Islam now exemplifies the permanence of a catastrophe, that a history of the 'history' leading to this persistent catastrophe needs urgent restatement, and that Islam in 'the West' has too often been discussed outside of a proper historical framework.

I therefore confront issues that many theorists have struggled with, particularly the intricate connections and disconnections of 'Islamic cultures' with the colonial cultures forced on them as well as the contemporary effort to "Occidentalize the West." The specific concepts compared here have not been brought together in a single study before: a genealogy of the difference between history and fiction; the genesis of historical thought in Europe; its revolutionary development during the 'Enlightenment' by Kant, Hegel, and Marx; the construction of Islam in the public sphere and modern philosophy of Western Europe; colonial and postcolonial battles over the location of Ibn Khaldūn's theory of history both in 'the West' and the Arab world and their connections to hegemonic appropriations and apologetic nationalisms, in addition to related philosophical and historical discourses in French, English, and Arabic.

But one must also acknowledge that the Arab-Muslim world has become plagued with nationalism, and that Arab nationalism has veered from the path of social justice and political responsibility, creating instead tyrannies, abuses of authorities, and a resurgence of despotic traditions of the worst form. We must stop thinking sympathetically and imagining that the Ottoman-ruled pre-colonial Arab-Muslim world was a safe haven. However, this "absolutist state" of corruption and political failure, to borrow Perry Anderson's phrase, is not an excuse for colonialism, for nothing justifies the ruthless usurpation of other people's lands and resources. But the Arab-Muslim part of the world certainly had its share of misgovernment and abuses of human rights, as my analysis elucidates.

Albert Hourani warns us against the danger of seeing modern nationalism in the Arab-Muslim world "as being no more than a new version of an 'Islamic' idea of political domination."[8] Arab Muslims must see through the ideologies of cultural pride, the affirmation of roots, and the drum-beating fanaticisms that characterize the empty speeches of their rulers today. Nationalisms capitalize on geohistorical notions of belonging to one's own place. In so doing, nationalisms create an illusion of continuity and stasis and enable social diseases like despotism and corruption to roam unchecked. There is no question that in a post-national era, most Arab-Muslim states will have to make serious choices. Some countries may choose simply to submit to their own version of 'modernity' and accept it as it is; others may opt to merge their own culture and identity in a larger, more dominant whole. Some may try to turn their back upon the so-called 'cosmopolitanism' and all the fashionable universalizations it stands for, choosing to withdraw to a lost theocratic ideal. Some may continue their autocratic practices of exploiting their people in the name of democracy and Islam. Yet some Arab countries may eventually transform their social forces from within and meet the 'globalized' world on equal footing. Other countries may choose to adopt some 'Western' ideas and merge them with their own traditional values, principles, and philosophies. While there is still much that Arab states aspire to achieve, especially on the political level, many try to adjust the balance between their own specific cultures and the cultures of Europe and America.

But in order for this to happen, we have to interrogate the multiple dimensions of political autocracy and economic stagnation in the Arab world, which cannot be separated from the hegemonies exercised mainly by the USA and to some extent by Western Europe. This hegemony, which began with Napoleon's invasion of Egypt in 1798, makes it evident that the forms of cultural exchange brought about by colonialism were themselves both the causes and effects of the modes of economic domination and political tyranny that constituted the basis of colonial relations in the Arab-Muslim world. It is therefore completely 'natural' that cultural hegemony and its satellite discourses, which forget their own violence and capture only the violence and antagonism of the so-called 'Islamic world,' would become the governing paradigm that continues to channel the passionate current political views on Islam in America and Western Europe today.

A crucial element of this crooked line of continuous hegemony is the transfer of colonial power from Western Europe to America during the 1950s, which is most exemplified in the latter's unflinching support of Israel in the latest incarnations of the Middle East conflict and the most recent involvements of the two Bush Administrations in oil-rich Iraq. Through complex legacies, the USA inherited British and French colonial paradigms in the Arab-Muslim world, with systems and policies of management that replicate the colonial tradition of the last two centuries, albeit with a different, more sophisticated technology: this is exactly the implication of the various accounts of Euro-American colonial continuity.

Therefore, it makes little sense to focus only on the image of Islam in 'the West' after September 11 and disregard the protracted and complex involvement of Western Europe and the USA in incessant acts of transnational (neo-)colonial aggressions against this part of the world. There is an insidious continuity at work here, and it must be broken asunder in order for us to have a more informed understanding of the relationship between Islam and 'the West.' This understanding can only be achieved through a responsible invocation of history, since the task of radical historiography, as Walter Benjamin argued, cannot be downgraded to a recounting of events in fixed time, but must "seize hold of memory as it flashes up at a moment of danger," and "grasp … the constellation that [one's] own era has formed with an earlier one."[9]

Ultimately, this book has one core goal: to examine the possibility of restoring the referent 'Islam' to a functional code of knowledge. In fact, at no other time has a careful examination of Islam and its relationship to the West, to historiography, and to the discourse of intellectual history been more compelling than in today's post-September 11 political environment. The attacks of September 11, which resulted in the deliberate brutal killings of thousands of innocent Americans, have raised many questions about Islam. Those questions range from investigations of the relationship of Islam, both as a religion and as a social practice, to the discourse of violence, to issues of democracy, liberalism, gender, secularism, and freedom, among others. More importantly, the events of September 11 have reopened old debates on Islam and 'the West' and brought to the surface 'inconvenient' questions not only about the position of Islam in relationship to modernity and the European understanding of world history, but also the implications of this understanding in the world today.

I hope this book does not fall prey to the ready-made ideological assumptions that because I am an Egyptian/Muslim/Arab, I must somehow be writing from a provincial position or represent the point of view of the Arab-Muslim world, supposing that this part of the world indeed has a single unified view on any one question, much less in general. Those assumptions are wasteful obfuscations that only serve to nourish the minds of conspiracy theorists who choose to ignore rigorous critique and divert attention from core matters and crucial issues involving our common humanity. Those critical issues raise a genuine and humanistic concern over the divide between the palimpsestic abuses of the past and an understanding of history as a rich and teachable discipline.

Engagement in arguments makes us all victims in a war of fruitless reasoning that is inevitably lost on all fronts. It is easy to take sides and to simply deny, prove, or dispute pro-Islamic or anti-Islamic positions, especially when there is no absolute standard or norm of grounding statement to which all can return. In this sense, the Muslim world's witness to Islam being anatomized and critiqued has divested the Muslim world of the means to argue. If a scholar seeks to prove a given statement about Islam as an empirical fact, say Islam's tolerance for coexistence, then the moral gravity of Islam as a dynamic religion based in ethics will be unnecessarily lost. If he or she attempts to demonstrate the bias present in anti-Islam campaigns, then the general and the universal value of the argument will also be lost, and so on and so forth. This is because radical revisionists of Islam deny not merely the referent of Islam, but its historical sense as well. In other words, a statement of spirituality and peace in Islam or a lecture on the beauty and loftiness of Islamic sophism is not enough to defeat revisionism and antagonism. It is no longer a matter of making others submit to the verification game, because, in a postnationalist global world, Islam *has become* a political and an ethical question.[10] How then in this already alienating globality can we speak about Islam? If there are no grounds, or, if the grounds have been shaken and questioned, how can we meaningfully write about Islam?

An important starting point for making sense of Islam today is contextualization. To learn about Islam is to situate it in relation to its non-Islamic correlatives. Since Islam will achieve its meaning, in fact its stamp of verification, through linkage to, or difference from, the non-Islamic, what other discourses, networks, or fields of knowledge and practices can one define as essentially non-Islamic or anti-Islamic? Modernity? Globalism? Cosmopolitanism? Humanism and all its offshoots of secularism, freedom, democracy, progress, and enlightenment? Is it also fair in this context to add colonialism as an anti-Islamic discourse? After all, most of the Arab-Muslim world was colonized for decades by European forces with 'civilizing missions' that symbolized the above differences. With all those fields of difference in mind, how can we link the current political and economic conditions of the Arab-Muslim world to European colonialism and global conflict? Approaching such questions requires serious considerations of global tendencies and connections. In the postcolonial, the differences between Islam and its others, or what Islam is the other of, are no longer seen from a strictly religious point of view that differentiates between 'right' and 'wrong' or 'truth' and 'error,' for those are passé, though in some discourses the dichotomies of 'good' versus 'evil' have never broken down. They are rather viewed from the trendy 'globalizational' standpoint of acceptability, whether Islam is suitable or unsuitable, useful or superfluous, sophisticated or obsolete, worldly or nihilistic for a world moving rapidly towards internationalism.

Some recent and contemporary studies have in fact raised the question of Islam in relationship to globalization. A number of scholars approach this topic as if the Arab-Muslim world's recent history had not passed through colonization,[11] or as if the experience of imperialism had somehow shaped a common concern of an imaginary Muslim "*ummah*,"[12] or even as if the culture of Europe had set the standards against which Muslim national cultures must measure themselves.[13] We would have learned nothing from the last three decades of theory and cultural studies if we did not question assumed coherences and wide generalizations, especially when many spaces within the Arab world have not yet achieved complete cultural decolonization. As I elucidate in the Epilogue, I take issue with the 'global,' the 'cosmopolitan,' and their associated '-isms.' The first because it normalizes relationships among world's nations and assumes a homogeneity that is at best questionable in a world of political rifts and economic hierarchies, and the second because ours is unfortunately a world completely different from Aldus Huxley's *Brave New World*; there is simply not enough "soma" to entertain the bourgeois idea and produce the "historical amnesia" and the "identitarian reconditioning" necessary for the fresh cosmopolitan start.

In a post-September 11 political world, 'global' research on Islam has unfortunately mainly been focused on the study of its relationship to violence and terrorism. Notions like Islamdom, Islamism, political Islam, the rise of the new *umma*, and the revival of the Caliphate have been viewed as phenomena facing 'western modernity.' In her important work on the Islamic revival and feminism in Egypt, the anthropologist Saba Mahmoud draws attention to this syndrome by arguing that "the neologism 'Islamism' frames its object as an eruption of religion outside the supposedly 'normal' domain of private worship, and thus as a historical anomaly requiring explanation if not rectification." Because of September 11, Mahmoud continues, there is now powerful support "to strengthen the sense that it is secular-liberal inquisition before which Islam must be made to confess."[14]

While those and many "Islamism" studies that Mahmoud critiques and that clutter our bookshelves and libraries could use some radical unpacking, most of them come as a consequence of or a reaction to current political thought about Islam in a "new world order," where the 'global' becomes coterminous with 'the political' and inextricably linked to the notion of secular modernity which followed the European Enlightenment. In this context, the most prominent religious culture that does not portray itself as 'global' is that of Islam. In this universally 'democratic' cosmo-politicality, Islam is seen not just as an "inquisition-able" religion that refuses to immerse itself in a global environment, but as one whose refusal to assimilate automatically implies that all its adherents could pose significant threats to the world at large. By accepting this limitation, we narrow our research and miss opportunities to broaden the discussion and engage with more informed studies on Islam and 'the West'. Despite the anti-Islamic scare tactics of people like Daniel Pipes and Martin Kramer, Middle Eastern and Islamic Studies now is at its heyday in the Western world, and could in fact be the transnationalizing vehicle with which to escape obsolete apologetics, biased polemics, or the return of vicious forms of knowledge like ethnocentrism. Therefore a meaningful approach to Islam cannot dissociate itself from the wider historical and cultural European and North American contexts embedded in the contours of various political, economic, and social traditions.

There are many scholars and historians in 'the West' who study Islam discursively as part of a rigorous intellectual endeavor spanning both 'the West' and the Arab-Muslim world. Not only have a number of those scholars contributed influentially to Islamic studies, but they have also raised the bar for quality scholarship on Islam both within and outside the Islamic world, maintaining the primacy of evidence over all theory, some of whom are native to the Arab-Islamic world and normally write in English or French (such scholars include Edward Lane, Arnold J. Toynbee, Franz Rosenthal, Jacques Berque, Wilfred Cantwell Smith, Albert Hourani, Mohammed Arkoun, and many others). We must take into consideration the fact that numerous studies have dealt with ways in which the West perceives Muslims and Arabs and vice versa. Works like Said's *Orientalism* (1978) and Ḥasan Ḥanafi's *Muqaddima fī 'Ilm al-Istighrāb* [Introduction to Occidentalism] (2000) create a continuity thesis on Orientalism, although the two have different ideas about the response. Even before Said and Ḥanafī, Hourani had already taken broader steps in theorizing the divide between the East and the West. Hourani's incisive analysis of major Western writers ushers us through the intricate and daunting task of a historian like Marshall Hodgson, whose *Venture of Islam* Hourani examines very closely in *Islam in European Thought* and discovers intriguing similarities between Hodgson and Ibn Khaldūn. Hourani's talent also exposes the anti-Islamic bias of eighteenth-century thinkers like Voltaire, Diderot, Comte de Boulainvilliers, and Schlegel as well as Orientalists like Henri Lammens and Sir William Muir.[15] Many years after the writing of *Arabic Thought in the Liberal Age*, Hourani acknowledges that he may have been "wrong in laying too much emphasis upon ideas which were taken from Europe, and not enough about what was retained from an older tradition."[16] On the contrary, Hourani illuminated many dark corners in Islamic and European cultures; only a rare scholar like him can successfully navigate the rough terrain of Arab-Islamic and European exchanges in the eighteenth and nineteenth centuries. But we should not take Hourani's acknowledgement lightly, as it does point to a constitutive lack in Islamo-European studies. In trying to explain to post-September 11 readers not just the history of Islam but Islam as a condition enabling historical thinking, especially that of 'the West,' one must be aware of two interlocking forces working simultaneously: that which Western schools of thought and philosophies of history tried to impose upon world readers, and that which an Arab-Muslim society with a long tradition of historical thought was producing from within itself.

There are also those who are mere accomplices to power, who already know the argument before they read the text, and can produce and promote ideas tailored to serve an existing political agenda. They are usually the ones who play the role of Othello's Iago, the knowledgeable villains in a tragedy they may not have sparked but are sure to orchestrate to the end. It is a tragedy whose most diabolic script can best be shown in Daniel Pipes' following statement:

> There is no escaping the unfortunate fact that Muslim government employees in law enforcement, the military, and the diplomatic corps need to be watched for connections to terrorism, as do Muslim chaplains in prisons and the armed forces. Muslim visitors and immigrants must undergo additional background checks. Mosques require a

> scrutiny beyond that applied to churches, synagogues, and temples. Muslim schools require increased oversight to ascertain what is being taught to children.[17]

As history continues to disrupt the neatly ordered speculative structures and theoretical assumptions we cast on ourselves and on others, we yearn for a firm and trusted ground to stand on, especially after Islamic fundamentalism had stood out as extremely hostile to the new world, allowing people like Pipes to inaugurate a new age of "thought police" against all Muslims inside and outside America. While 'Islamism' has received its due of scholarly and non-scholarly attention over the last few years, a critical examination of the mechanics of the production of history between Islam and 'the West' and the logos of rationalism and positivism is long overdue.

Thus, this book's argument is structured around the development of intellectual history in Western Europe and its distinctive academic ramifications as we encounter them in studies of Islam and the Islamic world. I build this framework not simply around contested definitions of history, or around Europe's transition from a modernity of 'historical progress' to a coloniality of legitimation, but more importantly around some highly loaded historiography of "encounters" between East and West, whether those encounters were colonial, personal, or even textual, since texts too are a viable form of hegemony.

One final cautionary question. How can one write a book on Islam, modernity, and 'the West' without being apologetic or polemical, or without being labeled as Islamophilic, or pro-Islam, or anti-Western? I have tried to avoid the often truncated and abusive reference to the 'Muslim world' which includes Muslim populations in the Arab world, as well as wherever they live in small or large numbers outside of this region. I say "Islam *and* the West," which are not two totally distinct entities, in order to refer specifically to the intricate encounters in modern history that brought the two together, or one to the other. But I also assert the 'Arab' and 'Arabic' part of Islam in this book, as I elucidate below, to specify not only the original language of Islam, but also the part of the world that uses this language today, which I will refer to as the 'Arab-Muslim world' throughout this study.[18]

My view of the West's impression of Islam is that it was shaped in struggle and that thoughts about the lost empire in Africa and Asia, the 1979 Iranian Revolution, the rise of militia wars and political strife in Lebanon, the

Palestinian question, and the deadly chess game of peace negotiations in the Middle East were all perceived to have been largely influenced by the actions of the Arab-Muslim world. The transformative events of Western history itself – the depression of the 1890s, the "scramble for Africa," World War I, the depression of the 1930s, World War II, the rise of bipolar global politics, the rise of the United States as a superpower – all had a tremendous impact on the Arab-Muslim world that deserves careful consideration. The 'West' was reacting to a wide range of real and imagined threats: fear of the colonies fighting back as well as fear of pan-Arabism, pan-Islamism, pan-Africanism, the 'Red Sickle,' to name a few. As they colonized the Arab-Muslim world, both France and England, to choose two major European colonial powers, had different polices but similar objectives. France aimed to expand and annex the Maghreb while England invested in indirect ruling and building up the middle class. Both colonial powers, however, endeavored to 'contain' and redirect Islam in the Arab colonies. In places like Egypt, Sudan, and Algeria, at least, Islamic resistance to colonialism had already proven wrong any simulations of order and containment in the colonies.[19] We must ask harder questions about how the discourse on Islam in the West was produced and maintained. In assuming coherence rather than attending to silenced voices, we will never be able to see through the cracks of an all-knowing imperial apparatus.

While it is not my intention to either make this book about Arab-Muslim nationalism and anti-colonial movements or blame 'the West' for everything that went wrong, I do hope to bring out the extent to which colonial history was part of intense and ramified encounters and demonstrate that there still persist some intellectual remnants of those encounters that behove us to interrogate the logical frameworks and specific cultural discourses that produced and sustained them. Although I believe that a careful examination of colonialism in the public spheres of both the colonized and colonizers has much to say about contemporary politics and impressions of Islam in the West, this is not a book about postcolonial conditions, nor does it attend to the extensive work done by writers like Dipesh Chakrabarty, Homi Bhabha, Gayatri Spivak, Achille Mbembe, and others.

Many of my examples are drawn from Egypt, a country that I know very well, not only because I was born and educated there, but because I have studied it a great deal. Egypt in particular provides for an excellent case study of the book's central themes. Not only does the colonization of Egypt play a pivotal role in the genesis of theories of capital imperialism, but Egypt has also become one of the classic cases of European expansion and a ground for contended histories and theories of colonialism from J.A. Hobson to Roger Owen and from Jacques Berque to Timothy Mitchell.[20] In this book, the invasion of Egypt raises an important set of questions over British perceptions, and equating, of the misery of modern Egypt with that of biblical Egypt as well as colonial violence and penal codes in the colonies, especially with reference to Denshawai, a central yet less widely studied event in British-Egyptian colonial relations.

Even though my approach foregrounds intellectual history and in some of its chapters deals with problems of historiography and colonialism, this book is a product of the present and reflects not only the current state of knowledge, but also the preoccupations of the post-September 11 world, and in the process overlooks others, sometimes consciously. In the end, I argue that history is an organizing discourse and a powerful rhetorical practice, but not always in the blatant ways that the current focus on Islam might lead us to expect. In recent and current scholarship the term 'Islam' has been avoided as often as it was used. Terms currently used that show political correctness and specialization include: "Islamism," Islamicism," "Islamdom," "good Muslims," "bad Muslims," "political Islam," "radical Islam," "militant Islam," "islamicists," "global Islam," and others. But this does not mean that "anti-Islamism" (hate of all Muslims regardless of their political affiliations) vanished with the "academic" or official language in which it was condemned. This careful rhetoric *will not necessarily naturalize intellectual history*, especially when less than a century ago, the very names of Islam and the Arabs were used as a homogenizing and essentializing tool for imperial categorizational purposes.

The Structure of the Book

Since this study looks at Islam both as a religion and as a social practice, locating it within binaries with which it is typically associated, this chapter continues with a list of keywords and corresponding definitions that are of crucial importance for the reader's understanding of the bone of contention between Islam and the West. Those keywords are meant to draw attention to the pattern of Islam's being seen as an "Other" to modernity, globalism, cosmopolitanism, humanism and its offshoots of secularism, freedom, democracy, progress and so on. The goal of those definitions is to point to the importance of deconstructing the (perceived antagonistic) relationship that Islam has held *vis-à-vis* each of these concepts.

In Chapter 1, I examine the intricate relationship between the writing of history and the writing of fiction. As I interrogate and trace the borderlines between those two discourses since Aristotle, I argue that Islam has been caught in the fault lines between the fictional and the historical. I further argue that the problem of misunderstanding Islam began with European modernity, and that it is in essence a question of epistemology. Tracing three crucial moments in modern European historical thinking – the Enlightenment's concept of intellectual history since Kant, European modernity's re-appropriation of intellectual history, and the rise of the poststructuralist critique of European modernity – this chapter points to the gaps that Europe's contending 'history' of intellectual history creates in relationship to itself and to the Arab-Muslim tradition.

In Chapter 2, I critique the Aristotelian/non-Aristotelian theses that now inform most Western criticisms of Ibn Khaldūn. I show how modern and contemporary Arab writers, while they challenge the ethnocentrism of Western intellectual history, expose their own proto-nationalist biases and one-dimensional thinking. This dialectic alerts us to a new kind of war, one in which the discourse of intellectual history has become a variation on the theme of colonial conquest. I use the case of the Arab-Muslim historian Ibn Khaldūn as my guiding example. I argue that conflicting critiques of Ibn Khaldūn reveal a major issue in scholarship on cultural heritage: the problem of Islamic thought as "Other" and as "Othering," namely, Islam as constituted in the West where a "thinking" "Self" distinguishes and distances itself from an alien "Other," and Islam as it constitutes itself in the Arab world against the colonial West in the same dialectical movement.

Chapter 3 focuses on the place of Islam in Hegel's philosophy of world history. Islam and the Arab world represent a palpable gap in Hegel's understanding of history. In Hegel's scattered references to Islam, he paid more attention to a dominant or received impression of Islam without attending to its original texts, subsequent developments, or contemporary living expressions, and without careful documentation of his sources. I emphasize a major difficulty in grasping Hegel's concept of history, namely, that the *real* to Hegel is not what is out there in the phenomenological world. *Geist* (the mind or the spirit) is the only reality for Hegel and history is primarily a mental process. Using Perry Anderson's *Lineages of the Absolutist States* as a point of reference, I investigate the historical framework that 'shaped' Hegel's views on Islam in world history and the recycling of those views in contemporary critiques of Islam.

Chapter 4 focuses on the evolution of Islam in modern British thought. I examine the cultural productions which allowed 'interest' in Islam and the Arab world to thrive and become symptomatic of a broader historical positioning of the Arab-Muslim world in nineteenth-century England. I argue that even before the emergence of anti-Islamic bias in the works of Edward Lane or Mary Shelley, the eighteenth century served as a clear predecessor to an imminent condition of coloniality. This condition indicates that many writers' and travelers' accounts of the non-European world in nineteenth-century Britain stemmed not only from a general position of antipathy and confrontation, but also from an *inherited* cultural and religious bias.

In Chapter 5, I take the French and British occupations of Egypt as a springboard for examining the contradiction between the liberal ideals imported from Europe and the denial of fundamental rights in the colonies. This chapter raises an important set of questions over the double standards of colonial penal systems, with particular reference to the incident of Denshawai, a central event in British–Egyptian colonial relations. In the postcolonial Arab-Muslim word, the depredations of colonialism have been transformed into nationalist memories of the brutal perpetrations of colonial Europe. Every time those memories are invoked today (in museums, TV series, or Friday sermons), a sense of resentment and indignation is rekindled. I further argue that if colonial Europe's influence on Islam is hemmed by a number of complex issues, including the conflict between modernity and traditional culture and the protracted, conflict-ridden process of the emergence in the postcolonial Arab-Islamic world of versions of modernity and nationalism, then it must follow that these narratives will offer an alternative history that cannot be ignored.

Lastly, in the Epilogue, I discuss restoring Islam to a code of knowledge. Through a return to the overlap of fictional and historical representations of Islam, I draw attention to false continuums and constructed ideologies that took shape and continued in the post-September 11 political climate. I particularly investigate the positioning of Islam in relationship to fashionable concepts like globalization and cosmopolitanism and the effects those concepts have on the cancerous growth of Islamophobia in Europe and America today.

Definitions

While each of the following terms is the subject of numerous volumes that vary in their comprehensiveness and emphases, I limit my coverage of each term to what is most relevant to this book. My point here is not to offer a general introduction to each of these terms but to highlight the specific aspects of their developments that are relevant as background. In presenting these definitions, I also aim to shed light on the ways in which continuously used terms are not used to refer to the same referents over time. Where important terms like 'Islam,' 'Arab,' 'religion,' and 'nation' are used, they stand for ideas that have histories and are never simply stagnant (even if some wish to paint them this way for ideological reasons).

Arabic and the Arabs

The Arabic language, together with Hebrew and Aramaic among others, is classified as one of the Semitic languages within the Afro-Asiatic family of languages. Today, the word 'Arabic' is used in English to refer to the Arabic language, but in Arabic, the word for the Arabic language is a feminine definite derivation from the stem ʿ-r-b, namely *al-ʿarabiyya*. Many historical linguists consider this triliteral root to be related to the root of the word Hebrew (עברית) through metathesis. Others believe that this triliteral root derives from the name of the first man ever thought to have spoken the language, the folkloric figure Yaʿrub ibn Qaḥṭān. He is also known as the father of the lands of Yemen, where the aboriginal Arabs, among them Ismāʿīl (Ishmael), son of Ibrahīm (Abraham) by his Egyptian wife Hājar (Hagar), are said to have lived (at least according to the famous Arab lexicographer and philologist Ibn Manẓūr in his renowned dictionary *Lisān al-ʿArab*. In pre-Islamic times, Arabic was spoken mainly in the Arabian Peninsula, where it was the medium of a great tradition of poetry, also known as *fann al-ʿarabiyya al-awwal* (the first art of the Arabic language), which was mainly preserved and transmitted orally.[21] Although Arabic writing was known in Arabia during the pre-Islamic era, tombstones as early as the third century attest to Arabic being written in gradually evolving forms as Aramaic-based script, a script which eventually evolved into the present Arabic script.[22] It was not, however, until the fourth century that Arabic was written in Aramaic script. In the fifth century, the city of Mecca gained commercial prominence and began to organize poetry competitions at an annual fair known as ʿUkāẓ. Poets from every tribe would gather there and recite poetry

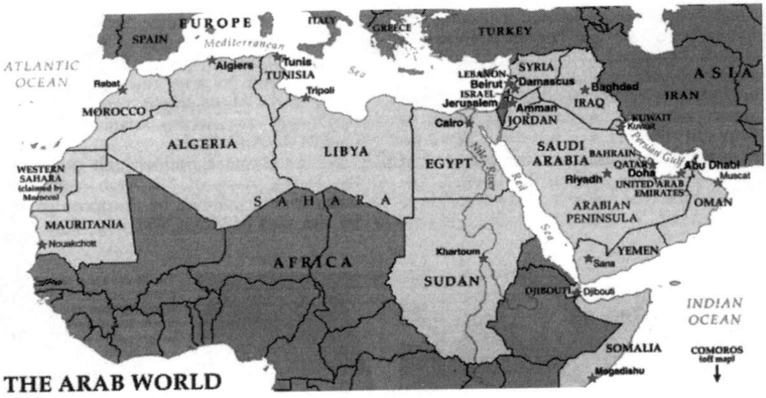

Map 1 The Arab world, shaded here in light gray

exalting the deeds and exploits of their respective ancestors. It was at this fair that the Arabic language reached a high level of mastery and perfection, especially among the poets of the famous tribe of Quraysh. Before long, members of the tribe of Quraysh became, as Ibn Manẓūr writes in *Lisān al-ʿArab*, "the most proficient speakers of Arabic in history." It should not escape us here that Ibn Manẓūr's admiration of Quraysh's Arabic could possibly be dictated more by the social and political concerns of his time than by scholarly evidence and consultation of sources from earlier centuries.

With the advent of Islam in the seventh century and with the revelation of the Qur'ān in the Qurayshī dialect, Arabic gained an even higher degree of perceived sanctity. The fact that the Qur'ān was revealed in Arabic and ritual prayers and public worship were performed in the same language made its study and cultivation a sacred endeavor. The hegemony of *dawlat al-Islām* (Islamic rule) affected the peripheries of the Arabian Peninsula, causing Arab pastoral nomads from the north and center of the peninsula to move into the countryside of the area now known as *al-hilāl al-khaṣīb* (the Fertile Crescent), which includes modern-day Iraq and Syria. As Islam spread, so did the Arabic language. Aramaic, Syriac, Coptic, and Pahlavi (Middle Persian), in addition to older diminishing languages like Assyrian, Babylonian, Chaldean, and other Canaanite languages of that area, slowly began to fade away owing to the rapid expansion of Arabic under the aegis of Islam. Not only was Arabic the language of the Qur'ān, but it also became the language of *al-sharīʿa* (Divine Law),[23] of *al-sīra al-nabawiyya* (the record of the events of Prophet Muḥammad's life), and of *al-hadīth wal-sunna* (the sayings and practices of the Prophet). With the growth of Islam and the subsequent dominance of the Islamic Caliphates, Arabic became the language of government and administration. As the center of Islamic rule moved from Mecca to Damascus to Baghdad, then splitting into multiple smaller centers of power in al-Andalus, North Africa, and Egypt, peoples who accepted Islam had to learn Arabic for purposes of work, trade, and communication with their governors in addition to religious reasons. It was no coincidence that the science of the Arabic language would emerge and develop at the hands of scholars whose first language was not Arabic and who had to acquire the language through practice and studied it in comparison with their mother tongues. Among those scholars is the famous Sībawayh (d. 793 CE) who is regarded as the founding father of Arabic grammar although he was Persian.

Today Arabic is the official language of 22 countries,[24] with a combined population of about 300 million people extending from the Persian Gulf to the Atlantic Ocean, across Southwest Asia and North Africa.[25] Spoken in many different dialects, Arabic remains the predominant language in Saudi Arabia, Iraq, Kuwait, Qatar, the United Arab Emirates, Bahrain, Yemen, Egypt, the Sudan, Libya, Tunisia, Algeria, Morocco, Mauritania, Syria, Lebanon, Jordan, and Palestine. Arabic is also used in countries in Africa, Southeast Asia, and elsewhere.[26] Although every Arab country has its own dialects that differ from Modern Standard Arabic (MSA) in pronunciation, grammar, and vocabulary, educated Arabic speakers usually use MSA in formal discourse and in writing. The multiplicity of dialects that co-exist alongside MSA in a diglossic situation reflect and reinforce the importance of local identity in an environment where historically a push for unity that used language (*Standard*-ized Arabic) as an instrument was never accepted as the sole identity of the Arab world's peoples. Local identities still play a major part within Arab countries. If you ask a Syrian where s/he is from, you're more likely to hear 'Aleppo,' or 'Damascus' rather than 'Syria.' To complicate this further, many speakers of Arabic who live in the Arab world do not think of themselves as Arabs, such as the Maronites of Lebanon and the Copts of Egypt.

The English word 'Arab' is thus derived from a very rich root in the Arabic language that has a variety of complex meanings. For example, the Arabic word *'arab* (Anglicized as 'Arab'), which generally refers to the Arab peoples, is different from the word *a'rāb* (Arabized or nomadic Arabs), used historically to refer to the peoples who lived in the outskirts of the Arab Peninsula but were not considered *'arab*. Historically, there were considered to be two kinds of *'arab*. The first are known as *'arab 'āriba* (autochthonous), and the second *'arab musta'riba* (Arabized), often used to refer to those who have become Arabs or Arabized after mixing with the Arabs for generations, not to be confused with *muta'arrib*, (de-Arabized), an obsolete derogatory word that referred to someone who left the metropolitan life of central Arab cities like Mecca and went back to live in the desert. Contrary to the argument that the word Arab is used in the Qur'ān exclusively in the Bedouin sense and never to refer to the people of Mecca, the Qur'ān actually uses two different variations on the stem '-r-b. The first is the adjectival *'arabī* (Arabic), usually modifying the noun *lisān* (tongue) or Qur'ān to underline the fact that the Qur'an is revealed in "an exemplary clear Arab tongue" and to distinguish it from being *a'jamī* (foreign). Examples could be found in chapters like *The Bees*, *The Poets*, *Yūsuf*, *Fuṣṣillat*, *The Thunder*, and *Ṭāhā*. The second variation on this root used in the Qur'ān is *A'rāb* (Arabized or nomadic Arabs). This word is often used to alert the Prophet to the hypocrisy and lack of faith of some tribes from the desert and far oases who announced their conversion to Islam for the sake of receiving alms and charity, not for the love of God. The reference is meant to distinguish them from *al-'Arab* (the Arabs). Examples of this reference can be found in chapters like *The Repentance*, *The Parties*, and *The Rooms*. Moreover, according to Ibn Manẓūr, the Arab historian al-Azharī is reported to have said that "he who does not distinguish between *al-'Arab* and *al-A'rāb* (the Arabs and the Arabized) is ignorant and biased against the Arabs."[27]

The fall of the Ottoman Empire (a.k.a. the Porte) and the rise of colonialism in the Arab world have complicated the meaning of Arabness as well as of the Arab world, which is not coextensive with the Middle East. The latter is an exclusively political term of Western origin that is often taken to include non-Arab countries like Israel, Turkey, and Iran. Following World War I, major European forces, particularly Britain and France, divided Africa and Asia into smaller areas of interest. As the Porte disintegrated at European hands that then grabbed its pieces and made colonies and spheres of interest out of them, Arab identity started to go through a series of important changes. Once these regions became independent countries, identities within the Arab world grew to encompass many layers: ethnic,

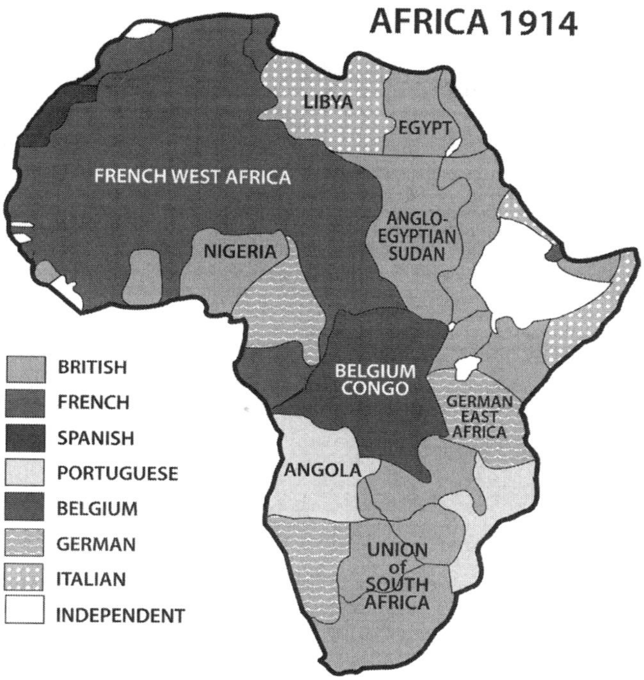

Map 2 Africa in 1914

religious, national, local. Meanwhile, the word 'Arab' began to assume a different character and became almost a monolith, especially in Western eyes.

Islam

The Arabic root for the word Islam consists of three letters: s, l, m. This root is rich in meanings. Among words with this root are "peace," "surrender," and "submission;" pre-Islamic meanings included such nominal, verbal, and adjectival variations as "purity/purification," "sole ownership," "safe," "to deliver from harm/evil/vices," "to deliver to a destination," "to return something back to its original owner," "to receive something by hand," "elevation/ascension/sublation," and "welcome and greetings."[28] Although Islam is neither the first nor the only religion in the Arab world, to speak of the Arab world today is to refer not only to countries that share a language and other cultural traditions, but also to countries whose demographics, ideologies, and political identities have in many ways been formed and informed by the predominance of the Islamic faith. As Islam spread, it came to be practiced in diverse ways by diverse cultures both inside and outside of the Arab world today.

But the religion strongly retains its Arab substance and character. The message of Islam was brought to the world by Prophet Muḥammad, himself an Arab. The nature of Islam's emphasis on communal ties and social ethics is fundamentally rooted in the Arab experience and therefore cannot be fully understood without reference to its setting of origin. As the most effective ideological force governing the Arab world for more than a millennium, Islam has no doubt left indelible marks on the way it has defined itself. In the eighteenth and nineteenth centuries, for example, major Islamic movements, including Wahhābism, Mahdism, and Sanūsism, rose in response to changing political dynamics and social practices in certain Arab regions. Although these movements' heydays are now long past, their legacies remain alive in the minds of some proponents who appear sporadically in different parts of the Arab world.

Nothing has roused Arab Islam to action in recent history more than the external threat and political challenges posed by European imperialism in the nineteenth and twentieth centuries. By the end of World War I, a predominantly Muslim Arab world found itself in the grips of an alien culture that challenged its fundamental principles and values. The pressure of this foreign modernity with its military superiority and ostensibly secular values contributed to the rapid development of a sense of Arab nationalism centered on Islam that spread throughout Africa and Asia.[29] The struggle was harsh and long, and the results of European colonialism have been colossal. The geopolitical map of the Arab-Muslim world changed dramatically as Arab countries began to assume their independence from foreign rule. All independent Arab nations successively became members of the Arab League, which at its inception in the 1950s was controlled by Gamal Abdel Nasser, the Egyptian leader who disseminated the ideology of pan-Arabism. The movements of pan-Arabism, pan-Islamism, and Arab nationalism, sought to unite massive populations on various bases. A strong sense of historical consciousness makes it plausible to argue that the rise of political Islam is not a postcolonial phenomenon, but indeed an anti-colonial one *ex post facto*.[30]

Modernity

Even when we limit ourselves to the institutionalized European modern period that is said to have extended roughly from the late 1850s to the late 1920s, there are still a multiplicity of definitions of the modern, of modernity, and of modernism: early, late, high, political, philosophical, and literary. There is modernity that is defined in relationship to the classical traditions of the nineteenth century, and another that is defined as a stylized and individualist version of the so-called Enlightenment, one that resists its myth of progress and challenges modernity in the name of modernity; a third one is seen from the point of view of the postmodern or from whose point of view the postmodern is (re)defined, not to mention the unpacking of modernity into other offshoots like modernization and modernism, or literary and artistic modernity with its various subcategories of impressionism, dadaism, surrealism, avant-gardism, futurism, and so on.

On the semantic level alone, there are crucial debates on what is modern and what is modern*ist*, on modernism, modernity, and modernization.[31] Add to this the fact that there is a Western fashion of defining the term modern departmentally: in philosophy, modernity is a rejection of mainstream logic of thought from Descartes through Kant to the epistemological trajectory of German idealism. Philosophical modernity celebrates Nietzsche in its rejection of metaphysical realism. In architecture, modernity rejects monumentality and elitism and embraces pastiche and subjectivity.[32] In literature, modernity is generally a reaction against mimeticism and functionalism, one that troubles the terrain between literature and life by making it difficult to say whether art represents, exaggerates, or deforms reality. For example, the English literary modernism of figures like Eliot, Pound, and Woolf follows the footprints of the French Mallarmé, though without admitting it, in mobilizing difficulty as a mode of privileging its own aesthetic sensibility, and therefore celebrating a kind of complexity and irony appreciable only by the cultural elite.

This leaves us with the impression that modernity is still an enormous field of study, one that has been given numerous definitions by the historian, the philosopher, the cultural theorist, the art historian, and the literary critic, without even including mass culture, popular literature, gender, and the non-European. For purposes of intellectual history, I choose to define modernity as a condition that Europe had carefully employed to serve its own expansionist purposes. This condition entailed ruthless critique of the present as well as the formation of native political powers, in addition to the rise of national identity, the secularization of values and norms, and freedom from any external authority.

In the process, however, European modernity instrumentalized human history in a fashion that served Europe's present aims, as I will discuss in Chapters 2 and 3. This dematerialization led to the confusion of interpretations with facts. Those attained facts are sometimes based on biblical knowledge and sometimes, paradoxically, on scientific data. As a result, European history was often written in one of the following four modes: a continuous mode, namely, one that pertains to unverifiable memory of the past; a demonstrable mode, that is, one that relies on positivistic, protoscientific language that assumes objectivity and detachment; a reflective mode, i.e., one that mirrors the impression that an existing power would like to give itself; and a terminal mode, namely, one which views history as a progress towards an end, be it biblical or, again, scientific.[33] All this tells us that modernity had a clear historical function. Ironically enough, nothing is more historical than modernity, even in its very construction of history. Modernity, often treated as a period of time that has long elapsed, cannot prove itself without being part of the continuity of history, even though it could establish itself as a violent discontinuity with history.

The West

The term 'the West' has been used loosely and inaccurately. Some use it as a geographical marker to refer to Western Europe. Sometimes it is easy to find an anchor in the term 'the West' to help the postcolonial critic lump together that dominant and powerful imperial part of the world, namely EuroAmerica, in discussing postcolonial ideas and themes. Some even believe that if one unpacks the word 'Eurocentrism,' it will somehow yield 'Europe,' 'ethnocentrism,' and 'the West,' which one can use interchangeably. This is unfair and incorrect. Like Islam, which has become an ideological category – although many still pretend it is solely a theological one – 'the West' too has turned into an ideological label among postcolonial critics hiding underneath the garb of geography. Observing this new semanticization of 'the West,' Raymond Williams remarks that "the west (to be defended) is notoriously variable to geographical and social specifications."[34] Interestingly, Williams also notes that after the eleventh century "the *West* [Williams' italics] as Christian or Greco-Roman," which he emphasizes are not the same thing, came to be used "by contrast with an *East* defined as Islam."[35] Thus, the invention of 'the West,' much like the invention of Islam, positions it as both a location and an empire at once. But if, as Williams implies, 'the West' is a historical category and not a geographical construct, then we must regard the construction of 'Islam' too as a fixed civilizational category. These constructions inevitably result in dehistoricized and dematerialized understandings of Islam and the so-called 'West.'

'The West' in the Arab-Muslim world, very much like Europe's idea of the Orient, has also been misconstrued. In the Arab-Muslim world, 'the West' has come to mean 'the modern.' This association inevitably opposes 'Islamic culture' to 'Western culture' and corresponds to the rise of pan-Islamic nationalism.[36] In that sense Islam became the momentum that fueled Arab nationalist thought in the colonial age. In his study on the emergence of nationalism in colonial India, the postcolonial critic Partha Chatterjee offers a significant account of similar, though not wholly religious, stages of national thought. Chatterjee prefers to refer to those stages as decisive "moments" in which nationalist modernity is produced in the colonial context. "Nationalist thought at its moment of departure," Chatterjee argues convincingly, "formulates the following characteristic answer: it asserts that the superiority of the West lies in the materiality of its culture, exemplified by its science, technology and love of progress. But the East is superior in the spiritual aspect of culture."[37]

A principal factor in this epistemological attitude towards 'the West' and its difference from Islamic cultural history concerns geopolitics, which led to the emergence of terms like 'Eurocentrism' and 'Euronormativism.' Ironically enough, both Eurocentrism and Euronormativism are themselves specifically geopolitical constructs: calculated moves designed to insert the newly established *idea* of Europe (although such geopolitical categorization is neither adequate nor precise in capturing the constitutional complexity of European politics and culture) into a world imperial system, dominated mostly by England and France, but which certainly includes Germany, Holland, Italy, Portugal and Spain. Such geopolitics, however, came about in circumstances completely different from those of September 11. What is most at issue here is not the scholastic environment of European epistemology (on which Edward Said and others have often commented) but, as I discuss in Chapters 4 and 5, the fortunes of European supremacy at the moment when epistemology took a colonial turn.

In works by writers like Francis Fukuyama, Bernard Lewis, and Samuel Huntington, we find a tendency to situate the world's advancement into a globalized village and the distribution of capitalist economy in terms of the "backwardization" of Islam and "universalization" of 'the West.' In such views, both Islam and 'the West' are construed as civilizations. The unavoidable consequence of this mode of thinking is again a dematerialized and stagnant understanding both of Islam and 'the West.' This misunderstanding is in large part caused by the condition of modernity, which serves as the sociohistorical background to the speculative formalization of categories like 'the clash of civilizations' and 'the end of history.'

While none of these authors' analyses provide historical contexts to support their claims on Islam, they fail still to prove how the characteristics that distinguish 'the West' from the rest of the world have come about to be. They also fail to explain how 'the West' remains whole and resists any infusions, mergers, or adjustments. In part, this is also a problem of ignoring significant parts of history: the bloody chapters on slavery and colonialism in the book of modernity and the enormous wreckage caused in the Age of the Empire. Their absurd essentialisms prevent us from understanding Islam and from engaging critically with history and with 'the West.' The best critique of this essentialism is voiced by Arif Dirlik, who, in debunking Samuel Huntington's argument on the "clash of civilizations," lays bare the logic of dehistoricized Americo-Eurocentrism:

> He reifies civilizations into culturally homogeneous and spatially mappable entities, insists on drawing impassable boundaries between them, and proposes a fortress EuroAmerica to defend Western civilization against the intrusion of ... unassimilable Others. What is remarkable about his views is his disavowal of the involvement of the "West" in other civilization areas ... [he denies] the legacies of colonialism, [and insists] that whatever has happened to other societies has happened as a consequence of their indigenous values and cultures.[38]

As evident from Dirlik's incisive critique of Huntington and his pool, there is a persistent denial, or perhaps even a selective amnesia, at work. Michael Hardt and Antonio Negri describe Huntington as a "secret-advisor," an "imperial *Geheimrat*" whose reduction of human civilization to "a conflict of the west against Islam" is nothing but a cheap attempt to get into "the ear of the sovereign."[39] Edward Said called Huntington's "clash of civilizations" a "Clash of Ignorance," while Paul Gilroy labeled him a "civilizationist" who dismisses any commitment to "cosmopolitan consciousness," and believes that any contact or mixture with the foreign "is risky" and will lead to "ontological jeopardy."[40] But maybe we should not put the blame wholly on government-connected scholars like Huntington, for they are not anomalous among the scholars of their setting. While Huntington is certainly worthy of criticism, worse still is the racism that is internally active and not outwardly distinguishable from one that is out in the open. Huntington gave Edward Said, Paul Gilroy, Timothy Brennan, Arif Dirlik, Mahmood Mamdani, Michael Hardt and Antonio Negri, and many others the chance to confirm their stand and reinforce their confrontations of the mentality of "mappable entities" and irreconcilable differences. Huntington's "clash of civilizations" symbolizes the tip of the iceberg of Islamophobia and administrative discrimination that is otherwise hidden and *practiced* quietly on a daily basis. This administered desk-top terrorism against "the unassimilable Others" is a variation on the theme of power, one that wears the uniform of national security and targets innocent civilians, constantly subjecting the un-rightful people of the world to surveillance, persistently investigating their backgrounds, and tirelessly monitoring their movements, not to mention the indefinite 'detention' of aliens in Guantanamo which many eminent critics, including Judith Butler and Paul Gilroy, continue to debate.[41] There are "good Muslims," as Bush once told us, but it sadly appears that there are a great deal of "bad ones," and it looks like it is difficult to tell them apart. It is "unfortunate," to echo Pipes' derisive adjective, that we live in a country divided by race and religion, that a country of freedom and a land of opportunity expected to be hospitable to its "non-Western" immigrants and visiting guests would fall into hostile barbarism and discriminate against citizens because of their religious and cultural backgrounds. It is disheartening that the terrorized would become the terrorizer and regard its own as time-bombs, "sleepers," "persons of interest," "terrorists-in-waiting." If this is what homeland security is predicated on, then this must be the moment when you know, as Mahmood Mamdani fearlessly puts it, that "Islam has become a political identity in post-9/11 America."[42] This is why a fully educated American like Huntington (who earned a B.A. from Yale in 1946, an M.A. from the University of Chicago in 1948, and a Ph.D. from Harvard in 1951, and served as the White House's Coordinator of Security

Planning between 1977 and 1978) is not an island unto himself or a "mad scientist" speaking to empty seats when he hypostatizes Western civilization and states that "A [sic] multi-cultural America is not possible because a non-Western America is not America."[43] If anything, Huntington is a victim, or, to be more diagnostically correct, a symptom of a certain malady in the sociopolitical order that produced him. His ideology is a sign of a malicious growth in an educational system that teaches history selectively and cryptically, treating it like a card game, shuffling it as the circumstance dictates. Certain historiographical methodologies in these institutions where Huntington received his education must somehow have enabled an essentialist like him to become who he is and think the way he does. It is those particularly supremacist factories of remapping global order, and which Said has once referred to as "latent Orientalism," that are responsible for generating Huntington-like mentalities of political antagonism, xenophobia, and civilizational essentialism, and which we ought to confront.

Islam, Modernity, History

Here I move from discussing individual terms to looking at how they converge and overlap. To reemphasize in different terms a point I mentioned above, the fact that the ground covered by the intersection of these three terms for example is so fecund only serves to indicate the rich lives of each of the terms on its own. This term and those that follow bring together concepts at intersections that will be again highlighted at crucial points throughout this book.

There are many instances where Arab scholars have struggled with existing conservatism in the Arab-Islamic world. From the very early days of the *Nahḍa,* Muslim intellectuals like ʻAlī Mubārak, ʻAbd al-ʻAzīz Jāwīsh, Rifāʻa al-Ṭahṭāwī (perhaps the first modernizer in the Arab world), and Muḥammad ʻAbduh have wrestled with the idea of modernizing Islam and of engaging with Western modernity at a time when Islamic culture was striving to match the new models of the West while seeking to preserve its own heritage. This tension is as evident in modern Arab-Muslim culture as it is so in the so-called 'West,' especially in the effect which the encounter with Islam has left on Western Europe. Other scholars have also addressed the emergence of a non-Western modernity in various cultural, philosophical, religious, sociological, and political fields of Islam. This list includes works by scholars like A.L. Tibawi (1961, 1966),

Abdallah Laroui (1976, 1977), Anouar Abdel-Malek (1963, 1969), Samir Amin (1988), Edward Said (1978, 1986, 1993, 2000), Ḥasan Ḥanafī (2000), Talāl Asad (1979, 1993, 2003), Timothy Mitchell (1991, 2000), and Zachary Lockman (2004).[44]

There are also instances where Europe "deconstructs" its modernity from inside its own contours (as I will further discuss in Chapter 1). The Marxist historian Perry Anderson, the Frankfurt School critic and cultural theorist Theodor Adorno, the poststructuralist French archaeologist Michel Foucault, and his deconstructionist student Jacques Derrida are remarkable examples of this inward turn and self-critique in Europe's modern intellectual history. But it is not enough that the critiques of modernity come from the inside. In *Poetics of Relation*, Edouard Glissant argues that "the West itself has produced the variables to contradict its impressive trajectory every time. This is the way in which the West is not monolithic, and this is why it is surely necessary that it [i.e., the West] move toward entanglement [in rough terms: interrelations between 'itself' and the 'non-West']. The real question is whether it will do so in a participatory manner or if its entanglement will be based on old impositions."[45] In the introduction to his study *The Burden of Modernity*, Carlos J. Alonso has this to say about cultural critics who "endeavor to change the perspective on the cultural exchange process between the metropolis and the periphery by proposing to look at it from the optic of the subordinate cultural party":

> The assumption here is that the work of recomposition done on a metropolitan discursive modality by its "savage" appropriation inevitably undermines the former's claims to being an organic discourse, which in turn is a way of questioning its authority. But the reality is that this maneuver does not entail any concrete exploration of the plurivocal, self-contradictory, and open-ended dimension of metropolitan discourse, which is therefore left to stand as the self-same, monolithic authority it purports to be, regardless of its supposed disfigurement in the periphery.[46]

Likewise, Islamic historiography in the West focused primarily on the difference between Islam and modern Europe with its Judeo-Christian tradition, especially regarding historical questions on the life of Muḥammad, the genesis of the Qur'ān, the spread of Islam, and more recently the relationship between Islam and 'secular' modernity.[47] Parallel interests took place in the field of anthropology with growing attention to comparative genealogy and techno-modernity. While the hegemonic role of secondary sources and reliance on translations within the study of Islam in the United States goes a long way toward explaining why scholarship on Islam is in numerous cases missing the vital tool of consulting original material and references, a full intellectual history of this post-Orientalist transition has to address more than this imitative dependency and turn instead to several developments in linguistics, philosophy, philology, demography, and history which in various ways continue to mark the "Islam discussion" and frame efforts to define Islamic Studies as a scholarly topic.

Often considered a 'benchmark of civilization' and a 'road to human progress,' modernity has been regarded by many as essentially European. While this is a heated debate in itself, it was at the acme of *its* modernity that Europe's "scramble for Africa" took place (to be discussed further in Chapter 5). This scramble was justified by an oppressive structure of attempted legitimation, one that employed many disciplines that ranged from anthropology to historiography in order to create documents in support of Europe's so-called *mission civilisatrice* in Africa. In this act of colonial expansion, the writing of history turned into a discourse of conquest. What began as an expansionist and muscle-flexing adventure for Europe in Asia and Africa became the central concern for the entire Arab-Muslim world in its colonial and postcolonial struggles to achieve self-rule and independence from the West. To consider the colonial aspect of this "modernity effect" from an Arab-Islamic perspective is to speak of a long overdue historical responsibility towards the Arab-Muslim world, the very world that was claimed to lie beyond the boundaries of enlightened Europe, excluded and silenced.

It would be impossible to contextualize the relationship between Islam and modernity without addressing European colonialism and its legacies. In the wake of the French Revolution of 1789 and the first Industrial Revolution of the following century, the Arab-Muslim world suffered the physical, material, linguistic, ideological, and cultural effects of European imperialism, its barbaric modernization and expansion in the form of cultural hegemony and military colonization. Napoleon, as part of his passion for the French Empire, was driven to occupy Egypt in 1798 before the English could do so. The case of Algeria in 1830 was analogous. The British example, particularly in Iraq and Egypt, is even more revealing and complex.

After signing their famous Mutual Accord of 1904, England and France, the two lions of the imperial herd in Asia and Africa, looked at the "Black Continent" and the Arab-Muslim world as a source of raw material, economic gain, political supremacy, and expansion.[48]

So in addition to 'Orientalist' and 'post-Orientalist' accounts I address in this book, I also look at 'Occidentalist' narratives derived from the two most remarkable colonial events in modern Egyptian history: the French Expedition (1798–1803) and the British occupation (1882–1922), as I will further discuss in Chapter 5. The first clash of Islam and the West in modern times, so to speak, and its accompanying cultural transformations is described by al-Jabartī in *'Ajā'ib al-Āthār fī al-Tarājim wa al-Akhbār* (1805–25).This account has played a significant role in defining European modernity as "Other" in Muslim eyes while portraying the complexities of the Napoleonic invasion in a charitable way that continues to challenge many Muslims into rethinking their basic impressions of France and Western Europe.

A second narrative draws on what we know about the characteristic conditions of imperial violence and exploitation of natives in the colonies, as it is exemplified in the Denshawai affair of 1906 (as I will discuss in Chapter 5) wherein the Egyptian village of Denshawai, located in the mid-Delta region, experienced the public hanging and flogging of fifty Egyptian peasants accused of stirring a riot and killing an English officer. I cite these 'historiographies' because the very idea of narrative, of telling a story – as opposed to the static, panoptic, and organized 'vision,' of history – destabilizes Eurocentrism's essentializing and exoticizing ideas about the Islamic non-West.

The Orientalism Thesis

A key starting point for a discussion of how Islam has been perceived in modern European history is Edward Said's *Orientalism* precisely because it spans pre- and postcolonial European political formations and explores the perception of Islam in the West. Such a prominent focus on Islam in *Orientalism* could have never been timelier. Written in the aftermath of the Cold War, the rise of the USA as the world's sole superpower, the discovery of oil in the Middle East, and a reshuffling of allies and foes in the political world regarding the Israel–Palestine question, Said's work puts Islam in a larger Orientalist context with the claim that Islam had to be integrated into any serious discussion of the core developments in modern European thought. Of course, his approach benefits from his training in comparative literature and his versatile knowledge of Arab and European history. But to articulate a critique of modern European intellectual history from his vantage point as an Arab-American humanist at a crucial turning point in the twentieth century makes his work all the more remarkable. Said's provocative thesis is that the subject of Orientalism is "not so much the East itself as the East made known, and therefore less fearsome, to the Western reading public."[49] Said's critique is grounded in the belief that starting from the late eighteenth century there existed "corporate institutions" that made the Orient their discipline, "dealing with it by making statements about it, authorizing views of it, describing it, by teaching it, settling it, ruling over it."[50] To extend Said's argument a bit further, while none of these "corporate institutions" were legitimate, they somehow managed to flourish especially under the auspices of colonial modernity which gave them the power not only to legitimate their authority over Islam and the Orient but also to disseminate their own historiographies:

> As a system of thought Orientalism approaches a heterogeneous, dynamic, and complex human reality from an uncritically essentialist standpoint; this suggests both an enduring Oriental reality and an opposing but no less enduring Western essence, which approaches the Orient from afar and from, so to speak, above. This false position hides historical change. Even more important, from my standpoint, it hides the *interests* of the Orientalist.[51]

These "interests of the Orientalist" that Said underlines were claimed to be objective in two ways: theoretical, written according to a set of so-called common universal and rational concepts; and anthropological, based on practical field studies and analysis of existing Arab and Islamic communities.[52] This proto-scientific objectivity raises an important question: could these theoretical and anthropological standards have been a decoy for the articulation of the "higher law" of a Western system of domination? Said's *Orientalism* attempts to answer this question by arguing that colonial culture is tuned by the dialogical nature of colonial and anti-colonial power relations.

This dialogical tension also means that the Arab-Muslim world would have different versions of colonial history. There is no doubt that those versions are also exaggerated. In fact, there is a problem among many Arab intellectuals who view history internally, that is, from a deeply damaging nationalistic mind-set, which contradicts the real situation in the Arab-Muslim world. This is not to say that Arab intellectuals suffer from "dishonesty," as someone like the Middle East scholar Kanan Makiya would argue.[53] While many Arab postcolonial scholars are prompted by the desire to set the records of history straight, so to speak, their writings are often curtailed by one-dimensionality, be it Arabist or Islamicist.[54] But for the sake of clarity, this particular mind-set is itself a product of many intertwined forces. While this is not the case among all Arab-Muslim intellectuals, there is no question that centuries of injustice and decades of despotism, with political oppression, censorship, persecution of liberal-minded intellectuals, in addition to sheer educational isolationism imposed by colonial powers and the autocratic regimes that followed them, have left negative marks on cultural and intellectual production in the Arab-Muslim world. Despite this, Makiya's accusation of Arab intellectuals as "silent" and ambivalent towards "real" issues of corruption and tyranny in their own countries should not dissuade us from probing for the historical reasons for this contempt. Not only is Makiya's argument unfounded (since many Arab intellectuals have indeed been critical of their ruling systems and suffered dire consequences in the process, including banishment, persecution and imprisonment),[55] but his condemnation of leading Arab intellectuals like Abdallah Laroui, Samir Amin, and Edward Said as 'inflammatory' writers who mislead more than guide their readers is erroneous. In what seems like an attempt to exonerate the West from any responsibility towards the Arab-Muslim world, including the recent US intervention in Iraq, Makiya accuses Said in particular of making a wrong and dangerous argument in *Orientalism.*

Makiya's concern is that Said's thesis with its anti-Western rhetoric was employed by Arab intellectuals to foster their sentiments against the West. While Said acknowledges that his ideas have been misunderstood by Arabs and Westerns alike, both according to their political affiliations,[56] this misunderstanding is at bottom political and ideological. While this is not the place to engage in an in-depth debate over Said's thesis, it is sufficient to argue that *Orientalism* does not imply that whatever Europeans have said or written about the Orient was racist or ethnocentrist. It would be a grave misunderstanding to say that Said's work appeased the Arab mentality or helped feed generations of young Arab scholars with deeply rooted populist feelings of resentment against the West. Regardless of Said's work, anti-Western sentiments have been and continue to be an essential internal component of fundamentalist Arab-Islamic politics in general, one for which Said should not be given credit.

This being said, there are some inescapable generalities and risky intellectual adventures in Said's argument. For example, Said specifies three interconnected types of Orientalism: first, Academia (as a discipline supposedly concerned with detached and scientific study of a particular area of the world, historically, geographically, and anthropologically); secondly, a predominant *épistémè* or mode of thought premised on a flat binary opposition between the 'Orient and the Occident'; and thirdly, existing corporations and institutions working from a position of power to promote this opposition and influence the objectivity of the academic work. This interconnection raises some concerns, especially with reference to scholars who studied the Orient with the scholastic will to know and understand rather than to dominate. While doubt and suspicion are essential for rigorous critique, it is not a compelling argument to assume that the Orient is simply above critique and that every Orientalist is biased and catering to the political interests of his country or the general spirit of his own discipline.

Apart from this extrapolation, it is crucial to emphasize that Orientalism is not an attack on European critics and contemporary scholars in the fields of Arab and Islamic Studies, however ramified or interlinked those fields are. Orientalism does not mean the Orient was misunderstood or transformed into an 'Arabian Night' in Western imagination, or that the Orient has no life outside Europeanized fantasy-narratives of Scheherazade. What Orientalism critiques is the pernicious apathy of Western intellectuals to the real Orient 'out there,' while they happily immerse themselves in a myriad of ideas and images that do not necessarily exist, images that they inherited, imbibed, and reproduced in flagrant distortions of local realities both inside and outside academia. For all those reasons, Said has been instrumental in unmasking the ignorance, prejudice, and sheer pervasiveness of the ideological formation called 'Orientalism.' If anything, Said's outlook on Islam in the West saved Islamic studies from the hidden 'interests' of 'scientific analysis' and laid the foundation for future studies guarding the 'Orient' from falling prey once again to neo-imperialism in its contemporary guise as 'globalization,' which is a term, as I explain in the Epilogue, oriented to serve urban academic elitism and is irreparably dematerializing and unhistorical in its approach to the so-called 'globe' or 'cosmos.'

In addition to the Orientalism thesis, scholarship of Islam will continue to benefit more from considering the overwhelming demographic development in the Arab-Muslim world of the postcolonial era, the constant emigration of many Muslims from the Arab world to Europe, North America, Australia and South Africa as well as to parts of South America, not to mention other European countries with large Muslim populations like France, Belgium, Germany, and Spain. This enormous emigration of Arabs and Muslims to 'First- and Second-World' countries, which I address in the conclusion of this study, is a crucial component of Islamic Studies now.[57] Over the last three decades, there have been writings that painted Islam's history as that of a backward civilization since the time of Muḥammad; there have also been writings about the writings that do so. Beginning in the last century, such biased scholarship has occurred continuously in the work of writers such as Renan, Massignon, and Lewis, thus engendering critique from respondents like Amin, Said, Arkoun, and many others. Orientalist allegations have typically addressed the stagnation and immobility in Islam, with the implication that the religion includes sufficient tenets to limit, resist, and eventually undermine any sort of humanistic developments, politically, democratically, and scientifically. Orientalist claims towards the end of twentieth century have involved theses regarding Islam's resistance to modernity and freedom, although some have also notoriously impugned aspects of Islamic culture as already anticipating if not laying the way for September 11. In fact, Islamic fundamentalism, and all its various offshoots, has been the most widely studied phenomenon in Western Europe and America since the era of decolonization and the rise of the Third World.[58] Moreover, Orientalist ideology across the divide between World War II and the emergence of national governments in the Arab-Muslim world effectively served polemical purposes in the context of cultural differentiation. That's why it is germane to this study to interrogate the relationship between the writing of fiction and the writing of history and to examine the level of autonomy from political influence in both discourses. Academia is allegedly free from the pressure of politics, although there is always the choice "to become the *Geheimrat*," to echo Hardt and Negri, and subordinate knowledge to political gains.

1

FACT OR FICTION?

How the Writing of History Became a Discourse of Conquest

> It is not because they don't know [*faute de savoir*] that Europeans do not read their history as a history of responsibility.
>
> Jacques Derrida, "Secrets of European Responsibility," *The Gift of Death,* 1995

In recent years a range of disciplines has been concerned with the question of the exclusion and the representation of Islam as the other of the West. My discussion of the foundations of intellectual thought in Europe (self versus other, Christendom versus Islam) reflects the way in which today's global politics maintains such a palpable polarization between Muslims and the rest of the world. For a better understanding of the historical specificity of anti-Islamic rhetoric in the West, we need to acknowledge that many forms of Western thought – colonial, scientific, revolutionary, secularist – have also participated in forming this antipathy.

Without a proper understanding of such forms of thought, we are at risk of losing the sense of how much these "ideas" of modernity both formed and continue to inform the present. "*Il y a de l'abîme*,"[1] says Jacques Derrida, an "abyss" located in the very nature of history and resisting any attempt towards confirmation, totalization, and naturalization.[2] This very abyss is what makes history fundamentally un-representational and fundamentally non-narrative. If European modernity misunderstood history, according to Derrida, it is not because modernity "emplotted" history, but because even if history must be admitted, history can never be acknowledged and remains a problem that cannot be resolved. If there has been such a crisis, then this very crisis will engender a practical need that can only be satisfied by rethinking the basic conceptual elements of modernity and its relation to history, or history and its relation to modernity both in Europe and outside if it. For all these reasons, what must be registered 'historically' is the fact that the confining of modernity exclusively to a Western tradition did exist and still exists now. If recent and contemporary anti-Enlightenment theories like "the death of the subject" (Roland Barthes) or "the death of man" (Michel Foucault) have any value to this particular moment in intellectual history, it is that they signal the end of a specific conceptualization of history with its transcendental individualism, inherent subjectivity, and telos-oriented categorical imperatives. One could suggest that recent revisionist theories of historical thinking, especially in the case of France, may not be so much a reaction to a rigid structuralism as they are a response to external factors like Islam, the Third World and the war with Algeria. In fact, many of these theories developed in an atmosphere conscious of the relationship of 'self' to 'other.' These theories provide the hope that (European) reason is still alive, that after reason there still comes a changed reason.

What conclusions does all of this have for the place of Islam in modern European thought? If modernity, as Timothy Mitchell shrewdly puts it, "is not so much a stage of history but rather its staging," then modernity is not just "a world particularly vulnerable to a certain kind of disruption or displacement."[3] In fact it is not even a "world" at all, but rather a condition that the West has carefully employed to serve its own purposes. One is also left with the impression that if history includes an inevitable fictivity that makes it an unreliable linguistic artifact in the vicious circle of knowledge and power, one's understanding of history has to change; the travelogue which was usually regarded as an eyewitness historical document runs the risk of being a suspicious genre or a kind of writing which works *as if* one had been there.[4] Ethnography too is in danger of becoming historical writing that operates in the same way, *as if* one had been there, but for a longer time (Lévi-Strauss); and finally universal history is in jeopardy of being exposed as ambitious writing produced *as if* one had not just been there, but everywhere, anonymously and omnisciently (Foucault, Ibn Khaldūn). This proto-scientific analogical notion of history is what constitutes the domain of positivism. This ascribed scientificity to the discourse of history is crucial to hold on to as it would play a significant role in legitimating European colonialism and the consequent denigration of Islam as "Other."

I will frequently refer to these reconstructions of history in what follows, but I am not interested in critiquing or theorizing positivism. There are several studies that have already done so.[5] What I particularly seek to investigate are not only the formative premises of historical thinking and their development from Plato's mimesis to Foucault's *énoncé*, but also the practical consequences of their uses and abuses in order to examine some of the ways history was constructed to channel European political orientations in the nineteenth and twentieth centuries. In the latter part of this chapter, I discuss some of the major twentieth-century works that drew attention to the consequences of modernity in reconstructing history.

Why modernity? Because only in modernity – it is argued, though this is still a highly debatable topic – has history become largely subversive of other discourses and spheres of knowledge. On this basis, and on the basis of other offshoots of modernity like literary modernism, one could best reinvestigate the modalities governing the production of the historical. As its very name indicates, modernity points to a break, in fact, a breach of a given tradition from within. This break marks history and 'fiction' as two questionable fields sharing the limits of recuperating what we could call "the absent referent." Neither of them can come into being without this "absence," and that is how they should be studied. From this perspective, fiction and history have always been fields of risk. Both are constituted by the attempt to cancel themselves before what they represent.

In order to understand the development of this duality and its connection to intellectual history – as it passes by modernity and intersects with colonial historiography – it is important to point to some of the major currents of philosophical reflections on intellectual history up to the twentieth century. The goal is not to reiterate a number of judgments on modernity, but to position it in light of another complex discourse, namely the Islamic tradition. My argument is that in order to reach any tentative assessment of modernity, one must extend the limits of the modern and test its defining tenets on other grounds. I aim to delineate a set of theses characterizing various modern philosophies of history in order to gain a wider perspective on the intellectual framework of modernity and its influence not just on the dynamics of exchange between literature and history but on the construction of the divide between 'East' and 'West'.

History and Fiction, *Les Fausses Amies*

History, as my senior high school teacher in Egypt used to say, does two things. It tells us about the past, not only its major events, but also ideas, images, ways of living and seeing things; and it introduces us to a particular way of thinking, which makes us aware of the inconsistencies, ambiguities, gaps, and prejudices inherent in any given historical source. Fiction, on the other hand, as my English professor, a Thomas Arnold specialist, told us repeatedly, is a "criticism of life," a way of writing that does not merely seek to record what was once present. Although fiction too includes its own history, it still extends beyond the limitations of a fixed reality and invests in the inventive "elastic powers" of the imagination. That is, if the field of history deals with events that are said to have happened in a particular time and place, the literary field is concerned not only with this kind of event, but also with events that never happened or that might take place.

However, the relationship between history and fiction cannot be understood without recognizing the similarities between the two. What is interesting about both is not so much the nature of the happening or non-happening of given events, but the extent to which fiction and history intersect and overlap with each other in the representation of those events. Without dwelling too much on the techniques and narrative structures used in their composition, one might propose that history and fiction share a representation of an absence. If history is a representation of an afterness (in the sense that it can only be written after things have happened), fiction is a capturing of a fleeting present, or an attempt to do so, invoked not *necessarily* by external happenings as by internal desire to reflect, represent, express, or be inspired by such happenings – by external events immediate or otherwise, or by its own happening. Both are enabled by an absent referent that can never be recuperated. Ironically enough, they are both representations of an absence and are also the absence of representation, since their representations are dictated by a given present, a present that implies a historically inflicted model that functions in the absence of the historical and with the fictive forms they seek to modulate. The two discourses "wish to provide a verbal image of reality."[6] But in their "wish" also lies their limitation. The two discourses *cannot but* provide a verbal image of reality.

Both history and fiction imply, and sometimes even invoke, a notion of memory and a notion of *inheritance* in the broad sense of the word, that is, a cultural knowledge of the past. Since inheritance cannot be anything other than history, fiction too is an inheritance, a kind of history that tends to find its roots in a remote past, as happens with the history of English literature, at least in Allen Tate's version of it, which claims to have its legacy back in *Beowulf,* and with Arabic literary tradition which traces its *adab* (literature) back to pre-Islamic poetry. History, many critics have argued, is fictive, or at least dwells on fictional language and techniques that make it "emplot" its events, tropologize its style, and concoct its narrative to the extent that an act of writing would become no less an affirmation of history than it is an affirmation of literature. In fiction and in history, there is a perpetual urge to write narratives that are not simply compensatory, but experimental and self-questioning. But some narratives, whether fictional or purportedly 'fact-based' versions of the past, can be related to questions of redemption; that is, they attempt to give the past its due right by representing it from an alternative angle that is no less legitimate than the mainstream version(s). With this overlap of history and fiction, it is hard to argue which of the two can claim more access to the real than the other.

Raymond Williams confronts this interweaving of literature and history on more than one occasion. In *Marxism and Literature*, he argues that the concept of literature as we understand it now "did not emerge earlier than the eighteenth century."[7] Williams' statement suggests that what we call literature is a recent invention of modernity. In *Keywords,* he makes the point that although history and fiction were seen to assume different functions, "the relations between *literature* (poetry, *fiction*, *imaginative* writing) and *real* or actual experience"[8] became much more complex during the nineteenth century. Later theories corroborate Williams's statement by arguing that in their exposition, historical accounts depend on coherent narratives drawn out of raw materials through "emplotment," which Hayden White defines as "the encodation of facts continued in the chronicle as components of specific kinds of plot-structure."[9] Emplotment is a use of the same techniques employed in creative writing and films. For example, the way any account of World War II is emplotted depends on the point of view. Some see the atomic bomb dropped on Hiroshima as an unrepresentable tragedy in human history, as in Resnais' *Hiroshima mon Amour*. Others see it as a post-Pearl Harbor revenge tragedy, as Spielberg does in *The Empire of the Sun*.

It is not unusual, given the remarkable affinities between history and fiction discussed above, for many contemporary critics to question the nature of the distinction between the two discourses. White, for example, argues that historical narratives are nothing but verbal fictions, the contents of which are as much invented as found, and the forms of which have more in common with literature than they have with the sciences.[10] Lévi-Strauss argues that "in a system of this type [i.e., that of history writing] alleged historical continuity is secured only by dint of fraudulent outlines."[11] The implication is that if the form that the historian imposes on his empirical data is an artifice, then history writing and fiction writing are not different from one another in the sense that they are both products of human imagination, though there is also another argument asserting the differences from the standpoint of the structure of narrativization. But this is not new or surprising. Before the twentieth century, a long tradition viewed history as a branch of fiction, or as an art form. Long before even Ibn Khaldūn, the first Arab-Islamic theoretician of history, claimed history to be *fann* (art), Herodotus made it clear that his *Histories* are written to be performed. In the early modern times, historians were distinguished from other scholars and antiquarians mainly because they were "artists."[12] From ancient times the questions of historical method have often been ones of narrative style and presentation. But since the relationship between language and its referent has been the preoccupation of twentieth-century literary theory, many scholars have resurrected the contention that history writing has always been a futile literary attempt to en-frame the real and that fiction, which some attempt to glorify over 'mere' imitation, impersonation, representation, secondarity – in short, mimesis – still carries germs of historical reality.

In the end, fiction and history are both narratives, by which I mean they follow a specific logic of sequentiality in relationship to a given time and event. Since narrative is inherently chronological, it could be argued that narrative contains only one concept of time. This concept is the time of the event that took place. When the event is represented in historical narrative, and when the narrative embodies this 'absent referent,' the act of historiography, that is the writing of the event, makes of the event a re-enactment in the present, and therefore never actually the past 'event.' This re-enactment necessarily forces the imagination to step in. The combination of both history and imagination owing to the absence of the referent results in narrative fiction.[13] This is not to say that historical narratives are 'mere' fiction, but at the very least they include both the potentialities of what actually happened and what did not. This is the realm of fictional narrative of history. If it were at all possible to dispense with the fictional in representing the factual, then fiction, which does not have the obligations of documentation and which functions solely from the domain of what might have been, would also comprise "the potentialities of the real 'past' and the unreal possibilities of pure fiction."[14]

If literary theory has been recently preoccupied with the issue of the historical, and to be precise, with the relationship between theory, literary periods, and history, it is because modernity – and its late nineteenth- to early twentieth-century offshoots of literary and other modernisms – has had a tremendous impact on reshaping the contours of this relationship. One among the vigorous debates has concerned the relationship between modernity and the discourse of intellectual history. But in order to better understand the role of modernity in this relationship, it is worthwhile to examine the dynamics of separation and exchange between fiction and history as they emerged in Greek philosophy. To stage this connection, one needs to begin with Aristotle's famous distinction between history and poetry as outlined in his *Poetics.*

Confused Alternatives, or, the War that Plato Started

To claim that the writing of fiction is different from the writing of history is to *admit* that both fields must have been treated as if they were the same. Aristotle sees poetry as an art created by an author who thinks in terms of "what might happen." In history, he argues, an event is written when it is accepted by the community to have actually taken place. He suggests that a historian does not create events, but reports them, often textually, by mentioning the event and its date. In Aristotle's vision of history, there is no room for creation, authorship, or even plagiarism. Aristotle's poet, however, is more involved in the task of rearranging or inventing historical facts to present what in terms of philosophical value could be much more inherently useful. Aristotle's theory of poetry makes it clear that the function of the poet is to relate not things as they are, but things as they may or should have been, that is, things as they are possible in accordance with the laws of probability and necessity. Poetry is more philosophical and more serious than history since it tends to speak of universals, whereas history speaks of particulars.[15] If the relationship between a language (or the sign) and its referent is based on the assumption that it begins in the real and seeks to identify this real with the linguistic sign, then any representation of the past, Aristotle's theory seems to suggest, must be tied to the particularity of the events, an idea whose implications send us back to the unavoidable question of mimesis.[16] Plato's mimesis creates a duality. First, there is the 'real,' the object itself incarnate, as an apparent phenomenon; then there is the imitation of this 'real,' the translation, transportation, representation, impersonation, imitation of it in another medium (painting, writing, and – in the modern age – lithography, photography, audio-visual media). This is the moment of creating a hierarchy between 'real' and 'real-like.' Since what is imitated is the real, what is imitating always ends up being inferior to the real in terms of its realness. But since this 'real' can never be recuperated, the challenge of fiction is to "invent" rather than subserviently follow a superior "real." Aristotle sees fiction as nothing but mimetic; still he regards the mimetic status of the non-historical to be more valuable than that of the historical.

In the wake of poststructuralism, Aristotle's claim has been seen as dealing with the difference between the integrity and intentionality of two modes of writing: one that founds an order of representation, and one that escapes this order. The schism between what in a narrow sense is the transcendental imaginative realm (Aristotle's poet) and the empirical domain of representation (Aristotle's historian) is connected to the divide between the so-called 'fictional' and 'factual.' In Aristotle, while both history and poetry are perceived through texts, neither of them could completely replace the other in a radical sense. If fiction enjoys more 'seriousness' and more philosophical freedom due to its investment in the realm of probability and imagination, then fiction, according to Aristotle, serves the truth better than history does. One could still argue that Aristotle's view on history innocently assumes that the task of the historian is to use language restrictedly to imitate or represent particular events as they have occurred. In contemporary critical thinking, historical writing has become far more problematic than Aristotle portrayed it.

Intellectual History and Positivism: The Modern Shift

In the twentieth century, understandings of Aristotle's ideas have been made more complex, especially with the emergence of the system of signification in structuralist and poststructuralist theories and their explications of the intricate relationship between language and its referents.[17] What Aristotle defines as "relat[ing] things that have happened" is always refracted through the mind of the historian, among many other things, including the particular notion of the 'mind' which is dominant in specific historical periods.

Other factors, such as personal inclinations, religious affiliation, experience, conviction, political interests, and the ideology of the time are significant determinants of those so-called 'particulars.' The 'facts' of history do not and cannot exist in pure forms. There are always new angles of vision that are inevitably destined to appear as time and the historian within it move by. In every way, the historian is part of the history he/she writes, and it is this history that inevitably constructs or refracts this representation.

In other words, there is no escape from the epistemological conditions that both govern and dictate the historian's intellectual inclinations and angles of vision over the past. At this point, it does not really matter whether the period treated by the historian is remote or close to his/her own time. Historical proximity and eye-witness accounts might serve to clarify vision in some ways, but they obfuscate it in other ways. Even as facts and documents are the substance of any historian, they do not themselves constitute history. This leaves us with the grim fact that the history we read, though based on archival documents and pamphlets, is always already ordered according to presuppositions. After Aristotle's *Poetics*, there was a major gap, at least in the West, in philosophical reflections on history. This gap closed when the French Revolution made it possible to conceive that a radical break from the past could happen. Although the West's reflection on history began well before the French Revolution, it was only during the Enlightenment that history began to assume a major role in the discourse of Western philosophy.

Since the Enlightenment, the meaning of 'history' has expanded and assumed a more objective and positivistic relationship with the past, thus divorcing itself from the subjectivity and fictionality associated with narrative.[18] New meanings will later serve to identify the articulation of the experience of history as indicated by a new relation – modernity – between the space of experiencing a historical event and the horizon of figuring/troping such an event. In light of a new political consciousness, many philosophers of the Enlightenment wondered whether reason should have an ethical and social responsibility that somehow forms and informs our understanding of history. And so, by the nineteenth century, it became customary among historians to identify truth with fact and to regard fiction as the opposite of truth, hence as a hindrance to the understanding of reality rather than as a way of apprehending it. Prior to this shift – which coincided with the rise of the Enlightenment – historiography was still considered a literary art, not only in the West, but also in the Arab-Muslim world.

Tārīkh and the Many Faces of History

It is useful here to recall some of the major changes that affected the definition of the word 'history.' The earliest meaning of 'history,' as Raymond Williams recalls in *Keywords*, was a narrative account of events, one that signified the account of both the imagined and the actual (factual) events.[19] In Greek, the word 'history' derives from *histos*, which means 'weaving.' In Arabic, the word *tārīkh* (history) has the double denotation of a sequence of events taking place and the writing down of those events.[20] In German and in French, the words *historie* (*Geschichte*) and *histoire* also give the double meaning of a sequence of events taking place and the relating of those events. In English, the word 'history' retains the twofold sense of 'actual history' and 'told history.' The Arabic word *tārīkh*, however, signifies precisely the relationship between a series of events and a series of narratives.

The word 'history' appears to have a somewhat stable definition shared by a number of languages both ancient and modern. However, 'history' is still a tricky term in its modern use, oscillating between sociohistorical processes, narrative accounts, and the so-called "major events" themselves. In using the word 'history,' one implicitly tends to acknowledge an overlap between a sociohistorical process (a given historical period), the knowledge of this process (narrative), and the inevitable reduction of this process to certain happenings (eclectic events within the period). This overlap is the result of various connotations of the "historical," which suggests that the (linguistically defined) boundaries in historical discourse are often quite fluid. The above definitions suggest that the word 'history' already lends itself to layers of irreducible semantic ambiguities, even before one starts to investigate the problematic distinction between an event that took place and its various representations – whether oral as in history telling, textual as in literary or historical narratives, or later visual as in photographic and cinematic narratives. But since not all words are concepts, as Kant would have it, it is not surprising that between the use of history as a word and the reference to history as a concept, many layers of theory have accumulated throughout the ages, and the inherent ambiguity of 'history' has caught the attention of many thinkers from Ibn Khaldūn to Hayden White. Some currents in these layers of thought, which still stand out today, can be traced back to European modernity

Broadly speaking, there are two historical arguments that can be made about the concept of modernity: either the term modernity is applicable to the whole world regardless of cultural specificities, or, alternatively, it can be applied only to Western Europe. For some, a characteristic feature of modernity has been its universality. For example, the German philosopher Emmanuel Kant (1724–1804) defines the Enlightenment as "man's emergence from his self-incurred immaturity" and describes immaturity as "the inability to use one's own understanding without the guidance of another."[21] The two principles that mark Kant's definition, universality and independence, open modernity to the entire world. By virtue of this definition, modernity is neither a geopolitical monopoly nor an inheritance passed down from one generation to the next. Nor, again, is modernity a permit granting so-called "enlightened nations" the right to have dominion over less- or non-enlightened ones under the pretext of delivering them from their ignorance.

If on the one hand we agree that universality and independence are the hallmarks of modernity, these values necessarily make modernity a relational term unconfined to a specific period or a specific place. The relationality of modernity tells us that even though it usually marks a break with the past, there can be many offshoots of modernity, each interacting with it from different perspectives and exposures, integrating it or eschewing it according to the relics of its own past and the dictates of its present. Inaugurated by the Enlightenment, modernity is not a fixed set of beliefs. "If it is asked whether we at present live in an *enlightened* age," argues Kant, "the answer is: No, but we do live in an age of *enlightenment*."[22]

But if, on the other hand, modernity were perceived as a developmental process, one that the Frankfurt School critic Jürgen Habermas problematically refers to as an "unfinished project," and if it were necessarily progressive and teleological, then its definition would *ipso facto* be impossible. In fact, many of the principles attributed to modernity via the Western tradition cannot capture the concept. Rather, they impose a set of principles that can only weigh it down and end up creating the bias they try to avoid. If modernity as a broad term figures the critical, temporal, and performative paradigm that makes certain works appear to have a form and a content representative of it, the present work seeks not just to provide an exegesis of a number of texts defined by a anti-colonial nationalist modernity, but also to see in what ways a comparison of these texts can confirm, redefine, or even further problematize our understanding of modernity.

The assumption here is that modernity will never be fully interrogated without including the non-modern and without incorporating other fields of cultural production and seeing how in our case the Arab-Muslim world, while forged by colonial influence, still considers itself to be a partaker in modernity, especially at its earlier historical stages. Paul Gilroy has demonstrated that different representations of popular cultures as well as literary and philosophical expressions coming out of African diasporas – whether in the African continent, in the Americas, or in Europe – testify to intricate engagements with 'Western' cultures. Those engagements neither deny the experience of Western modernity nor attempt to carve an independent or 'authentic' alternative path; put another way, there is the assumption of a *linear* progression to modernity.

Gilroy argues that the atrocities committed in the name of the modern, such as slavery, colonialism, and racism, gave those who lived through them access to modernity that clearly brought some nations economic advancement, political inclusiveness, and social acceptance. While Gilroy does not stress enough the fact that racism is a very broad term common to *all epochs and cultures,* he is right in making the argument that the 'black Atlantic' has become a critical transformative site of modernity.[23] If modernity then is acknowledged as an extraordinary break with extraordinary issues, and if human thought in general has been affected by this break, then this extraordinary quality invites us to question the provinciality and the myopic tendencies that equate the geographical with the geophilosophical and that centralize both in the geopolitical. The need to transcend these 'imaginary' contours of European modernity calls for another horizon outside Europe from which the inside of its modernity can be assessed.

A number of recent writers have come up with the notion of 'alternative modernities.'[24] These approaches foreground local and regional dynamics whose influence shapes the specific trajectories of their respective modernities. By not centering on that which is internal to the West, these ways of thinking provide new visions that acknowledge the differing contexts of non-European cultures. Some even entertain different forms of these modernities, ones that co-exist untenably with European modernity while seeking alternative historical paths that are remarkably, if not completely, independent of the West. This equivalence theory, however, harms rather than benefits our understanding of modernity. Instead of defining modernity by constructing notions of 'other' independent modernities, we should speak neither in favor of a unique modernity whose uniformity subsumes all other histories according to its own condition, nor of nationalistically-driven pluralisms that undercut the definition of the modern and risk misunderstanding the idea itself. It is therefore useful to break away from local monolithic definitions of modernity and open the term to its wider trans-European implications. This is an approach that has opened new avenues in the humanities since Edward Said's *Orientalism*. This approach also opens history, the history of Islam and the West, which cannot be studied *separately*.

The central question Said raises systematically throughout *Orientalism* is this: how is reliable knowledge possible? The phrase 'theory of knowledge' and its synonym 'epistemology' were coined in the nineteenth century, but the retrospective subject from whose point of view knowledge is produced is the European subject in general. Using this logic against itself, that is, as a theoretical reason that can dialectically ascertain not only its own validity but its limits, Said manages to subject the Western apparatus of knowledge production to a radical investigation of its own formative methodological principles. But before Said, and to be more precise, before Foucault, the critique of knowledge was still conceived in reference to a system of cognitive faculties that included practical reason and reflective judgment, especially in the writing of history.[25]

European Modernity and the Relocation of Islam in History

When Cairo was conquered by the army of 'Amr ibn al-'Āṣ during the caliphate of 'Umar ibn al-Khaṭṭāb in 641 CE, the Arab-Muslim soldiers, who thought of themselves as "not merely an army of occupation," but also "representatives of God's good orders among mankind,"[26] did not tear down the Sphinx or the pyramids, nor any of the other Pharaonic artifacts scattered around the Nile Valley. Reasons for this vary. Some believe that most of the Egyptian *'aṣnām'* (statues and artifacts), so to speak, were buried under the sand and invisible to the Arab-Muslim army which was too busy fighting the Romans to seek them out and destroy them. Others think that early Egyptian Muslims did in fact try to destroy the Sphinx and the pyramids, but because they were built over generations of structured hard work, they were just too colossal to yield to primitive equipment.[27] A third group believes that since the ruins of ancient Egypt are part of its history, Muslims under 'Umar saw no harm in leaving them alone. Whatever the reason, the monuments are still standing, although given the case of the Taliban's unforgivable destruction of Buddhist statues a few years ago, it is not at all far-fetched to suggest that some thick-headed fanatic Muslims are still out there boycotting the pyramids or even planning to blow them up some day.

Two centuries after *fatḥ miṣr*, as Arab Muslims call it (literally 'the opening of Egypt,' a euphemism used to describe the Muslim conquest as a liberating event), most Egyptians converted to Islam.[28] Nowadays, many Muslim Egyptians look back with contempt at the idolatrous practices of their *jāhilī* (pre-Islamic) ancestors. But the Egyptian Ministry of Tourism thinks otherwise. Not only are those 'idolatrous stones' a major source of national income for Egypt, but the Egyptian government insists that all the antiquities ever taken outside Egypt's borders are hers. Although the latter may seem contradictory to the aforementioned contempt of idolatrous practices, one does not need to approve of Lord Cromer's imperial lootings of Egyptian antiquity to think that there is something to be said about giving people the opportunity to see the art of one of the world's great civilizations displayed in its own national museums. But herein lies the paradox of modernity: Egypt, a country forced by Islam to disown its ancient heritage, is now the main agent for its promotion and preservation.

The incongruity between Islam and the dictates of modernity has been a major topic in scholarship over the last few decades. In his book *Islamic Liberalism*, Leonard Binder argues that since the Enlightenment the Islamic world has been faced with the burden of modernity, a burden that can only be alleviated through mutual dialogue. Binder maintains that since the European Enlightenment, and regardless of the increasing number of what he calls "responsive Muslims" who willingly/eagerly adopt the Enlightenment's advancements, there remain a significant number of Muslims who steadfastly argue that it is possible to progress without paying such a heavy cultural price."[29] According to Binder, both Islamism and liberalism have a common future goal: to promote civil society and democracy.

There is some truth to this argument. In more than one instance, Albert Hourani's *Islam in the Liberal Age* points to the numerous phases Islam underwent to modernize its thought in the age of liberalism.[30] In fact, one of the *fin de siècle* intellectual attempts at *Iṣlāḥ* (reformation) in the Arab world, which took place in Egypt as a response to the tension between colonial supremacy and Islamic radicalism and extended to the 1940s, called precisely for liberalism as a mediatory solution for the country's hitherto undecided political future. It is interesting that revisionist Muslim scholars who make sensible non-orthodox arguments about Islam are known among Egyptians as 'enlightened.' Although most of those scholars had different intellectual and political affiliations, they all agreed that repositioning Islam and *al-Sharq* (the East) in relationship to Western modernity was inevitable if the Arab world were to survive and compete in a changing world order. One can distinguish two groups: the first consists of figures like 'Abd Allāh al-Nadīm (d. 1896), Imām Muḥammad 'Abduh (1849–1905), Jamāl al-Dīn al-Afghāni (1838–97), and 'Abd al-'Azīz Jāwīsh (1876–1929).[31] The major concern of that first group was to advocate a modern and politically engaged form of Azhari Islam[32] in public life in addition to unconditional love of one's homeland, regardless of religion or race, in defense of national identity against foreign powers.[33] The second group consists mainly of expatriates who received Western education in the West, especially in France. They include Qāsim Amīn (1863–1908), Muḥammad Ḥusayn Haykal (1888–1956), and Tāhā Ḥusayn (1889–1973).

In fact, Ṭāhā Ḥusayn's controversial work *Fī al-Adab al-Jāhilī* [On pre-Islamic poetry] has been a revolutionary work in Islamic reformation and remains influential in the Arab world. Ḥusayn's study called for reconnecting Egypt with its pre-Islamic past and advocated a controlled and entirely cultural role for religion in Egyptian society, one that could still be moderately demonstrable in politics and social life. Although this spirit of liberalism was not a naive mimicry of colonial rule, as Ḥasan al-Banna would have it, but a reaction to a growing fundamentalism aiming at a religious totalization of Egypt, the tension between Islam and modernity in Egypt has remained unresolved. In the spirit of intellectual history, how do we then assess the gravity of this tension between Islam and the West? Here I call to mind two phenomena. The first is the rapid 'Westernization' of everything Arab-Islamic, especially in advanced technology and consumer markets. This onslaught has not been easily welcomed or accepted by traditionalist Arab-Muslim intellectuals, who still believe that a Muslim renaissance is yet to take place and change the hierarchies of this new world order.

A well-known Egyptian proponent of this wishful 'renaissance' is the philosopher-academic Ḥasan Ḥanafī who, in an effort to turn the page of history against Western modernity and its so-called eroding effects on Muslim communities, points to the urgent need of a new science: Occidentalism. Ḥanafī calls upon the Arab-Muslim world to 'Occidentalize' the West in the same manner the West Orientalized the Arab-Muslim world. He goes on to define Occidentalism as an epistemological study of the West by the Arab-Muslim world. In his over-600-page *Introduction to Occidentalism*,

Ḥanafī begins by cautioning his readers that his project is not to be misunderstood as the product of a closed-off "traditionalist Salafī"[34] mentality, since his intention, as he clarifies, is not to reject or eschew the West, but to awaken a sense of creativity and leadership in the "Orient[al] self" and shake it out of its slumber and passive subordination to the "Western other." "It is high time," Ḥanafī maintains, "the West became the object of study rather than the source of knowledge. This is what Occidentalism is all about."[35] In other words, Ḥanafī is repeating the Huntington mistake of civilizational wars by advocating a hierarchical and exclusivist form of thought.

The second phenomenon is the so-called 'revelation' versus 'reason' problematic, which I will illustrate through an analogy. Think of a man spending all his life trying to figure out the way the human mind works, how it perceives and understands the real world, how it causes things to happen, and how it passes judgment and tells the difference between the beautiful, the nauseating, and the sublime. Now compare this man to another pondering a text and trying to make the phenomenal world fit into the sacred word of God, or one involved in the theological task of determining whether or not the blood of a flea, if it touches a man's body, would invalidate his ablution. To put it in even more concrete terms, think of a man contemplating the pyramids, without having seen them, reflecting on the magnificence of those man-made structures, and wondering how they put phenomenality itself into question. Think of this man at pains trying to put the human mind's ability to apprehend and comprehend reality, which are two different mental processes, to the test of magnitude and measurability because of the Egyptian pyramids, only to conclude that they must be "sublime" and must be regarded with awe and admiration. Now compare him to another man beating his brain to find the best way to destroy those pyramids and level them with the earth because somehow they count as *awthān* (pagan relics) and offend the sensibilities of his faith.

The first man is Kant, the father of German idealism, who reached far beyond the scriptures of his eighteenth-century religiosity and looked into the human tradition at large in his search for a concept of God. Kant has the following to say about the pyramids in his *Critique of Judgment*:

> Hence can be explained what Savary remarks, in his account of Egypt, viz. that we must keep from going very near the Pyramids just as much as we keep from going too far from them. For if we are too

> far away, the parts to be apprehended (the stones lying one over the other) are only obscurely represented, and the representation of them produces no effect upon the aesthetical judgment of the subject. But if we very near, the eye requires some time to complete the apprehension of the tiers from the bottom up to the apex, and then the first tiers are always partly forgotten before the imagination has taken in the last, and so the comprehension of them is never complete.[36]

So much for phenomenology if Kant bases his critique of judgment on someone else's account of the pyramids, notably M. Savary's *Lettres sur l'Egypte*, but I will discuss this proxy idealism at length in a later chapter. The second kind of man in this comparison is no less than al-Khalīfa al-Ma'mūn himself, the champion of the Islamic scientific renaissance of the ninth century. These two contradictory variations on the theme of the Egyptian pyramids are sure to complicate the relationship between Islam and modernity, but they should in no way dissuade us from a more intense and nuanced analysis of the 'differences' between the Arab-Muslim world and 'enlightened' Western Europe.

One should not hastily blame al-Ma'mūn or praise Kant: both acted according to their own convictions not only in two cultures, but also in two completely different epochs. Al-Ma'mūn behaved according to the imperial dictates of a ninth-century caliph of *dār al-Islām* (the abode of Islam), followed 'revelation' meticulously, and emulated Prophet Muḥammad's anti-statue *sunna*; and Kant acted on eighteenth-century Western European grounds of aesthetic judgment and the Age of Reason. The continuing challenge is to reconcile these views or mediate between them. A productive focus on the relationship between Islam and the West does not lie in giving up before seemingly insurmountable oppositions, but in de-icing frozen historicities, in investigating the space between cultural *épistémès*, and in interrogating the subtleties of convictional and ideological differences.

Two Defining Moments in Intellectual History

In broad terms, one can distinguish two specific phases or modes that have had a conspicuous impact on the philosophy of history in the West. The first appears with the Renaissance and the second with the Enlightenment. Foucault described the Renaissance as the period that witnessed the birth of the *épistémè* of resemblance, which presumes a non-problematic relationship between the sign and its referent, an epoch that treated language as a simple transparent system able to name things.[37] Though European in essence, this early mode of modernity, which took place roughly between the fourteenth and sixteenth centuries, developed mainly from Europe's relationship with the outside world as it coincided with the European discovery of the Americas and with the beginning of European dominance over the rest of the world.[38] Trans-geographically, the Renaissance also signals the birth of a new theory of history established by the Arab historian Ibn Khaldūn. Ibn Khaldūn's work, which I address in more detail in the next chapter, later served to essentialize the colonial geographics of Europe and to legitimate as well as territorialize what is now known as 'Eurocentrism.' If the Renaissance marked a significant break in human history, "it is precisely because, from that time on," as Samir Amin argues forcefully, "Europeans become conscious of the idea that the conquest of the world by their civilization is henceforth a possible objective… . From this moment on, and not before, Eurocentrism crystallizes."[39] This early modernity had the same tenets as the one that followed it two centuries later, although with different consequences. It too destroyed its relationship with the past, celebrated the present, regarded its knowledge as the triumph of proto-scientific observation, and admired its own "newness." In short, it pushed man and the human mind to the center of history.

Before the Renaissance's division of the world into East and West, the Middle Ages held a view of history rooted in theology, whether in the form of a 'circularity' as in Ibn Khaldūn or of history as salvation as in St. Augustine.[40] The Renaissance, often labeled as a turn to secularism, carefully moved away from this religious view of history by developing a humanistic curiosity for everything 'new.' While 'newness' was not equally appreciated in all fields of knowledge, it still remained the supreme value of modernity. A spirit of exploration set the groundwork for the idea that human thought progresses from one enlightenment to another. A fuller development of this trend soon dominated the discourse of human sciences in general, and the discourse of history in particular, marking the emergence of the second mode of modernity to crystallize in the Enlightenment. If the Renaissance, or "the ideology of adventure,"[41] as Michael Nerlich calls it, was able to overcome the opposition between religious circularity and scientific linearity, the Enlightenment carries the concept of history to new dimensions. Such dimensions include the birth of the idea that history should not be exclusively associated with the past or linked to the present and the future, but more importantly, the idea that history is above all a structure of legitimation, one that projects the future as an authentic fulfillment of a foundational past. This shift was made possible by the emergence of the assumption of continuity in positivistic thinking which mainly, but not exclusively, resulted from the dominant scientific spirit of the age.

As a field of experiments and objective verification, science relies on objectivity in emphasizing the relationship between the referent (in this case, history) and the signifier (language).[42] This is the time when history, as a discourse, as a discipline, and as a practice, begins to separate itself from the arts to claim a more 'objective' access to the so-called 'truth.' In the second half of the nineteenth century, for instance, utilitarian theories of history followed the path of Auguste Comte's notion of positivism. Driven by the new spirit of mechanism, 'objectivity' dictated the philosophy of history and channeled its trajectory, which not long before was still considered closer to literature than to science. Accordingly, a profession was born, and new so-called 'professional' historians assumed that the past was a tangible reality independent of their own consciousness. This hypothesis of a 'real' recuperative writing made their task simply the business of reporting their findings from research in primary sources. According to Peter Gay, the shift was mainly a stylistic one imposed by the demands of impartiality: "This pressure toward objectivity," comments Gay, "is realistic because the objects of the historian's inquiry are precisely that, objects, out there in a real and single past."[43] The same principle is confirmed by Perry Anderson as follows:

> The premise of this work is that there is no plumb-line between necessity and contingency in historical explanation ... there is merely that which is known (established by historical research) and that which is not known: the latter may be either the mechanism of single events or laws of motion of whole structures. Both are equally amenable, to adequate knowledge of causality [and to] rational and controllable theory in the domain of history.[44]

Anderson's elucidation of the difference between the 'known' and the 'unknown' results in a massive re-examination of the contours of political history in Europe, which I shall address in more depth in the next chapter. For now, Anderson's argument makes it clear that this assumed and 'practiced' objectivity ignores the problematic connection between the historian's act of writing and the so-called historical pamphlet. If the historian works with pamphlets and documents substantiating his/her writing, then the writing of history must, so it is claimed, be substantially different from that of fiction. This notion has dominated the profession for three centuries. Not only has its false empiricism formed the illusion of separating history from literature, but it has also given rise to new approaches to history based entirely on a deterministic logic of narrative causality. The main limitation of this kind of logic is that it consists mainly in using a posited effect (the present assumed to be the effect of a past that preceded it and (therefore) caused it) as a new cause to determine an unforeseeable effect in the future, and so on. If teleological thinking was indispensable to the Enlightenment mentality, it automatically gave rise to what could be called the sophism of the Enlightenment, that is, the fictitious hypothesis of a continuous historicity conceived through an ill-formed syllogism of a concatenation of causes and effects. Reductive as it is, this fabrication of an end (future) based on an imaginative (or pseudo-scientific) connection between a beginning (a certain point in the past) and a middle (the present) renders the empiricist project of historical narrative more fictional than it ever desires it to be. Collingwood refers to this process as mere fabrication:

> We fabricate periods of history by fastening upon some, to us, peculiarly luminous point and trying to study it as it actually came into being. We find our eyes caught, as it were, by some striking phenomenon (Greek life in the fifth century), or the like, and this becomes a nucleus of a group of historical inquiries, asking how it arose and how it passed away, thus we form the idea of a period, which we call the Hellenic period; and this period will resemble the Byzantine period or the Baroque *in being a period,* that is in having a luminous center preceded and followed by processes whose only interest to us at the moment is that they lead to and from it.[45]

Collingwood's reference to the theory of period-resemblance points to another important aspect of teleological thinking, that is, the expansion of telos to include humanity at large. This logic left remarkable impacts on major intellectual and theoretical movements of the time, passing from Kantian idealism through Hegelian absolutism to Marxian determinism.

Take, for example, Kant's essay "The Idea of Universal History with Cosmopolitan Intent." This text reflects the aspiration of the Enlightenment to a collective human project of reaching a natural teleology of progress through what he refers to as the "hidden plan of nature." Kant's essay propagates a natural telos of historical progress. His 'Idea' is based on the premise that, unbeknownst to particular individuals, humanity as a whole is inevitably moving forward towards a universal future and a cosmopolitan world order. Kant still believes that this presumed fictivity will eventually turn out to be fact rather than fiction. Therefore, "the philosophical attempt to work out a universal history of the world in accord with a plan of nature that aims at a perfect civic union of the human species," Kant continues, "must be regarded as possible and even as helpful to this objective of nature."[46]

In many respects, the writings of Kant stand at the center of this development, and his influential thought leads in different directions, but he is particularly important as a fountainhead of transcendental history and the notion of continuity essential to the idea of European modernity. Kant's philosophy not only expresses the teleological biases of metaphysics, but it also raises the position of the subject, as does Descartes', to the level of transcendence and renders him out of touch with everything else except his own selfhood.

With another act of force, Hegel adds to the development of modernity and historical thinking a new conception of temporality in the form of dialectical teleology that arrives at its end. With Hegel, history is *complete*, and there is no possibility of going beyond it, much less beyond Hegel himself. In *Reason in History*, he alludes to this completion by asserting the unavoidable fact that before a historian undertakes the task of writing history, he must enter/conform to a mode of thinking subordinate to "the data of reality, which guides his historical discourse."[47]

To Hegel, whose relationship to Islam is very problematic as I argue in a later chapter, history could be written from multiple perspectives: as an origin, as a reflection, and as a philosophy. Those methods correspond to one fact: history is *a priori*. Based entirely on anteriority and presuppositions, the writing of history has so far been in constant resistance to the given data.[48] In Hegel's philosophy of history, any of these approaches would necessarily do violence to history by shaping it according to a ready-made structure that precedes it. On more than one occasion, Hegel also emphasizes that history is to be understood as governed by a circular motion.[49]

With Marx, historical thinking reaches a different climax. Insisting on the existence of a model of exploitation and a model of class struggle in every society, Marx invested in the notion of historical determinism in which history becomes a history of class struggle. His theory even offers a view of the historical event as already determined. The historical event, argues Engels, "may be viewed as the product of a power which works as a whole unconsciously and without volition."[50] This continuous and unconsciously functioning power is the power of a material dialectic and of class struggle, a struggle which, according to Marx, will eventually end, leading to the liberation of the proletariat. But it is here that a theory of Marxism is also in danger of falling into Eurocentrism and *unconsciously* becoming complicit with the dominant master-narrative of European modernity, including that of colonialism. Marx sees history as a force driven by human labor and socioeconomic relations. In Marx's eyes, history is nothing but the history of human industry which goes through stages of development until it reaches maturity.

This maturity somehow manages to mark "the end of history." In short, it is the material conditions of any society that determine the trajectory of historical development. In this sense, Marxism's approach to history appears to be 'vulgarly' reductionist as well as totalizing, and Marx himself becomes a thinker whose ideas were in sync with those of other thinkers of his time. As Foucault put it, "Marxism exists in nineteenth century thought like a fish in water: that is, it is unable to breath anywhere else."[51] Foucault's view on Marx is shared by a number of postcolonial theorists. Robert Young argues that "Marxism as a body of knowledge itself remains complicit with, and even extends, the system to which it is opposed... . Marxism's standing Hegel on his head may have reversed his idealism, but it did not change the mode of operation of a conceptual system which remains collusively Eurocentric."[52] Tsenay Serequeberhan observes that Marx celebrates the "globalization of Europe" at the outset of the *Communist Manifesto* and therefore is a fitting cog in the wheel of Eurocentrism along with his precursors Kant and Hegel. "No matter how differently they view the historical globalization of Europe," argues Serequeberhan forcefully, "what matters is that European modernity is the *real* in contrast to the *unreality* of human existence in the non-European world."[53]

What is at stake in such deterministic narratives of history is the very notion of teleology. The positivistic philosophy that enabled the concept of determination subjects the thinking of history to limited horizons, especially by reducing the range of historical events to Europe alone, and by looking at history as a predetermined process of cause and effect functioning within the contours of teleology. The problem of Marx's counter-Hegelian theory, a "death-defying leap from existence in theory to existence in practice,"[54] as Pierre Bourdieu once described it, lies in the fact that it still suffers from the symptoms of the very 'theory effect' it is critiquing. To sociologists like Bourdieu, Marx's theory contradicts itself by trying to materialize a kind of 'reality' and a future that remains unknown. Bourdieu's reservation is part of a larger discourse that dismisses deterministic theories of history as simply "fictional," capable only of producing a flat objectivity that judges the future before it takes place. Marxism falls within this category as a movement that envisions history as a project based on causal laws accounting for objective facts. This approach does not really distinguish Marx from Kant and Hegel. To a greater or lesser degree, they all see history as an Other of an already determined future. Like Kant and Hegel, Marx is the son of the very modernity he criticizes. To subject history to methods of observation and verification is to disregard the inherent retrospectiveness of its discourse and to dismiss the very principle that enables history and distinguishes it from other lab experiments, that is, the absence of samples.[55]

In addition, there is disregard for the fact that history is an act of writing that presumably gets its impulse from the desire for truth and not from its establishment. The teleological principle of the Enlightenment allows for the division of history into periods and for connecting these periods into a linear sequence. The resulting narrative usually works syntagmatically, that is, taking the present as its point of departure, and not paradigmatically, where the historical event is viewed as that towards which historical narrative is made to tend through a renewed process of emplotment. In syntagmatic historicity (a view of history adopted by major French structuralists like Lévi-Strauss and Greimas), the end of a happening is that from which a historian starts in order to reach its probable genesis through a series of logical presuppositions. This awareness of the difference between the development of historical logic and of historical development *as logic* is critical to the understanding of the Enlightenment's teleological principles of historical construction.

Metaphorically speaking, the Enlightenment provides two diametrically opposed modes defining the movement of history: the arrow and the cycle. The cycle, Ibn Khaldūn's model, is a trope for a continuous pattern of changes, but changes that are endlessly repeated, a kind of history that "educates men," to borrow White's phrasing, "to the fact that their own present world had once existed in the minds of men as an unknown and frightening future," one that tells them that their existence has already been performed, thus creating "a sense of the absurdity of all human aspiration, and at the same time, a sense of the necessity of such aspiration."[56] All religious and faith-based historiographies are written in the spirit of history as envelopment, not development. Historians like Ibn Khaldūn and Vico, writers ranging from eighth-century Muslim poets like Abū al-ʿAtāhiyya to eighteenth-century English authors like Samuel Johnson or Thomas Gray belong to this almost sermonic and epigrammatic belief-based vision of history. The arrow, on the other hand, is the new product of modern Western thought, one that allows for more continuity than the cycle. The arrow becomes the root metaphor for the notion of a receding telos and the gradual revolutionary advancement in the course of history. The arrow embodies the idea that the past not only moves in the direction of a positive future, but moves continuously, without major breaks or gaps.

Poststructuralism and the Undoing of Modernity-based History

The twentieth century witnessed the emergence of a somewhat sympathetic self-doubt and a recognition of the perils of the categories of totality and progress characterizing the modern understanding of history in Western Europe. Many intellectuals began to take upon themselves the task of exposing the misunderstandings and relapses inherent in all progressive concepts of history. Though many of those theoreticians cannot argue away the phenomenon of modernity with its social and historical distinctiveness, they are still able to provide new ways of understanding its condition of possibility. In his insightful work *Metahistory*, Hayden White revisits nineteenth-century European discourses of history (both the theory and the practice) demonstrating that this history is nothing but an imaging or an imagination of history. Re-examining major figures such as Hegel, Burkhardt, and Nietzsche among others, White's study comes to exemplify a movement in the historical profession that challenges historians to reflect on the writing of history as a literary endeavor.

Much of White's later work touches on the same idea of the literariness of written history from different critical angles. According to White, historians shape historical evidence into literary tropes (metaphor, synecdoche, metonymy, and irony), which not only yields a sense of coherence, but also renders the evidence itself a fictive act.[57] At the bottom of White's theory is the structuration of literary criticism and tropes laid down by Northrop Frye in the late fifties. Frye's modes of literary emplotment are romance, tragedy, comedy, and satire. By projecting Frye's *Anatomy* onto historiographical narrative, White expands rhetorical analysis into the historical field, thus raising many questions concerning the tropological nature of historical writings in general.[58]

Striving to resist the social scientific tendencies of professional historical training in the twentieth century – which naively assumes that the past can be related objectively – White not only analyzes historical texts, but also attempts to write, as the book's subtitle indicates, a history of historical consciousness in nineteenth-century Europe.[59] Furthermore, White identifies the history that historians make with their written texts and shifts the ground of discussion from history to histories, defining the historical work as "a verbal structure in the form of narrative prose discourse that purports to be a model, or icon, of past structures and processes in the interest of *explaining what they were by representing* them."[60]

White explains how thoroughly the historical discipline differs from a purely descriptive science and how much it owes to literary art. Focusing mainly on narrative structures and tropological acts by which the historian "prefigures the historical field," White underscores a "deep[er] structure," a rhetorical determinism that helps him shift the attention of historical discourse from what is most manifest in historical narratives to what is most latent and hidden, sometimes from the historian himself. This method solidifies White's argument that there is a repressed historicity in non-historical texts and that there is no essential difference between the works of the great historians and their counterparts in philosophy. Essential for White's own purpose is the fact that the deep structures of historical thought are actually more accessible in non-historical texts than in the histories themselves. White's four major books are more or less variations on the same theme: the constructedness of the historian's craft and the linguistic and rhetorical nature of the project of history in general:

> In short it is my view that the dominant tropological mode and its attendant linguistic protocol comprise the irreducibly 'metahistorical'

> basis of every historical work... . What remains implicit in the historians is simply brought to the surface and systematically defended in the works of the great philosophers of history. It is no accident that the principal philosophers of history were also (or have lately been discovered to have been) quintessentially philosophers of language.[61]

This "view" of history, especially in nineteenth-century historical writings, contributes significantly to our understanding of the intellectual tendencies in modern Europe. White's idea that history is something made (not found) by historians finds echoes in Michel de Certeau's theory of history.

Like White, de Certeau contends that history is entirely narrative. De Certeau does not investigate what type of discourse history is as White does; rather he seeks to situate history within the cultural need it must fulfill, and it becomes the job of historiography to fulfill this need by repressing any evidence of it. De Certeau regards historiography as an operation that can only be understood in terms of a function within a specific cultural field. But in order to have a full grasp of de Certeau's take on historiography, it is important to situate him in relationship to the cultural atmosphere of the time.

European colonialism of the Arab-Islamic world began with France's occupation of Algeria from 1830 onwards and its partial dominion over Tunisia. This occupation lasted more than a hundred and thirty years, ending on July 5, 1962. It is no wonder that postcolonial France has been occupied with this recent past. Pierre Nora, a prominent French historian, argues that France, presumably because of a sense of "duality between a monarchy and a revolutionary radicalism," has been a nation obsessed with its own history, continuity, and identity. "It is surely one of the reasons," comments Nora, "why France enjoys such a unique and central relation with its past, with its memory, or, to put it another way, with its history and with its politics, which are forever charged with the mission of patching up the torn robe of the nation's past."[62] This preoccupation with the national past has found an important echo in diverse aspects of France's intellectual life, including literary theory, cultural studies, films, and literature. In the introduction to a multi-volume work on French history, *Les lieux de mémoire* [Realms of memory], Nora also speaks about both the preoccupation with a certain tradition of national historical memory and the sense that it is being lost. According to Nora, "we [the French nation] speak of memory because it is no longer there."[63] This observation leaves no doubt that the recent reflection on the French past betrays the attitudes and desires, the uncertainties and fears, of the present. New interests in marginal histories and of history from below, as opposed to the discourse of the 'center,' began to appear at the hands of a dissident group of writers who worked against the grain and sought to resurrect moments and events ignored – perhaps even repressed – by the official records of French history. This act of looking in from the outside of discourse and of observing one's own culture with the alienated gaze of someone who does not belong to it (though in epistemological terms, it is arguable that there is no such thing as outside discourse) becomes the standard position of poststructuralism in general. Foucault and de Certeau belong to this model of non-identical (re) thinking. The latter, both a historian and a member of the *École Freudienne*, finds an analogy between the writing of history and the unconscious. De Certeau contends that history is to the present what the unconscious is to the conscious. History to de Certeau is the absent Other of the present. Historiography is thus "an odd procedure that posits death in order to deny it." In this way historians allow the dead to have a voice only so that they can inter it; that is, historiography is a "double operation, a labor of death and a labor against death."[64]

An understanding of the dynamics of this "double operation" and its relation to France's long colonial past is crucial for a better assessment of the poststructuralist vogue in modern France. It is not at all a coincidence that the postcolonial critic Gayatri Spivak embarked on the translation of *Grammatology*, the first major work of the Algerian-born French philosopher Jacques Derrida, which debunks the major premises that constituted the idea of Europe and the intellectual presuppositions that led to the Europeanization of world culture.[65] In *The Writing of History*, de Certeau seeks to investigate this same positing of the death of the Other, although he goes further by questioning what happens when a Western historian, usually in the form of a travel narrative, writes on the occasion of or in relation to the Other. De Certeau's project is to deconstruct a specific "conquering and orgiastic curiosity," as he argues, one that is "so taken with unveiling hidden things," and that "has its symbol in travel literature: the dressed, armed, knighted discoverer face-to-face with the nude Indian woman."[66] To de Certeau, the writing of history has become a "discourse of separation,"[67] for not only does it separate the present from the past, but it also "forces a silent body to speak and bases its mastery of expression upon what the other keeps silent."[68] Writing thus converts the "seen body into the known body and turns it into the semantic organization of a vocabulary."[69]

Western writing of history did enjoy this power of transforming tradition into text, "of emptying out the other into a blank page that it should itself be able to write."[70] History, de Certeau tells us, "would fall to ruins" if we studied it without paying attention to "the connection between the act that it promotes and the society that it reflects." Otherwise, history would be nothing "more than a fiction (the narrative of what happened) or an epistemological reflection (the elucidation of its own working laws)."[71]

De Certeau's critique is primarily set against the first modernity outlined in the Renaissance, where European colonialism may be said to have started, notably with the Portuguese sailor Vasco da Gama's discovery of the route to India and East Indies around Africa in 1498. During those world discoveries, Europe underwent what might be called an identity crisis, a repositioning of its sense of self and non-self. This reevaluation was greatly influenced by the acquisition of new geographical knowledge; in fact, the most dramatic findings in this realm occurred in the late fifteenth and sixteenth centuries. As the colonizing West gained a relational superiority to other newly explored regions, it was given the power of a God-like authority to create history and to mark the beginning of the civilization of the Other through those acts of discovery. Many discoveries of that era were made by British, French, and Dutch explorers whose accounts of what they saw were taken unquestionably as the accurate testimony of the circumstances witnessed.

However, the difficulty of naming the unknown (as well as claiming to know what a new thing is) arises from a mode of perception. Linguistically, this would imply that it is the signifier that shapes our perception of the signified, not vice versa. In short, the relationship between knowing, seeing, imagining, and writing revealed major insecurities and put the historiography of early European modernity into question. De Certeau writes: "If therefore the story of what happened disappears from scientific history (in order, in contrast, to appear in popular history), or if the narrative of facts takes on the allure of a 'fiction' belonging to a given type of discourse, we cannot conclude that the reference to the real is obliterated. This reference has instead been somewhat displaced."[72] De Certeau here points our attention to the connection between vision (the characteristic feature of modernity) and writing, and to the effect that such a connection has on the field of historiography. What the mind recognizes is not always the same as what the eye sees, much less than what the hand writes. The name given to a totally foreign object must have originally referred to an already decoded signifier in the historian's own system. European historiography, de Certeau argues, has ignored the possibility of what existed outside of its discourse.

While it is true that objects are 'seen,' these objects are described in terms of existing *lexemes* and a designated linguistic framework. Historiography's very efforts to describe the unknown in terms of the known, to install ready-made signifieds on brand-new signifiers or vice versa, have indeed created a rupture in the relationship between seeing and writing, between the act of observing and the objects observed. The strong insistence on vision and the visual appropriation of space is manifest in the desire to possess the other through vision. *Voir* (seeing) is an act that necessitates a split between subject and object, which in turn results in two modes of visual objectification: objectification of the past, and objectification of the Other. Historians maintain control over the object by constructing both the Other and the past as outside, that is to say, as objects of vision "over there."

The Cartesian equation of being with seeing and consequently of seeing with knowing has given many European historians and philosophers the authority to construct reality. *Histoire* then becomes a scriptural resultant of *voir* and *savoir*, of seeing and knowing and of containing the Other under the historian's assumed epistemological panoptic position. This duality of vision and knowledge still haunts modern epistemology:

> The eye is in the service of a "discovery of the world." It is the front line of an encyclopedic curiosity that during the sixteenth century "frenetically heaps up" material in order to posit the "foundations of modern science." The frenzy of knowing and the pleasure of looking reach the darkest regions and unfold the interiority of bodies as surface laid out before our eyes.[73]

These are some of the tools de Certeau uses to criticize Jean de Léry's *Histoire d'un voyage fait en la terre du Brésil.*[74] He begins "Ethno-Graphy," chapter 5 of *The Writing of History*, with a note on the rectangular precepts of ethnography, namely, "Orality," "Spatiality," "Alterity," and "Unconsciousness." These four concepts gave rise to "transformations in which the basic scheme will always remain apparent"[75] and from which historiography developed in the opposite direction of "Writing," "Temporality," "Identity," and "Consciousness." Significantly, writing is the most metonymic of the four elements, since it is the only one that combines the other three together in one single form.

Chapter 5 in de Certeau's book is a good example of the specificity of a given other, the Tupi, who managed to resist Occidental classification. The argument of de Certeau's chapter follows the line of the ironic implication that what the ethnographic project tried to reduce emerges as irreducible in the very text of the Western historian. Indeed, de Certeau understands historiography as a written "action against the past," and as a rhetorical strategy aimed at "erasing its own relation to time." He sees writing as the only viable source of work that creates the demarcation between "over here" and "over there."[76] When a historian writes, de Certeau maintains, he produces place and time, unaware of the fact that he himself is in place and time. The very locus from which a historian writes and which he refuses to leave necessitates the elimination of the 'other':

> Still more characteristic is the nature of the rift. It does not result essentially from a selection between [primitive] error and [Christian] truth. Here the decisive element is the possession or privation of an instrument that can at the same time keep things in all their purity [as de Léry will remark further on] and stretch all the way to the other end of the world. In combining the power to keep the past [while the primitive fable forgets and loses its origin] with that of indefinitely conquering distance [while the primitive voice is limited to the vanishing circle of its auditors], writing *produces history*.[77]

As it is manifest in this quote, and as argued earlier, the idea that (modern) writing produces history preoccupies French postcolonial thought. The grim implication is that Western historiography has condemned the Other to a state of perpetual entombment. The Other – and in our case what could be more Other than Islam in modern Western thought? – has become "the phantasm of historiography, the object that it seeks, honors and buries."[78] The emphasis on place creates a centrality in the subject position in relation to writing: "in order for writing to function from afar, it has to maintain its relation to a place of production, even from a distance."[79] What appears to be at stake here is that the historian as subject refuses to be decentralized;

and writing, instead of maintaining its relation to a place of production, becomes faithful to the *center* of its production. This centrality is what silences or even irreparably effaces the voice of the Other:

> At least in this way appears one of the rules of the system which was established as being Occidental and modern: the scriptural operation which produces, preserves, and cultivates imperishable 'truths' is connected to a rumor of words that vanish no sooner than they are uttered, and are therefore lost forever. An irreparable loss is the trace of these spoken words in the texts whose objects they have become. Hence through *writing* is formed our relation with the other.[80]

With this quote in mind, it is easy to make the analogy to today's Islam and see how in some Western historiographies Islam has also functioned as an *hors d'oeuvre* in the double sense of the word, both as an appetizer and as an outsider. In other words, an Islamic topic – say the Qur'ān, the *sharī'a*, the *sīra* (biography of the Prophet), or even Islam itself – would start the historian's text, make it possible in the first place by becoming raw material for thought, but would still remain an outsider. Even when there is a slight opportunity for Islam to stand out as 'different' and *unappropriable,* this slim chance for its irreducibility is transformed by some polemics into a hierarchical difference between norm and aberration, either between Christianity and its other, or secular modernity and its other. The inability of some Western historiography to accept the reality of what is 'out there' poses a fundamental limitation. Here again de Certeau's example of late sixteenth-century French historiography is useful, as he shows us through de Léry's account how the 'Other' runs the risk of appearing negatively dissimilar, i.e. amputated, distorted, and incomplete in relationship to a perfectly normal and whole Western self:

> In this landscape the figure of dissimilarity is either a deviation from what can be seen 'over here' or, more often, the combination of Western forms that seem to have been cut off, and whose fragments seem to be associated in unexpected ways. Thus, among the four-footed animals (of which there exists 'not one' that in any or every aspect in any fashion can resemble our own'), the *tapiroussou* is 'half-cow and half-donkey,' 'being both of one and the other.' Their picture of the

> world [is] covered with countless broken mirrors in which the same fracture is reflected (half this, half that).[81]

If this critique is to teach us something about sixteenth-century Western historiography, it would be to expose its limited and narrow understanding of history by showcasing its own narcissistic norms and inability to expand its categories to include cultures and religions outside its own. One is not calling for a resurrection of a transcendental signifier or the recuperation of a lost referent. In fact, it does not really matter whether or not we are able to retrieve what has been lost, or repressed, or emptied out in many texts written on Islam. The task is neither ethical nor apologetic, for this is to no avail. What matters is to point from afar to some erasures that took place and to warn against the lapse into a polemic of historiography that hides under the garb of rational objectivity and scientific positivism in order to re-colonize Islam in the very act of writing about it. For 'writing,' as de Certeau warns us, is no small task, it is an "an archive, it declares, it goes beyond the end of the world, toward those destined to receive it according to the objectives that it desires," and with writing, "the Westerner has a sword in his hand which will extend its gesture but never modify its subject."[82]

De Certeau's interrogation of the axioms of modernity and its historical discourse finds great support in the writings of Michel Foucault. Like de Certeau, Foucault is opposed to the main tendencies of modern European historiography, namely, its realist assumptions about the past, its totalizing frameworks, and its empiricism. But more like Samir Amin and Hayden White than de Certeau, Foucault takes the Enlightenment as a breaking point and works against the notion of Romantic historiography, albeit from a different angle. Romantic historians thought of history as a way to restore contact with origins and to reconstitute some sort of a fractured totality. In this spirit, the task of the historian was to connect the specific experience of the subject to a totalizing historical experience. Jules Michelet, for instance, connects French political struggles in the middle of the July Revolution to his history of ancient Rome, a task described later by White as a tendency to "[*emplot*] his *Histories* as dramas of disclosure, of the liberation of a spiritual power fighting to free itself from the forces of darkness, a redemption."[83] Foucault's criticism does not specify this Romantic attitude towards history, but rather moves towards a broader rebuttal of all histories of ideas that focus on continuity, authorship, and novelty.

To Foucault, most histories end up in contradiction, for in seeking the roots of certain ideas (a consequence of the fascination with historical continuity), they paradoxically perform what prevents those very ideas from being truly new. In the face of this assumption of continuity and the focus on authors and novelty, Foucault suggests looking for discontinuities (which he defines as ruptures), impersonality, and irregularities in discourse, whose main nucleus is the statement, or *énoncé*.[84] Against the notion of a subject-based historiography, Foucault proposes the *archive*, a "historical a priori," which he defines as a machine generating social, as opposed to linguistic, meaning. The *archive* becomes the first law of what can be said; it takes history away from its dependence on the subject. An archivist, another word for an archaeologist in Foucault's diction, does not busy himself with personalities, as the Romantic historian would do; he does not seek to find out who writes what to whom and then to subsume all this under totalizing universal laws. The aim of history writing in Foucault is to save history from falling into anthropologism and to cleanse it "from all transcendental narcissism."[85]

Foucault tries to be an example of what he preaches. Many of his books present us with several different periods of history, focusing on the differences in thought and practice from one period to the next. Historical discontinuity is the centerpiece of Foucault's method. This method is pronouncedly clear in his earlier work *The Order of Things*, where he invokes the concept of *épistémè* to describe the intellectual conditions of possibility during certain ages.[86] In *The Order of Things,* Foucault deals with the development of modern thought from the late sixteenth century to the present. As usual, he sets out to invert the customary approach to the study of history: "It seems to me that the historical analysis of scientific discourse should at least be subject, not to a theory of knowledge, but to a theory of discursive practice."[87] In his Foreword, Foucault opposes archaeological analysis to traditional approaches of human sciences which privilege a self-reflective subject anterior to discourse, a subject that claims to be the sole origin of meaning. Foucault's archaeological method tries to uncover what he calls a "*positive unconscious*" of human knowledge, which is best defined in what he refers to as "*épistémè*":

> What I am attempting to bring to light is the epistemological field, the *épistémè* in which knowledge, envisaged apart from criteria having reference to rational value or to its objective forms, grounds its

> positivity and thereby manifests a history which is not that of its growing perfection, but rather that of its conditions of possibility; in this account, what should appear are those configurations within the *space* of knowledge which have given rise to the diverse forms of empirical science. Such an enterprise is not so much a history, in the traditional meaning of the word, as an 'archaeology.'[88]

Foucault's *épistémè* is defined as the condition of the possibility of a discourse, and consequently of history, at a certain time. It is an *a priori* set of rules that allows the discourse to function and that allows different themes to be spoken at a certain time, but not at another. As sex is different from sexuality, so too the *épistémè* should not be confused with epistemology. Epistemology reflects on knowledge in order to explain how things are ordered, what principles things follow and the particular order that has been established. The *épistémè* is different in that it is anterior to such epistemological forms of reflection. The *épistémè* is determined by *a priori* rules of discursive formation. The *épistémè* is the "middle region" between the "encoded eye" (empirical knowledge) and reflexive knowledge necessary for an understanding of the conditions of history: "This middle region [*épistémè*], then, in so far as it makes manifest the modes of being of an order, can be posited as the most fundamental of all: anterior to words, perceptions, and gestures, … between the use of what one might call the ordering codes and reflections upon order itself, there is the pure experience of order and its modes of being."[89] Any *épistémè* in the service of the subject, it must follow, whether this subject is medieval or modern, gives way to another *épistémè* to which the subject no longer lays claim.

In the aftermath of the Enlightenment the modern theory of the subject has considered itself the definitive truth of European intellectual history. The archaeological approach that Foucault offers makes it possible to dispense with the conception of the sovereign subject as the source of historical knowledge, since – to Foucault – the subject as a product of discourse is not a stable category after all. The treatment of the history of thought in terms of individual intellectual biographies is, therefore, inadequate to describe the density of discourse. The implication is that historical knowledge is not the grasping and ordering of phenomena by the mind, but instead history becomes the very phenomenon that produces the mind. The mind is theoretically reducible to the conditions of its production. To privilege the subject as the pre-discursive origin of historical knowledge is to disregard the fact that the subject itself, its situatedness, is determined by factors beyond its transcendental consciousness:

> If there is one approach that I do reject, however, it is that (one might call it, broadly speaking, the phenomenological approach) which gives absolute priority to the observing subject, which attributes a constituent role to an act, which places its own point of view at the origin of all historicity – which, in short, leads to a transcendental consciousness. It seems to me that the historical analysis of scientific discourse should, in the last resort, be subject, not to a theory of the knowing subject, but rather to a theory of discursive practice.[90]

According to Foucault, language established itself in the late seventeenth century as a means to knowledge, and knowledge was already discourse; in the eighteenth century, it was understood that to know was to 'know' nature and to build upon the basis of language a true language, one which reveals the conditions in which all language was possible. Though too broad, Foucault's centennial periodization is based on discontinuity. This discontinuity manifests itself in the rediscovery of other patterns of reality, that is, the beginning of taxonomy and the definition of abstract characteristics. To sum up, Foucault's method singles out three different modes of the *épistémè* that characterize three periods in history. First, the Renaissance's *épistémè* was "*resemblance*," which "played a constructive role in the knowledge of Western culture."[91] Foucault infers that the interpretation of things was guided during the Renaissance by a perception of the resemblance between things. This "resemblance" structured the exegesis of things to the extent that any search for meaning was the bringing to light of a similitude. The utmost teleology was to discover that things are alike. On the contrary, the Classical Age that followed favored order and a unified system of taxonomy. Knowledge in the seventeenth and eighteenth centuries was based on a "universal science of measure and order."[92] The focal issue was how language as a sign system could adequately account for the nature of the world. In other words, the shift in language was from a Renaissance sameness to a classical age of representation, from language as a simple transparent system capable of naming things unobtrusively to a complex set of operations based on binary classical classifications.

Following the same logic, the end of the classical age would, in Foucauldian terms, mark the beginning of a new *épistémè* that breaks away from the representational and taxonomical paradigm of the seventeenth and eighteenth centuries. In the nineteenth century, discourse itself becomes the subject of discourse. The author no longer uses language and then stands outside of it, but language is also conceived as inside the creating subject and as having its own producing effect. If language becomes divorced from its referent, it still paradoxically remains the only medium through which the thing can be known. A production of anything (from commodities to literary discourse) is no longer conceived as structured around individual consciousness, but rather around the age, or as Foucault prefers to call it, around "the discourse" that creates not just individuals but events as well. Language, therefore, takes on a whole new mode of existence; it creates the role of the metaphysical mediator/revealer of philosophical truths and becomes more and more self-referential. Hence, Foucault regards not only language but also the human species and its major events as a mere product of a certain period of "those figurations within the *space* of knowledge:"

> It is comforting, however, and a source of profound relief to think that man is only a recent invention, a figure not yet two centuries old, a new wrinkle in our knowledge, and that he will disappear again as soon as that knowledge has discovered a new form.[93]

Foucault's thoughts on the historical event are subsumed under the umbrella of what he refers to as 'periodization.' He argues in "Nietzsche, Genealogy, History" that "all knowledge rests upon injustice," since outside their temporal function and periodization, such rules would confirm the idea "that here is no right, even in the act of knowing, to truth or foundation for truth." In this and other writings Foucault attempts to appropriate the traditional concept of history by a basic reformulation of its substance into process and discourse, or into a structured *épistémè*, driven by an intellectual *tour de force* to demystify the notion that history is continuity. Foucault deals the notion of continuity another sharp blow when he critiques origins. Foucault explains that the search for origins should be avoided "because it is an attempt to capture the exact essence of things … because this search assumes the existence of immobile forms that precede the external world of accident and succession."[94]

Foucault's discursive method invites a radical reassessment of the historical event. According to him, the field of the so-called modern scientific historiography emerging from eighteenth- and nineteenth-century Europe has produced a kind of linearity in historical thinking. This linearity regards any event that lies outside its normal course as abnormal, a concept that both de Certeau and Derrida later investigate. The imaginative sense of directed movement through time led to the emergence of a philosophy of progressivity based on the principle of 'forward movement,' embracing the false belief that history deals with 'facts' only in order to reach the 'truth.'

Even if he is not a historian in the strict sense of the word, Foucault manages to restore to the study of history the idea that a historical event is no longer a secularized happening, but a larger *statement* that would only make sense if seen through sociological, political, educational, and cultural possibilities, so that an event in history will be considered only as a participant in an institutional activity that transcends its particularity.[95]

Why does all this matter to the treatment of Islam in the West? The answer is simple. All the aforementioned theorists agree that history is not an objective or a transparent or even a continuous undertaking. Anyone who believes that the self-glorifying historical project of Western Europe during the Enlightenment which categorized Islam as barbaric and uncivilized is an objectively true narrative that 'gets it right' will find these writers an annoyance. As for the question of 'constructing' the history of Islam in a way that serves Western supremacy, its reality or unreality becomes almost irrelevant. History, Roland Barthes tells us, "is not so much *the real as the intelligible*."[96] Interestingly, if we follow this formula of rethinking history, we will find that Islamic history or Islam as history interrupts the rigid tradition of European modernity as much as modernity interrupts, indeed shakes, the tradition of Islam in its definition of itself; we will find that there exists, as Mohammed Arkoun once put it, "a liberal, critical Islam open to change, an Islam still little known and rarely taken into consideration."[97] While this history of Islam still needs to be written, the predominant mode of writing about Islam in the West points to a grave historiographical misunderstanding, one that is neither accidental nor produced by lack of knowledge.

2

POSTCOLONIAL BATTLES OVER IBN KHALDŪN

Intellectual History and the Politics of Exclusion

> Learn that the art of history is one of great pursuits, enormous benefits, and honorable ends.
>
> Ibn Khaldūn, *Muqaddima*

What happened to Ibn Khaldūn between the fourteenth and twentieth centuries? How does his reputation grow? How is his theory used in the Arab-Muslim world? Is there any tension between assessments of Ibn Khaldūn in the pre-colonial period and the ones in the heydays of European imperialism? Has Orientalism transformed the translation, reception, and understanding of Ibn Khaldūn? It has been widely accepted that imperial expansion was deeply implicated in the reconfiguration of European culture and science in the colonial era. Attention to the ways in which European investment in the Arab world has at once cancelled out the Ottoman Empire and been shaped by it is at the heart of Europe's reception of Islam in the nineteenth and twentieth centuries. The historian Róbert Simon acknowledges that "the refusal of the knowledge of the *other* [Islam] has not been loosened by the two hundred years of Crusades and the European presence of the Ottoman Empire, but it was even more enhanced."[1] Many scholars, including Monneret de Villard, Johann Fück, Norman Daniel, R.W. Southern, Maxime Rodinson, Benjamin Kedar, Albert Hourani, and Edward Said have written extensively on the image of Islam in Western Europe over the last century.[2]

Therefore, a focus on the reception of only one Arab-Muslim intellectual's work may not do justice to the scopic dimensions of such a vast field. While one does not seek to repeat the varied concerns of all those studies, it is useful to confront them by examining recent and contemporary debates over Ibn Khaldūn's intellectual legacy. I argue that the account of Ibn Khaldūn's reception in recent and contemporary scholarship in the West is not simply shaped by implacable monolithic Eurocentric hegemony over Islam; it is just as much a story of multifaceted engagements with an outstanding Islamic historian that also becomes a story of various engagements with the history of Islam and with intellectual history at large. My argument thus is not centered on the merits and drawbacks of universalizing or particularizing Ibn Khaldūn, but on the ways in which he has been harnessed and mobilized for particular colonial and postcolonial projects. In fact, there have been many rival claims on Ibn Khaldūn. First, there are writers like M. Kamil 'Ayyād and E. Rosenthal who emphasize his secular thinking and modern ideas on history. A second group, represented by H.A.R. Gibb, Franz Rosenthal, Mustafā al-Shak'a, and Sa'īd al-Ghānimī, study Ibn Khaldūn in a Muslim context, stressing his faith, historical setting, and judiciary career. A third group, notably H. Simon, M. Mahdi, and F. Gale, emphasizes the influence of ancient Greek philosophy on Ibn Khaldūn. A fourth one, represented by Wlad Godzich and Hayden White, deals with Ibn Khaldūn exclusionally, underscoring his difference from European modes of thought; and a fifth group, including Ḥasan Ḥanafī, Muḥammad Jābir al-Anṣārī, and Sa'īd al-Ghānimī, looks at Ibn Khaldūn with nationalistic eyes and regards him as an inspirational restorative figure of lost Arab glory and a memory of the future.[3] Each of these schools of thought faces critical challenges. The first group of secular thinking ignores Ibn Khaldūn's profound and genuine religious convictions; the second "faith" group fails to explain the incomparably structured rationality of his theory and how it was able to conceive of historical thought differently from his orthodox Muslim predecessors such as al-Baghdādī, al-Māwardī, and Ibn Taymīya. The "Aristotelian thesis" group faces the challenge that Ibn Khaldūn decidedly divorced himself from Greek philosophy, harshly disapproving of the Muslim Aristotelism and neo-Platonism of al-Fārābī, Ibn Sīnā, Ibn Bājja, and others. Those who compare his philosophy of history to the Western one(s) tend to de-emphasize both the context and the content of Ibn Khaldūn's work. Arab nationalists as well ignore the universal and transnational implications of his theory.

One is therefore left at a loss, while massive and conflicted research on Ibn Khaldūn could easily lead to a seemingly irreconcilable mass of sources. For this reason, I would like to start by offering a brief account of Ibn Khaldūn's theory of history, then proceed to look at broader themes in Ibn Khaldūn scholarship and return to the details after sketching the larger trends in order to guide the reader.

Ibn Khaldūn and the Craft of History

Two great achievements distinguish Ibn Khaldūn (1332–1406). First, he made history a new science on which he based his historical model of civilization. Secondly, he theorized a historical pattern of cyclical movement in Islamic dynasties. In his famous *Muqaddima*, Ibn Khaldūn introduces unique perspectives on the philosophy of history in connection to the modern notion of *ʿumrān*[4] and consistently associates history writing with *fann* (art), making the connection between fact and rhetoric an essential one.[5] While Ibn Khaldūn's philosophy of history supports recent and contemporary theories like Hayden White's view that historical representations are inevitably tropological,[6] Ibn Khaldūn's book on universal history *Kitāb al-ʿIbar* [The book of examples/histories] is generally recognized to have established a science of history some five centuries before the emergence of historiography as a recognizable field of knowledge in Western Europe. The book is divided into several parts: *al-Muqaddima* [The prolegomena], the most translated and analyzed text in which Ibn Khaldūn develops his theory of history; *Tārīkh al-ʿArab* [The history of the Arabs]; and *Tārīkh al-Barbar* [The history of the Berbers]. At the very end of his work, Ibn Khaldūn includes his autobiography, *al-Taʿrīf*, where he acknowledges all his teachers, with a short biography of each, following the traditional Islamic historical rule of *isnād* (chain of transmission).

Ibn Khaldūn's philosophy of history gives importance to structural representations and logical deductions based on the notion of causality. His vision is one of closure and finality; it could be said to derive directly from the Islamic tradition, though some claim the influence of Greek thought is very apparent in his writings, especially Aristotelian thought, whose logic not only survived the Dark Ages but also assumed a universal importance as a functional tool claimed to have honed the minds of many medieval intellectuals. Crucial to this study is the observation that Ibn Khaldūn benefited from Aristotle's syllogism and his concept of time with its connectedness to causation and divine creation. Arabic-speaking Muslim intellectuals were among the first to engage with Aristotle's philosophical ideas. A long concatenation of medieval Muslim philosophers who did so begins with Abū Naṣr al-Fārābī (874–950), who as far as we know is among the first to comment on Aristotle's philosophy in Arabic, and passes through Ibn Sīnā (Avicenna; 980–1037), al-Ghazālī (1058–1111), Ibn Bājja (1082–1138), Ibn Ṭufayl (1109–85), to Ibn Rushd (Averroës; 1126–98).[7] This Greco-Islamic background of medieval scholasticism began at least three hundred years before Ibn Khaldūn, who was the only exception to a strict tradition of binary oppositions between reason and revelation in Islam.[8] As Samir Amin argues, "[Ibn Khaldūn's] advances in the direction of scientific social thought are unequaled before him and unsurpassed until the eighteenth and nineteenth centuries."[9] By making history subject to *nawāmīs al-sababiyya* (laws of causality), Ibn Khaldūn was able to rescue Islamic historiography from falling into falsity. As it emerged in the fourteenth century, Ibn Khaldūn's philosophy of history cannot be separated from the theological shadow under which it developed. The image of a revolving mechanism and a repetitive pattern that begins, grows, weakens, and dies is an Islamic idea as well as being a generally human one.

An hour's worth of reading of Ibn Khaldūn is enough to allow us to understand how his theologically informed anthropological vision helps establish the genealogical as well as the generational relations in his concept of history. If language and theories about language have always informed the definition of history, Ibn Khaldūn is no exception. Like many historians who have argued for the centrality of narrative language in the writing of history, Ibn Khaldūn took a linguistic turn in his theorization of history. The title of his work *Dīwān al-Mubtada' wal-Khabar*, can be read in three different ways: The Treasury Book of Beginnings and Historical Accounts; The Book of Subject and Predicate; or The Book of Historical Causes and Their Effects.[10] The third definition finds great support from Ibn Khaldūn himself who explains the title as covering early events and their subsequent histories. More important still, the emphasis on the textuality of history is evoked in the technical use and grammatical function present in the Arabic words *mubtada'* (subject) and *khabar* (predicate).

In addition to the linguistic play in the title, Ibn Khaldūn's historiography has a modern feel to it in two specific senses. First, it shuns the mainstream tradition of Islamic historiography, which centers on the life and deeds of Prophet Muḥammad and major Muslim rulers. Ibn Khaldūn was quite aware of the colonial influence that Islam had been exercising over other nations' histories. Ibn Khaldūn's critique of the writing of history recognizes the silencing of minority voices through the effacing act of Muslim historiography. Ibn Khaldūn regards traditional Muslim historians as fanatical one-dimensional writers who see history and time only through the binary opposition between a *before* and an *after* established by the advent of Islam. Secondly, Ibn Khaldūn's theory of history holds some grains of the connection between power and knowledge. In seeking to interrogate history within a broader epistemological framework, Ibn Khaldūn becomes the first historian to overtly criticize the Arab sense of *'aṣabiyya* (feelings of blood solidarity) and to expose the Arabs' injustices. Ibn Khaldūn's *Kitāb al-'Ibar* is ostensibly an apology to the Berbers who, while still having their own *'aṣabiyya*, had long suffered from the Arabs' degrading view of them. To Ibn Khaldūn, the Berbers are brave people worthy of glory because "the strength that they have revealed throughout time makes them fearless; they are as brave and as powerful as the other nations and peoples of the world, such as the Arabs, the Persians, the Greeks, and the Romans."[11]

Through the example of the Berbers, Ibn Khaldūn manages to establish innovative and corrective principles for writing history. Ibn Khaldūn was driven to write his history in response to an existing crisis in Islamic historical thinking. In the *Muqaddima*, for example, he sets out to introduce rational criteria in writing history with a view toward promoting historiography based on a corpus of sociogeographical knowledge. This awareness helps avoid falling into myth that inadvertently leads to the perpetual burial of the referent and the death of the historical fact. In this "rationalization" process, Ibn Khaldūn's main aim was to de-sacralize the dominant practice of history by exposing what appears to him to be the greatest distortions committed by Muslim historians. Ibn Khaldūn refers to these errors repeatedly in the *Muqaddima*:

> The writing of history requires numerous sources and greatly varied knowledge. It also requires a good speculative mind and thoroughness. If he [the historian] trusts historical information in its plain transmitted form and has no clear knowledge of the principles resulting from custom, the fundamental facts of politics, the nature of "'umrān," or the conditions governing human social organization,

> and if, furthermore, he does not evaluate remote or ancient material through comparison with near or contemporary material, he often cannot avoid stumbling and slipping and deviating from the high road of truth. Historians, Qur'ān commentators, and prominent [ḥadīth and history] transmitters have committed frequent errors in the stories and events they reported... . They did not check them against the principles underlying such historical situations. Also they did not probe (more deeply) with the yardstick of philosophy, with the help of knowledge of the nature of things, or with the help of speculation and historical insight.[12]

Here and in many similar examples throughout his book, Ibn Khaldūn warns us against the lapse of history into fiction and *khurāfa* (myth). History, Ibn Khaldūn tells us, could very easily be "fiction," that is, untrue, if the historian ignores the sociohistorical circumstances that must govern his writing of history. In positing this, Ibn Khaldūn's text breaks away from the religio-political centrality of traditional Muslim understanding of *tārīkh*, as a discipline, as a tradition, and as practice that sought to sacralize the meaning of (Islamic) history. In this sense, Ibn Khaldūn is the first Arab-Muslim philosopher of history to introduce a reason-based theory of history.

The first principle he mentions, "resourcefulness and greatly varied knowledge," does not distinguish him from the general body of medieval Arab historians who were very sensitive to both the collection of oral traditions and the documentation of their chains of transmission. A classic example of those historians is the famous Ibn Jarīr al-Ṭabarī (d. 310/923). In the introduction of his book *Ta'rīkh al-Rusul wa-l-Mulūk* [History of prophets and kings], al-Ṭabarī explains his historiographical method of *naql* (uncritical transmission) versus *'aql* (logical processing) as follows:

> Let the reader of this book learn that in everything mentioned here I am entirely dependent on *akhbār* [accounts, news, history] I received from the works of predecessors, since knowledge of past generations is only available to me through their texts. So if the reader finds any piece of news that he does not like or that is inconsistent or illogical, let him know that this is not the product of my own reasoning, but of the *akhbār* I collected from *al-ruwāt* [the narrators], and that I only wrote down what was transmitted to me.[13]

As one can see clearly from al-Ṭabarī's disclaimer and insistence on an 'objective' unmediated transmission of historical writing, the quality that distinguishes Ibn Khaldūn from al-Ṭabarī and other traditionalist historians is the insistence on the role of the good, speculative mind of the historian, namely the necessity to adhere to the logical practice of subjecting whatever evidence may be available to rational analysis. The pains that Ibn Khaldūn goes through to differentiate between *khurāfa* (legend) and *tārīkh* (history) are owing to his concern over the confusion that may arise, since both of them are aspects of the same "absent referent." Ibn Khaldūn was successfully able to discover, establish, and apply those rules of authentication to his own work. A reliable *isnād* (chain of transmission) was the major criterion for the establishment of authenticity in Arab historiography. Ibn Khaldūn added a hitherto unknown logical dimension by which to judge the reliability of this *isnād* in its reporting of *akhbār* (accounts). He is a pioneer precisely because his work opens the door for a new method of historical thinking. Like any innovator and creator of a new field, Ibn Khaldūn had to work hard to find appropriate language and terminology:

> Famous Muslim historians made exhaustive collections of historical events and wrote them down in book form. But, then, persons who had no right to occupy themselves with history introduced into those books untrue gossip which they had thought up or freely invented. Many of their successors followed in their steps and passed that information on to us as they had heard it. They did not look for or pay attention to the causes and conditions of those events, nor did they eliminate or reject illogical stories.[14]

Ibn Khaldūn's criticism in this passage is aimed directly at historians like al-Ṭabarī who have no qualms about arguing that there is no room in *ta'rīkh* (writing history) for mental speculation and logical appropriation, thus allowing history to be a crude literal record of transmitted *akhbār* without any responsibility on the part of the historian. If there is blame, as we have seen in the case of al-Ṭabarī, then it goes to *al-ruwāt* (oral narrators). To Ibn Khaldūn, the likes of al-Ṭabarī unduly restrict the role of the historian to mere accumulators of events without questioning their validity. Ibn Khaldūn's understanding of the process of *tārīkh* is radically different, for he aims to free history from its passive dependence on the primordial irrationality of *akhbār*, thus achieving an epistemological quasi-scientific leap in the field of Islamic historiography.[15]

Furthermore, Ibn Khaldūn uses his terms carefully – verbs such as *dawwana* (to write down in book form), *saṭṭara* (to write down line by line), as well as *dīwān* (book) and *ṣaḥīfa* (manuscript, paper) – when he discusses history. These instances of precision and their symbolic intimations of intellectual authority and reason distinguish Ibn Khaldūn as a sensible critic of history and historiography. History to Ibn Khaldūn is not an irrelevant discourse, but one that has weight and significance; it becomes a '*dīwān*' – what we would today call 'a text.' Here perhaps one could juxtapose the term '*diwān*' to Foucault's notion of *énoncé* (statement), as opposed to 'document,' which to Foucault becomes "the elementary unit of discourse."[16] Ibn Khaldūn's '*dīwān*,' very much like Foucault's 'statement' in this respect, carries within itself the value that makes it serve as a *système d'énoncés* (a system of statements). This textual attitude towards history pushes Ibn Khaldūn to insist on editing the historical *khabar* (piece of news/account), removing the inaccuracies and consistently establishing a grammar for a more probable historical discourse. Ibn Khaldūn's early call for Muslim historians to rely on the expansive logic of epistemological historiography represents a pathbreaking moment in modern historiography:

> Historiography came to be considered the domain of common people. Therefore, today, the scholar in this field needs to know the principles of politics, the nature of existent things, and the difference among nations, places, and periods with regards to ways of life, character qualities, customs, sects, schools of thought, and everything else. He further needs comprehensive knowledge of present conditions in all such respects. He must compare similarities or differences between the present and the past (or distantly located) conditions. He must know the causes of the similarities in certain cases and of the differences in others… . His goal must be to have complete knowledge of the reasons for every happening, and to be acquainted with the genesis of every event.[17]

As we can infer from these methodology-oriented ideas, Ibn Khaldūn works to establish an independent science of history writing. In his own work, he tries to deduce from the histories of kingships a deeper structure of historical movement. In studying early Islamic dynasties, he concludes that the history of their rule is rhythmic and manifests its rhythm in a recurring circular structure at work in the rule of these dynasties. These cycles are causally recurrent to the extent that one can measure their movements in terms of generations based on repetitious causes and their inevitable effects. Ibn Khaldūn's cyclical theory leads from political strength to decadence, beginning with the founder, then the maintainer, passing through the imitator, and finally the destroyer. In the *Muqaddimah* he explains this process quite explicitly:

> It [the prestige of a dynasty] reaches its end in a single family within four successive generations. This is as follows: the builder of the family's glory knows what it cost him to do his work, and he keeps the qualities that created his glory and made it last. The son who comes after him had personal contact with his father and thus learned those things from him. However, he [the son] is inferior to him [the father] as a person who learns through study is inferior to a person who learns from experience. The third generation must be content with imitation and, in particular, with reliance upon tradition. This generation is inferior to the one of the second generation inasmuch as a person who relies upon tradition is inferior to a person who exercises independent judgment. The fourth generation then is inferior to the preceding ones in every respect… . He keeps away from those in whose group solidarity he shares, thinking he is better than they are. He trusts [that they will obey him because] he was brought up to take their obedience for granted, and does not know the qualities that made obedience necessary. Therefore, he considers them despicable and they, in turn, revolt against him. They transfer their allegiance from him and his direct lineage to some other related branch, in obedience to their group solidarity.[18]

As we can see in this quotation, Ibn Khaldūn's narrative logic of history can be critiqued for its structuralist/didactic reductionism. He was, however, careful not to consider this cycle of four generations an absolutely rigid rule or discount the possibility for variations. While the main structure of the cycle remains, Ibn Khaldūn concedes that variations are likely to happen:

> The rule of four [generations] with respect to prestige usually holds true. It may happen that a 'house' is wiped out, collapses, and

> disappears in fewer than four, or it may continue into the fifth and sixth generations, although in a state of decline and decay. The four generations can be defined as the builder, the one who has personal contact with the builder, the one who relies on tradition, and the destroyer.[19]

As we can deduce from this extract, Ibn Khaldūn's theory of history, unlike that of Foucault, is more speculative than "periodizational." Although all theories run the risk of not pinpointing particular referents, there remains for Ibn Khaldūn the matter of the structural logic of historical circumstances, of which the particularity of the event becomes the premise for a universal theory of history. In the end, he leaves behind a remarkable heritage that alludes from a distance to many of the modern and contemporary issues of intellectual history raised by prominent figures like Michel de Certeau, Michel Foucault, and Hayden White.

Ibn Khaldūn, Colonialism, and the Politics of Interpretation

The second half of the twentieth century witnessed a revival of Ibn Khaldūn's work of history, especially following Franz Rosenthal's pathbreaking translation of his work into English, which I will address in more detail in what follows. Two intriguing volumes appeared in the early 1980s to commemorate Ibn Khaldūn's 650th anniversary and assess recent and current research on his work: Ahmed Abdesselem's *Ibn Khaldun et ses lecteurs: Essais et Conférences* (1983) and Bruce B. Lawrence's *Ibn Khaldūn and Islamic Ideology* (1984).[20] They are both significant contributions within the realm of Ibn Khaldūn scholarship and deserve our attention.

In his book, Abdesselem points to Muhsin Mahdi's *Ibn Khaldūn's Philosophy of History* as the most thorough and up-to-date engagement with the Aristotelian thesis in Ibn Khaldūn's philosophy. Abdesselem's essays overlook Aziz al-Azmeh's *Ibn Khaldūn in Modern Scholarship* (1981), a valuable study that questions Mahdi's as well as Pines' tendency of attributing Ibn Khaldūn thought to Greek influences.[21] To its merit, Abdesselem's volume situates Ibn Khaldūn more contextually within the Islamic tradition of political philosophy and traces his influence on nineteenth- and early twentieth-century Arab scholars, especially the Tunisians Khayr al-Dīn and Ibn Abī al-Diyāf. Abdesselem contends that those scholars found in Ibn Khaldūn a theory of justice and balance that regards *qawānīn al-Ṭabīʿa* (natural laws) rather than *sharī'a* as the standard of government in a post-Muḥammad era. In this sense the *Muqaddima* was to many Arab and Turkish scholars an explanatory text of human progress despite religious conservatism.

As in the case of Abdesselem's work, Lawrence's volume also gives little attention to al-Azmeh's major contribution, perhaps because of the latter's critical approach to Orientalist scholarship on Ibn Khaldūn. Instead, Lawrence in fact argues the opposite: that "Ibn Khaldūn is a product of Orientalism," i.e., that the image the world now has of Ibn Khaldūn is in essence a creation of European scholarship.[22] This is a highly debatable argument, since valuable discussions of Ibn Khaldūn's work had already been raised among his own contemporaries and disciples, not to speak of oft-neglected Turkish scholarship starting from the seventeenth century as well as the various contributions of many Arab scholars until the nineteenth and twentieth centuries when renewed interest in his work took a major leap.[23]

Lawrence's examination of Ibn Khaldūn's place in Muslim *salafiyya* scholarship of the late nineteenth and early twentieth centuries reveals interesting results. Lawrence hurriedly argues that traditionalist and reformist Muslims relied on their own political and ideological standpoints in examining Ibn Khaldūn. Lawrence cites Muḥammad 'Abduh as an example of a writer who embraces Ibn Khaldūn because of his revolutionary and progressive thought. According to Lawrence, 'Abduh was a modernist (thus implying that Ibn Khaldūn was also a modernist), whereas his more conservative student Rashīd Ridā did not think highly of Ibn Khaldūn because of the latter's views on non-Islamic *'asabiyya*. Lawrence also believes that 'Alī 'Abd al-Rāziq, on the other hand, writes very positively of Ibn Khaldūn because 'Abd al-Rāziq's provocative views on Islamic Caliphates found great support in *Kitāb al-'Ibar*.[24]

To complicate Lawrence's argument even further, the French-educated Egyptian thinker Ṭāhā Ḥusayn, contemporary of both Riḍā and 'Abd al-Rāziq and an arch enemy of Islamic fundamentalism owing to his 'European' and 'secular' views, argues in his 1917 dissertation that Ibn Khaldūn was not original in his theory of history. Defining Ibn Khaldūn's oeuvre as that of "encyclopedic writings," Ḥusayn refers to works of fourteenth-century Muslim encyclopedia writers like al-Nūwīrī, al-'Umarī, and al-Qalqashandī to claim that "it is most likely that such encyclopedias were invaluable sources that supported and helped extend Ibn Khaldūn's core thesis on history."[25]

In his own contribution to the volume, Lawrence asks the following 'rhetorical' question: "[A]part from 19th-century European scholarship, would Ibn Khaldūn have become more than another footnote to Islamic historiography, inferior to such Muslim writers as al-Tabari and Abu Fazl and incomparable with seminal intellectual figures of the Western world, whether Hegel, Engels, Marx, Durkheim or Toynbee?"[26] This position invites one to ask how 'Western' scholarship on Ibn Khaldūn is indeed innocent of ideology, when only one of the eight contributors to Lawrence's volume, Franz Rosenthal, is an Ibn Khaldūn specialist.[27] In fact, it was Franz Rosenthal who called for a contextual study of Ibn Khaldūn in "his own time," emphasizing two major shortcomings in recent and current research on Ibn Khaldūn in the West, whether by Westerns or by Arabs educated in the West. First, most work on Ibn Khaldūn was written as doctoral dissertations (S. Van Bergh, Ṭāhā Ḥusayn, G. Bouthoul, K. Ayad, E. Rosenthal, M. Mahdi, S. Bacieva, N. Nassar, M. Rabīʿ, P.V. Sivers, Ali Oumlil, Aziz al-Azmeh). To Franz Rosenthal, this does not mean there is no serious scholarly effort exerted in these monographs, but he makes the argument that most of them are written by younger scholars whose theses are not well developed enough, thus lacking comprehensive knowledge of classical Islam and world history, two components essential for a thorough grasp of Ibn Khaldūn's work.

A second problem Franz Rosenthal addresses is the "pioneer phenomena." Since the renewed emphasis on Ibn Khaldūn's work in the nineteenth century, many scholars have come to consider him the founder of a certain branch of knowledge or a number of disciplines, including but not limited to sociology, anthropology, and intellectual history. According to Franz Rosenthal, this type of research does not usually do justice to Ibn Khaldūn, since scholars would limit their arguments by laying down the founding principles of a given science, trace it back to Ibn Khaldūn, and compare him with modern European thinkers (say Machiavelli, Durkheim, or Weber) who developed a given science until it reached its current mature status. In addition, there is the phenomenon of "schooling" Ibn Khaldūn, that is, relating him to Marxian, structuralist, or poststructuralist schools of thought because of their possible affinities with Ibn Khaldūn's line of thought.

While there is some truth in Franz Rosenthal's critique,[28] one must admit that many doctoral dissertations on Ibn Khaldūn are undoubtedly groundbreaking, especially al-Azmeh's rewarding thesis, which restituted

Ibn Khaldūn's work to its original core as a transformative study of human history.[29] In so doing, al-Azmeh debunked – though without much elaboration – the illicit uses of "alien cultures" to which Ibn Khaldūn was subjected, starting from the colonial eclecticism of de Sacy, to the mālikite *faqīh* theory of H.A.R. Gibb,[30] to the "inductive sociology" of Ernest Gellner[31], and ending with the Greek crypto-rationalization of Muhsin Mahdi.[32]

Inadvertently or not, by counterposing what he describes as a reactionary and ideology-charged 'Arab' scholarship to a supposedly dispassionate, scientifically based and thus universally 'correct' European one, Lawrence risks reducing intellectual history to stereotypical triteness. Moreover, his reference to early Arab-Muslim twentieth-century scholarship on Ibn Khaldūn as ideological and polemical ignores the fact that most 'Western' scholarship (to follow his binary oppositional logic) was not immune to colonial ideology. Lawrence's 'European scholarship' started two centuries ago when France occupied the Maghreb. Let us examine this 'scholarship' in its historical context.

One of the earliest Europeans to work on Ibn Khaldūn was Silvstre de Sacy (1758–1838), the founder of French Orientalism, who published several parts of *al-Muqaddima* and argued in the first volume of his three-volume work *Chrestomathie Arabe* (1806) that Ibn Khaldūn was perhaps the only Arab historian worthy of attention.[33] De Sacy's writings and work on North Africa flourished at the beginning of Western colonial interests in Africa when 'scientific' requirements of Oriental studies were just developing. Commenting on early nineteenth-century French Oriental studies, Rodinson remarks that "the school of French historians that flourished between 1820 and 1850 based its analysis on the internal dynamics operating between social groups in conflict. This view, however, garnered no interest among Orientalist scholars for whom the essential conflicts were between races and religions."[34] It was within this colonial context that de Sacy took interest in Ibn Khaldūn and introduced his work to European society. De Sacy's work on Ibn Khaldūn, however, is also imbued with religious and racial bias where the Orient becomes the vulgar and uncultured other, thus marking the emergence of Orientalism as an organized discourse. In his famous critique of de Sacy, Said rightly describes his revisionist and "compilatory" work on the Orient as a reflection of "a Western authority deliberately taking from the Orient what its distance and eccentricity have hitherto kept hidden."[35]

When the French occupied Algiers in 1830, colonialist France did not consider West Africa worthy of study, except perhaps for military gain. As an expansionist colonial power, France cared a great deal about issues of land and property. The need to study rural Islam, property laws, the structure and demographics of the tribes and their power relations became increasingly dire. So, just as Napoleon's savants had produced the *Description de l'Egypte*, his counterparts in North Africa produced the *Exploration scientifique de l'Algérie* (1844–67), edited by Pellisier de Reynaud and modeled on the *Description*. In this period, feuds among the Muslim natives and the "colons" escalated, and the higher military administration felt the need to gather accurate information in order to understand, control, and achieve cultural monopoly over the locals. This is the time when *les Bureaux Arabes* was created in 1844 under the leadership of General E. Duamas (1802–71), who endeavored to support the French-Kabyle alliance against the Arab Muslims.[36] This is also the time when de Sacy's work on Ibn Khaldūn became useful. Officers in the *Bureaux* took cultural research and translation assignments. Among them was William Mac Guckin de Slane (1801–78), an ardent student of de Sacy. The French War Office first assigned de Slane the translation of Ibn Khaldūn's autobiography and parts of *Kitāb al-'Ibar* in order to help the French army understand the topography and cultural practices of Arab Muslims. It was in 1868 that de Slane was finally able to issue his three-volume translation of *al-Muqaddima*, which remained in vogue among many scholars for almost a hundred years until Franz Rosenthal's English translation was published in 1958.

Postcolonial Battles over Ibn Khaldūn: Intellectual History and the Politics of Exclusion

The "Aristotelian thesis," posited in a number of studies on Ibn Khaldūn since Franz Rosenthal's famous translation of his *Muqaddima* (as the *Prolegomena*) in 1958, raises an interesting question about Western scholarship on Arab-Islamic cultural heritage. The question concerns the belated discovery among Western scholars of Ibn Khaldūn's oeuvre and its location in intellectual history. Does his theory of history stem exclusively from the Arab-Islamic tradition, or does he belong to a much wider and universal pool of intellectual history anchored in the Greek tradition, especially that of Aristotle's? In other words, how original is Ibn Khaldūn's work when compared to Western theories of history? All these questions center around one basic idea: the place of the 'other' in historical thinking, or, to be more precise, the location of Islamic thought in European intellectual history. Over the last century, certain tendencies have developed in a number of Western European history books to exhibit a concern for tracing historiography to a presumably pure and continuous European tradition that disregards influential non-Western figures. These works are important because in their very essentialism they serve to unmask a long tradition of European historical thinking that has formed Europe's relationship with its non-European Islamic other.

Conflicting opinions on Ibn Khaldūn within this body of scholarship effectively highlight these tendencies, revealing a fatal intellectual conflict between two opposing poles: Islamdom and Christendom, Islam and European modernity (whose proponents do not necessarily have to be Westerners), and philosophically, especially since Hegel, Islam and Greece: the one perceived as chaotic, rigid, and self-contradictory, the other transcendental and capable of total self-understanding and self-criticism.

But this is not new. Academic research on Ibn Khaldūn has a very long history of critical tension both in the Arab world and abroad. Most scholars who have recently studied him seem to have pre-conceived ideas of what their critiques are set to prove or disprove. Almost all modern Arab intellectuals, including but not limited to Lūwīs 'Awad, Aziz al-Azmeh, Muḥammad Jābir al-Ansārī, Muḥammad 'Ābid al-Jābrī, and Sa'īd al-Ghānimī, argue that Ibn Khaldūn is the father of the 'science' of history, of sociology, and even of Marxism *avant la lettre*.[37] In the Western world, however, Ibn Khaldūn's case is far much more complex. Some scholars, notably A.J. Toynbee, Muhsin Mahdi, Yves Lacoste, and Edward Said, regard Ibn Khaldūn as a pioneer of social sciences. Toynbee, for instance, decribes Ibn Khaldūn's work on history as "the greatest work of its kind that has ever been created by any mind in any time or place"[38] and places him among avatars of historiographical thinking like Herodotus, Thucydides, Polybius, Josephus, St. Augustine, Gibbon, and Turgot. He even argues that Ibn Khaldūn is the most modern of all, specifically because of his inclusion of sociology in his theories of history. Said, likewise, refers to Ibn Khaldūn as "the great fourteenth-century Arab historiographer and philosopher," whose perspective on social life cycles and the human discourse makes an excellent comparison to Michel Foucault's theory of discourse analysis in *L'Ordre du discours* and *L'Archeologie du savoir*.[39]

Other recent and contemporary Western scholars have been somewhat perplexed by Ibn Khaldūn's work on history, mainly because he remained largely unknown to Europe until the nineteenth century. Other reasons for this bafflement range from linguistic barriers to geopolitical orientations in critical and historical thinking. Ibn Khaldūn's work on history was rediscovered in Egypt during the nineteenth century when the Muslim scholar Rifā'a Rāfi' al-Ṭahṭāwī ordered the printing of *Kitāb al-'Ibar* in seven volumes in Būlāq in 1867. The Egyptian edition of the *Muqadimma* was first translated into French and published without an introduction by Firmin Didot Frères in Paris by Academie des Inscriptions et Belles-Lettres a year after the appearance of the Būlāq edition.[40] In 1950, a selected translation of Ibn Khaldūn's work by Charles Issawi appeared in England under the title of *An Arab Philosophy of History: Selections from the Prolegomena of Ibn Khaldūn of Tunis*. However, it was not until Franz Rosenthal's three-volume translation of Ibn Khaldūn (1958) that historians in Europe and North America began to engage with Ibn Khaldūn's work more seriously.

More generally, one could distinguish two major rival claims. A group of critics, mostly guided by Franz Rosenthal's introduction to the translation, argue that Ibn Khaldūn's precedence as a historical thinker is a result of the tripartite cultural tradition in which he grew up and lived, which consisted of 'Asharite theology, Islamic jurisprudence, and, more importantly ,early Islamic philosophy's engagement with Greek philosophy.[41] The second group questions Franz Rosenthal's assumptions and contends that the precepts of Ibn Khaldūn's theory of history are radically different from the ones that characterize Greek and Western historians for various theological and philosophical reasons.

In his book *Ibn Khaldūn in Modern Scholarship*, Aziz al-Azmeh refers to this problem when he argues that the "decline of oriental societies" perceived by the West led to the renewed interest in Ibn Khaldūn, and that such a theme of decline would have not taken place "had the fourteenth century not coincided with the beginning of the Renaissance and of Western expansion, had not Europe started becoming, from the European standpoint, the territory where 'hot' history was being enacted."[42] Al-Azmeh further argues that Ibn Khaldūn's work was appropriated by nineteenth and twentieth century scholars "of the flag," namely pro-colonial Orientalists who wanted to advance the argument that Ibn Khaldūn's work was an exception to a predominantly dogmatic Arab-Islamic tradition.[43] But to complicate al-Azmeh's argument further, even postcolonial studies of Ibn Khaldūn still insisted on the same position of Ibn Khaldūn's exceptional status as an Arab-Muslim historian, leading one to wonder what exactly this academic insistence represents in the postcolonial.

Scholars like Edward Said, Samir Amin, and Albert Hourani were able to describe some of the major problems regarding the critical assessment of Arab-Islamic culture and tradition in the West, showing how they appear throughout various critiques. In *Orientalism*, Said critiques the effect on the image of the "self" that was created by an "imaginary geography." This "imaginary geography" is what constructs the so-called Orient as the historical and cultural other of Western identity. This virtual connection renders the West–East divide nothing but a symbolic space whose mapping lacks a specific geographical point from which it could function. Although Said does not further investigate the foundations of this space as an imaginary formation, the spatial metaphor he dwells on makes it possible for the West to argue that "Islam is now the primary form in which the Third World presents itself to Europe, and that the North–South divide, in the European context, has been largely inscribed onto a pre-existing Christian–Muslim division."[44]

How does this dynamic affect texts and their reception? To answer this question, let us return to our telling study of Ibn Khaldūn's *Muqaddima* and the way that various scholars dealt with it. To begin with, note that in Franz Rosenthal's translation, terms and insertions useful to modern and contemporary debates on intellectual history are sometimes translated misleadingly or left out altogether. Among these words are key concepts like *'umrān,* appearing in Franz Rosenthal's translation of Ibn Khaldūn as 'civilization,' and *fann* (art), which is left out altogether. A year after its publication, Hayden White wrote a review of Franz Rosenthal's translation in which he includes this interesting disclaimer:

> The Editor of this quarterly, assuming no doubt that Professor Rosenthal's translation would be reviewed by a number of Islamists as a monument of Islamic civilization, requested the present review from a non-Islamist who would approach it in terms of its place in philosophy of history. In advancing into a field in which the content of the work is alien to him, the reviewer has sought aid and counsel on a number of special problems which arose. He therefore wishes to thank Professors Willson H. Coates and R. James Kaufmann, of

> the University of Rochester, and Professor Isaac Rabinowitz, of the Department of Classics, Cornell University, for aid given in analyzing and presenting this evaluation of Ibn Khaldūn's work.[45]

Despite this clear disclaimer and White's acknowledged lack of familiarity with the Arab-Islamic tradition, he still argues against Ibn Khaldūn's legacy as a world historian in the body of his review.[46] This line of argument invites a dialectical reaction to Franz Rosenthal's Prolegomena as the basis of young White's remarks on Ibn Khaldūn's legacy among world historians. This dialectical reading is manifest in White's radical departure from Franz Rosenthal's Aristotelian thesis after perceiving a characteristic in Ibn Khaldūn's thought that he saw as divergent from that of Western historians: "[B]oth the Greek and Christian traditions retained a leaven of true humanism which forced the historian to the discovery and description of concrete, individual personalities as active, if not totally free, forces in the historical process. This feeling for the individual and the unique in history is lacking in Ibn Khaldūn."[47] White's Ibn Khaldūn is simply not the great pioneering philosopher of history that some may think he is. White supports his claim by quoting Professor von Grunebaum, who, according to White, "hit the mark in noting: 'the weakness of Arab historiography is its concentration on personalities and on military incidents and court cabals.'"[48] Because of this fundamental "weakness," White sees Ibn Khaldūn as a historian who "lacks true humanism," a property that distinguishes only "both the Greek and Christian traditions."

If White is correct and Ibn Khaldūn did not in fact attend to the 'humanism' and 'freedom' that characterize the unique position of the individual in history, then how is one to judge or define the criteria of true historiography?[49] What does one make of fields like sociology, intellectual history, and "history from above" that are also considered 'de-individualized' participants in the process of historiography? Would White likewise condemn/criticize 'Western' writers from the Greek and Christian camps (such as Herodotus, Thucydides, Augustine, and Hegel), who wrote history "above" the individual and above the "unique in history"? The history of critical reflections on Islamic tradition in the West is rich in such examples that define historiography according to pre-conceived norms. When it seems there is no better way to critique Islamic intellectual thought than by blaming it for dismissing "freedom" and "humanism," this willful misunderstanding of Arabs and of

Islam is worthy of consideration. It appears that there is a constructed mechanism of historical thinking in some academic disciplines that has already collected its own data for intellectual history and cannot accept any more, especially if new material seems incompatible with established theories.

Take for example Ernst Breisach's bulky work *Historiography, Ancient, Medieval, Modern*. An anthology of sorts, Breisach's book does not include a single reference to non-European contributions to medieval historiography. Intellectual history in the West is a 'science,' but although sciences should always be open to and challenged by new discoveries, it appears that the 'science of history' in the West is autoimmune, to invoke the Derridean complication of term, that is, it seeks to maintain and promote itself by marking its own turf and defending itself through biases and disciplinary restrictions, thus destroying itself in the very process of "self"-defense. It is interesting how White's later work would take a completely different stand in relationship to the discourse of history than the one outlined in his review of Franz Rosenthal's work, as I elucidate in the next chapter. But for now, this tension manifest in White's review of Franz Rosenthal's translation serves to exemplify certain historian-producing disciplines keen on tracing historiography to a presumably pure and continuous tradition where there is no credible place for the non-West.

For other scholars who feel that Ibn Khaldūn must indeed be acknowledged as a foremost figure in the tradition of intellectual history, Ibn Khaldūn is either quickly dismissed or redirected to fit the Greco- European pattern. An example of the first case is Wlad Godzich, who in his book *The Culture of Literacy* somehow concludes that Ibn Khaldūn is representative of Oriental historical discourse in general and jumps to the conclusion that his historical vision lacked causality. Godzich's thesis is that Ibn Khaldūn lacks the complex notion of causality that he associates with Western historiography, and that the same flaw is present in the entire tradition of Oriental historical thinking that Ibn Khaldūn 'represents':

> The specificity of the Western mode of historical discourse lies in the fact that it is concerned with the dimension of becoming as manifested in the past – that is, with the very movement of history, where the latter is conceived as a force or as a set of forces capable of effecting movement. Under such a conception, the paramount question is *why*, whereas in Ibn Khaldûn's view, the question is *how*.[50]

Here is another obvious example of exclusion, one in which Ibn Khaldūn's theory of history lies outside what Godzich confidently defines as a mode of historicity specific to the West, where history is "movement," and "a force," as opposed to stasis and stagnation. It is not certain *how* Godzich was able to reach this conclusion or *why* he used Ibn Khaldūn in particular to propel his argument. The important thing is that Godzich's criticism of Ibn Khaldūn's lack of causality is entirely baseless since Ibn Khaldūn's entire work is grounded in a theory of causality; as previously noted, all the latter really cared about was discerning a fundamental logic that governs historical "movements" and human cycles. Ibn Khaldūn's model for the causes of decadence in Islamic dynasties not only belies Godzich's analysis, but it also reveals the latter's bias in subjecting historical thinking to an imaginary mappable identity he calls "the Western mode of historical discourse."

The specificity of this subjection supports Samir Amin's idea that Eurocentrism is not a social theory integrating various elements into a global and coherent vision of history, but rather a prejudice that distorts social theories, one that masterfully foregrounds an idea while erasing another to satisfy the needs of intellectual supremacy.[51] The effect of this view not only renders the present better than the past, but it also creates an illusion of regional superiority when, forced by its own logic of continuity, it delves deep into its own past and attempts to draw for itself an imaginary narrative of developmental bias that separates West from East. This kind of linear bias towards history provokes critical responses by many poststructuralist intellectuals like Michel Foucault and Paul Veyne, thus laying the groundwork for a number of postcolonial theories, especially Said's *Orientalism*.

More recently, Stephen Frederic Dale added yet another dimension to contemporary Western studies on Ibn Khaldūn. Dale's essay investigates the structural tools that form Ibn Khaldūn's theory of history in relationship to Aristotle's theory of logic. In his essays, Dale describes Ibn Khaldūn as the "Last Greek and the First Annaliste," and makes a point of showing how the *Muqaddima* allows for a keener insight into what he calls the Aristotelian mind of Ibn Khaldūn than would be revealed on a surface, non-historically involved reading of the text:

> Despite the attention that scholars have lavished on Ibn Khaldūn's *Muqaddima,* the historiographical significance of that remarkable work is still not well understood... . In certain aspects, the *Muqaddima*

> still belongs to an Islamic historical tradition, yet its dominant intellectual lineage is the rationalist thought that stretches from the Peripatetic philosophers, and especially from Aristotle (384–322 BCE) through such Greco-Islamic thinkers as al-Fārābi, Ibn Sīnā and Ibn Rushd onward to European philosophical historians and socialists of the 18th, 19th, and 20th centuries ... he can be characterized as the last Greek historian.[52]

Dale's analysis makes one wonder how Ibn Khaldūn is Aristotelian since to Aristotle history is an inferior mode of inquiry. There is no question that a link between Islamic orthodoxy and Greek philosophy began as early as the first penetration of the Greek thought into the Arab-Islamic world through translation in the tenth century. But it is also arguable that intellectual tension reached a significant development with the publication of al-Ghazālī's *Tahāfut al-Falāsifa* [The collapse of philosophers][53], the first book written from an Islamic perspective to refute Greek philosophy. While Dale's argument is not new or original, it is difficult to ascribe Ibn Khaldūn's 'logic' to one school of thought over the other. In Chapter 24 of his *Muqaddima*, Ibn Khaldūn vehemently criticizes Aristotelian logic and dismisses it as "damaging" to Islam. This chapter is translated very clearly in Franz Rosenthal's version and the title easily sums up its thesis: "The Errors of Philosophy and the Corruption of its Followers." In this chapter, Ibn Khaldūn uses the Qur'ān to discredit human reason as it is embodied in Aristotle's philosophy, especially when it comes to opposition with divine wisdom:

> This chapter and what follows are important because the new sciences spread in our cities are damaging to religion. It is important that we address them and reveal their truth. It so happened that there is a rational group of the human kind that claimed that all existence is physical, and that whatever lies beyond, the causes and conditions of the meta-physical must be judged by rational criteria and mental standards. Those people are called *falāsifa* [philosophers], the plural of *faylasūf* [philosopher], which in the Greek tongue means "a lover of wisdom," because they looked for that and dedicated all their work to prove their point. They even designed a law that helps reason distinguish between truth and falsity and called it *al-mantiq* [logic].[54]

As can be deduced from this statement, Ibn Khaldūn has definitively taken the side of theology over reason. This does not mean that 'theology' is irrational but that according to Ibn Khaldūn part of faith is to acknowledge the limits of human reason, especially in its attempt to comprehend the totality of life experience as well as the secrets of divinity. He argues against philosophy and describes Aristotelian logic as flawed and conjectural at best. His further writings on prophecy and sophism complicate the claim to his use of Aristotelian logic. The *Muqaddima* states on more than one occasion that the bases of all material sciences are the Qur'ān, the Hadīth, and the Sunna. Ibn Khaldūn believes that "*al-'ulūm al-'aqliyya*" (intellectual sciences) are "*Ṭabī'iyya lil-insān*" (natural to humankind) as a result of the human's ability to think, and that those sciences are universal. He classifies them as the sciences of philosophy and wisdom (*'ulūm al-falsafa wa al-ḥikma*). Ibn Khaldūn further lists the seven philosophical sciences as follows: logic, arithmetic, geometry, astronomy, music, physics, and metaphysics. While he acknowledges the value of these sciences, Ibn Khaldūn does not see them to be necessarily the product of Greek thinking.

Published three centuries after *al-Tahāfut*, Ibn Khaldūn's *Muqaddima* takes al-Ghazālī's side in his attack against the Peripatetics. While it is likely in an age of religious fanaticism that Ibn Khaldūn could have opted to take sides and decry Greek philosophy and Aristotelian logic while still being influenced by them, it is not critically compelling to assume that this was simply the case. In fact, Dale's pronouncement appears to be effectively anti-Orientalist in its recognition of the enduring contact between Greek and Islamic thought in the medieval period. This is an incontrovertible fact the extent of which is perhaps not fully appreciated by modern intellectual historians and philosophers, especially Hegel, as I show in the next chapter. However, what is at stake here is neither the assertion nor the denial of this contact, but what is implied in both. The awareness of Aristotle in Ibn Khaldūn, as I have shown, is a debatable topic, especially when there is not enough scholarship on whether or not Arabic texts were translated into Greek during this period and whether or not there was a general cross-fertilization of ideas. In this particular example, Dale seems to have constructed his critical approach to Ibn Khaldūn rather innocently, without careful problematization of a highly contested issue at hand, taking Ibn Khaldūn's 'synthesis' of Greek reason at face value, which to Dale means one thing: influence. In framing Ibn Khaldūn in a theory of influence, Dale tries to delineate a set of reasons for his argument. But what his argument may also imply is that without Aristotle, Ibn Khaldūn would have been incapable of logical thinking and therefore incapable of modernizing historical thought.

The main theoretical difficulty inherent in historicizing intellectual history is the delimitation of borderlines that circumscribe the so-called European field of historiography by setting it apart from the different and unfamiliar. This explains the nervousness that any tampering with the European borders of intellectual history is bound to provoke. It is easy to argue that some scholars simply do not have a grasp on the topic they are talking about. It is also understandable that the essence of intellectual history is hard to fathom, especially when the Arabic language is less commonly taught and/or practiced in Europe, not to speak of the kind of Arabic Ibn Khaldūn used in his text. However, as I have been arguing here, a close examination of European treatment of these Arab-Muslim texts evidences an unwillingness to understand the relevant texts in a way that would result in their acknowledged inclusion in (European) intellectual history. We should treat the aforementioned shortcomings, which are clearly perceptible in published writings on Arab-Muslim texts in the West – such as White's review of Ibn Khaldūn – as symptoms of a deeper epistemic essentialism instead of dismissing them as isolated cases of biased intellectualization.

There is no doubt that research on Ibn Khaldūn has received a healthy push following Franz Rosenthal's 1958 translation, which despite some terminological issues remains a paramount achievement and a more reliable work than de Slane's French translation with its references to Machiavelli and Montesquieu, among other European thinkers. But translation is not a substitute for the original, and serious scholarship should not be at the mercy of pre-interpreted versions of the text in question. Before Franz Rosenthal, many relied on de Slane's translation, and not too many readers of the French text took Ibn Khaldūn's work seriously or understood his theories correctly. This does not mean that Ibn Khaldūn's theory is immune to criticism. There are problematic aspects of Ibn Khaldūn's theory of history that should not be overlooked, and many scholars from Ṭāhā Ḥusayn to Aziz al-Azmeh have pointed them out. But when it so happens that in the act of speaking of intellectual history one ends up speaking provincially and systematically of something other than intellectual history, then we must not disregard this something else. We must treat this intellectual 'tension' over Ibn Khaldūn as a sign of an existing and practiced pattern of thought, one that is prompted by a specific urge to use its own doctrinal 'history' tools (either utter exclusion or conditional inclusion) in order to safeguard a discipline which constantly threatens to dissolve into myth. One tends to perceive those 'essays' as careful revisionisms of past Islamic thought to keep a certain idea of history sheltered from the rest of the world.

Again, the particular mistake in which we find this kind of scholarship trapped – that of locating a Greek origin for "rational thinking" in everything, or of dismissing works upon accusations of their lacking that very origin – seems to dispel the thought from which it receives the very knowledge that allows it to pass judgment. In the case of Ibn Khaldūn, this contradiction reveals an unresolved tension in historical thought that could only occur in a state of crisis. I am not referring to the crisis of not knowing how to deal with a pioneering Arab-Islamic theory of history, for that is a different topic, but to the crisis of historical thinking in general, which reveals itself in studies that seek to re-establish contact with the self culture by looking for the origin of this "self" in linguistically and culturally foreign texts. White's and Dale's essays, for instance, despite their contradictory theses, are both exposed by their attempts at exposing Ibn Khaldūn's theory. This kind of thought is more revealing than the naive acceptance of its Eurocentrism, which asserts the impossibility of naiveté in modern mainstream Western attitudes towards the Arab-Muslim world. What one scholar may dismiss as a naive and undocumented reading, which seeks to assess the work of a medieval Muslim historian unproblematically on the basis of its inevitable influence of Greek philosophy or in sharp contrast with European modes of thought, is in fact a symptom of a larger *épistémè* that still persists in European and North American historiographical thinking in general. Said gave us a theory of Orientalism and Samir Amin examined the roots of Eurocentrism, but what begs to be written now is a history of misunderstanding, and in this history one of the rich chapters should not just be on Ibn Khaldūn but on the Arab-Islamic tradition from Muḥammad forward.

In examining Ibn Khaldūn in relation to these interpretive political projects, it becomes clear that the tenets of history on which we are so dependent are themselves cultural artifacts, built on institutional structures that erase certain kinds of knowledge, silence some, and valorize others. We are confronted with the obvious fact that every document of history – no matter how uninformed its author was of its language or society – is coated with the cultural grammar of the political moment.

Admittedly, Eurocentrism has come under new sorts of scrutiny as the production of what constitutes scientific, ethnographic, and colonial knowledge has been given more sustained consideration. But the fact remains that Western historiography in general has been tainted with elite efforts to produce or reproduce distinctions across lines of social and cultural interconnections between Islam and the West. There is no doubt that Ibn Khaldūn's legacy was affected by these distinctions, which are not just a thing of the past, but remain living realities. The very idea of 'Europe,' much like the idea of 'Islam,' is inevitably shaped by sharp contrasts to its others. This idea will continue to live as long as the tension between the exclusionary practices of pseudo-universalizing claims of intellectual history still dictate our critical choices.

3

HOW DID ISLAM MAKE IT INTO HEGEL'S PHILOSOPHY OF WORLD HISTORY?

Is the location of Islam in Hegel's philosophy indicative of any discursive tendencies in modern European views of Islam in world history? What does this placement tell us about the universality and atemporality of idealism (a view of reality as dependent on human perception) as a philosophical discourse? If Hegel's concept of Islam is predicated on the 'Orient' – in the sense this notion was understood in nineteenth-century Europe – how valid is this Hegelian legacy if employed by modern and contemporary scholars in re-examining Islam after September 11?

While answering these questions will not restore to intellectual history what was lost on the battleground of Eurocentrism, it would still help pinpoint the domains of power in which a hegemonic culture was mapped and its history was imagined and constructed. My attempt in this chapter is not to label Hegelian thought with Eurocentrism but to interrogate the intellectual premises that contributed to the emergence of the Eurocentric and Orientalist elements in his thought.[1] Let me begin by asking a clarifying question: why Hegel? Before I attempt to answer this question, I would like to caution that a clarification is not the same thing as a justification and that embarking on 'understanding' Hegel does not mean proving or conceding that he is right. Whatever the assessment of Hegel's philosophical position on Islam might be, there must always be room for second and third readings and a window for doubt in order not to fall into the vicious trap of misunderstanding again. I say this because a major difficulty in grasping Hegel's concept of history is that to him the real is not what is out there in the phenomenological world. *Geist* (the mind or the spirit) is the only reality for Hegel. Everything that takes place in the physical world must be brought into relationship with the mind/spirit; even revolutions must happen in the mind first: "World history begins with its universal goal: the fulfillment of the concept of spirit. The goal is the inner, indeed innermost unconscious drive, and the entire business of world history is the work of bringing it into consciousness."[2] History for Hegel is therefore first and foremost a mental process, an evolvement of self-consciousness and perception as the mind opens itself through human history and civilization.

Hegel died in 1831, leaving behind him a corpus of idealist philosophy that was to require centuries of unpacking and interpretations. Thanks to Hegel, an academic discipline of history rose to unparalleled heights in nineteenth-century Europe. Hegel left a tremendous impact on modern liberals, including Marx, who was a devout member of the Young Hegelians as a youth and deeply influenced by the new historical vein in Hegel's philosophy. Later on, Hegel's views on Islam as a religion that seeks "world dominion" while lacking particularity or nationalist inclinations would serve as a ground for Marx's analysis of Islam.[3] Hegel believed that the state is a "primordial institution of human life, like the family," and that it was "closer to the divine order than anything else on earth and therefore has the power to demand compliance."[4] Hegel also revolutionized transcendental philosophy through a radical self-critique of epistemology. In opposition to Kant, Hegel was able to demonstrate the phenomenological self-reflection of knowledge as the necessary radicalization of the critique of reason.[5] This radicalization resulted in a crucial moment in modern European thought when philosophy broke off the borders of its closed academic circles to become a commentary on the history of the world. In other words, theory and reality, transcendentalism and phenomenology, converged at this historic juncture. Or, to put it in Hegel's language, the rational-freedom became real.

Thanks to Michel Foucault, we now take it for granted that there is a direct relationship between power and knowledge, but it is worth pausing to question the bases and sources of that knowledge – not just how incomplete, but also how cryptic and obscure it can be. Only with closer attention to the mechanics of production of the historical *épistémè* and the narratives associated with it do we begin to discern not only the anecdotes and fantasies but also the politics that envelop the very source of such knowledge.

Hegel is not an exception to this rule and his use of terms like "absolutism" and the "Orient" has an intriguing historical context to it. This is what this chapter sets out to show.

The Roots of Hegel's Absolutism

In his intriguing work *Lineages of the Absolutist State*, Perry Anderson helps us dissect this Foucauldian axiom with reference to Hegel, albeit indirectly, through undertaking a topic many historians would shy away from: identifying blind spots in historical Marxism and philosophical Marxism, while attempting to synthesize both in an unrivaled comprehensive attempt to re-examine the European continent's modern political history, East and West, through the lenses of absolutism. To do so, he undertakes a radical historical contextualization of the spheres of knowledge in nineteenth-century Europe. What Anderson modestly refers to as "a comprehensive survey of the nature and development of the Absolutist State in Europe" turns out to be not just a survey, but an in-depth and thorough double-punch critique of Marxist empiricists who often neglect theory and Marxist philosophers who engage in the theoretical issues of historical materialism without paying much attention to the events of history.[6]

Anderson's study of "history from above," and of the "particular" and the "general" of Europe's lineages of absolutism, sheds significant light on "the first international State system in the modern world"[7] in a comprehensive way that help us understand and situate the discursive practices that informed Hegel's philosophy of world history, although Hegel himself is not a major aspect of Anderson's critique. According to Anderson, the issue that the serious historian must face is not only to detect forces and patterns of events at work in the formation of political thought, but also to resist chronological convenience and dominant customs of historiographic monism. Anderson thus writes his work against the grain of structured historiography, with its "common departure and common conclusion, spanned by a single stretch of time."[8]

The traditional view held by Marxism has been that history is a series of class struggles ultimately rooted in economic conflict, though these struggles may take political forms. These economic conflicts take place between an exploiting class and an exploited class. Pointing attention to the infamous ambiguity of Marx when it comes to the definition of 'class' and its retroactive applicability, Anderson contends that as much as "history from below" is beneficial to both Marxist and non-Marxist historians, "secular struggle between classes is ultimately resolved at the *political* – not at the economic or cultural – level of society."[9] To examine this "political level," he introduces a typology rather than a chronology of absolutism, one in which "periodization" is no longer the only criterion for historical judgment and should not obfuscate the similarities in the patterns and forces at work that produce the absolutist state in Europe. Spanish absolutism, for example, ended in the late sixteenth century; England's lasted till the end of the mid seventeenth, and France's till the end of the eighteenth, while Prussia's made it till the end of the nineteenth, and Russia's was only overthrown in the twentieth century. Still, Anderson maintains, such absolutisms share a common ground: recurrent absolutism. Anderson's point is that despite the temporal spacing of absolutism, there are essential thematic factors to be considered before we submit ourselves to truncated theories of history that reduce it to class struggle. In the case of Europe, and for the benefit of our approach to Hegel, these factors include the accumulation of capital, religious movements and reformations, formation of nations, the advent of industrialization, and the expansion of overseas imperialism.

For our purpose, it is most relevant to focus on the following questions that Anderson's study implicitly raises: why did Europe generate "monarchy," to use Montesquieu's terms, whereas the Orient, or the Asiatic, is only capable of producing "despotism"? What is so specific and unique to European forms of political domination? Why does Europe tend to dismiss its Eastern part when it writes its history? Was a warped line of Eurocentrism drawn in the public texts of the Enlightenment? If so, how did this attempt at demarcation influence the field of European intellectual history?

While it is easy to see why an 'advanced' Western Europe would want to sever itself from the continent's 'backward' regions, Anderson confronts us with the lamentable fact that historical research on Europe focused either on single countries or limited periods, and that historiography was conducted mainly within national bounds. For Anderson, as long as we are unwilling to interpret Western Europe's political thought in a comparative relationship to Eastern Europe and the Ottoman Empire, historical research, Marxist or not, will remain confined to limited national frames.

Anderson's contextual critique of absolutism is crucial for understanding how Hegel built his philosophy of world history and how he treated the non-European in his dialectical thinking, but more importantly how 'Europe' constructed its history in the nineteenth and twentieth centuries. As Anderson cleverly juxtaposes the genealogy of Europe's classical engagement with Greece and especially with its 'feudal' system and systematic segregation from the House of Islam, he puts into question the very foundations and formative premises of Europe's nineteenth-century sociopolitical and cultural heritage, making one wonder whether Western Europe's early nineteenth-century patronage of Greek nationalists against the Ottomans was an untimely sign of Orientalist animosity towards an Islamic state that happened to be in Europe. Anderson's line of argument seems to lead to this conclusion.

For example, he confronts the question of how it came about that "the Ottoman State, occupant of South-Eastern Europe for five hundred years, camped in the continent without ever becoming naturalized into its social or political system."[10] The Ottoman Empire, continues Anderson, "always remained largely a stranger to European culture, as an Islamic intrusion into Christendom, and has posed intractable problems of presentation to unitary histories of the continent to this day."[11]According to Anderson, the investigation into Western Europe's absolutism could benefit from comparisons with Eastern Europe, one in which the formation of Ottoman rule certainly stands out as a key example with which to contrast European absolutism for multiple reasons: the physical presence of Islam in Europe, the long history of military conflict between Islam and Christendom, and the self-understanding of Europe in relation to the "Orient." As I will explain below, the significance of understanding Europe's perception of itself in relationship to Turkey is particularly important for the positioning of Islam within the matrix of its intellectual history.

In Anderson's view, it was Machiavelli in early sixteenth-century Italy who, in two central passages of *The Prince* (published 1532), was "the first theorist to use the Ottoman State as the antithesis of a European monarchy" by explicitly condemning the Porte's autocratic bureaucracy.[12] A few decades later, Machiavelli was followed by Jean Bodin who, in his *Six livres de la République* (1576) describes the King of the Turks as the "Grand Seignior," a term used to describe despotism *avant la lettre*, due to his dictatorship and autocratic ownership of property.

Another important blow dealt to the Ottomans was in early seventeenth-century England at the hands of Francis Bacon (1561–1626). In *The Essays or Counsels Civil and Moral* (1632), Bacon distinguishes Europe from Turkey by emphasizing the latter's social absence of "hereditary aristocracy" that characterized European rule: "a monarchy where there is no nobility at all, is ever a pure and absolute tyranny, as that of the Turks."[13] The legacy of this distinction, argues Anderson, continued in figures like James Harrington and François Bernier who criticized Ottoman economy. In fact, it was in the *Commonwealth of Oceana* (1656) that Harrington further widened the gulf of distinction by arguing that unlike Europe, the economic foundations of the Ottoman Empire were based on matters of land monopoly.[14] Bernier's *Travels in the Mogul Empire* (1671), the work that is known to have invented racial classifications as such,[15] cemented Harrington's views and added a scathing eye-witness travelogue of the Islamic empire as "barbaric" and "uncivilized," where cronyism, favoritism, and land monopoly roamed unchecked. Bernier's account was the first to dwell on a relationship between biology and mental development and to leave a palpable mark on eighteenth-century European historiography and influence such major thinkers like the Baron de Montesquieu (1689–1755).

Despite Montesquieu's famous opposition to slavery and colonial expansion,[16] he still saw a sharp distinction between Europe and Islam as embodied in the Ottoman Empire: "There is no despotism so injurious as that whose prince declares himself propertier of all landed estates and heir of all subjects: the consequence is always the abandonment of cultivation, and if the ruler interferes in trade, the ruin of every industry."[17] In addition, Montesquieu went on to bestow a sense of geographical conditioning and atmospheric doom, fashionable at the time, on all Asians and Orientals.[18] Montesquieu's reputation as an 'enlightened' thinker was in every way conducive to making his *De l'esprit de lois* (1758) Europe's first geopolitical gospel of Orientalism. Although it was the despotic practices and corrupt reputation of the Ottoman Sultan, the "Grand Seignior," that triggered Europe's antagonism, this particularity did not prevent Muslim subjects and Islam in general from becoming the public target of Western enmity. With political despotism, economic corruption, and geographical fatalism now the fortifying walls separating Europe from Islam, Europe left the Orient with only a few branches of knowledge to claim as their own. Soon intellectual history would decide the battle, as Hegel, the inheritor of the Enlightenment and of Montesquieu's binarisms, would use history to widen the gap of disparity between Europe and the rest of the world. Now, if this indeed was the *épistémè* that granted Islam entrance into Hegel's philosophy of world history, and if one were to speak about the ideals of this history and grant oneself axiomatically the position of thinking and deciding those ideals, how are we to judge the validity of such ideals, especially when they were formed and informed by concepts of racial and economic supremacy?

Situating Islam in Hegelian Thought

The German intellectual Theodor Adorno once said of Hegel that his "genius relies in his mediatory philosophy and in his attempt to define the spirit that prevails over mankind but also prevails in them."[19] The literary critic Paul de Man also confirms the existence of unconscious Hegelianism in all of us:

> Whether we know it or not, or like it, or not, most of us are Hegelians and quite orthodox ones at that. We are Hegelian when we reflect on literary history in terms of an articulation between a Hellenic and a Christian era, or between the Hebraic and the Hellenic world. We are Hegelian when we try to systematize the relationships between the various art forms or genre according to different modes of representation. Or when we try to conceive of historical periodization as a development of a collective or individual consciousness.[20]

To both Adorno and de Man, then, Hegelian thought is an all-inclusive philosophical space in which currents of thought have been collected and preserved. Contemporary interpretations of Hegel's philosophy have also assumed this position of comprehensive totalization. Take for instance Adorno's provocative reading of Hegel's philosophy of history as consciously paradoxical:

> It is characteristic of Hegel's thinking that he really wants to have it all ways: that he really wants to include everything, even things that simply cannot be reconciled. By this, I mean that he adopts the standpoint of the universal. He tends always to claim, ideologically and in a conformist spirit, that the universal is in the right. But equally, almost as an afterthought, he would also like to be credited with wanting fair play for the individual. Incidentally, this comment applies with equal force to the entire Hegelian macro-structure since the whole point of his philosophy is that it not only teaches absolute identity, but also believes that non-identity – in other words, the very thing that cannot be included in identity – should somehow be incorporated into the concept of identity in the course of its elaboration.[21]

In this passage Adorno touches upon the core of Hegelian thinking, namely its antithetical inclusion or dialectical dynamism. According to this formula, Hegel has already accounted for everything, and even the opposite of his thought is a necessary component of the thought process. In other words, there is no outside Hegel.[22] And it is specifically in this context that we must examine his philosophy. On the one hand, there is the claim of universalism, the idea that Hegel's philosophy transcends time and space and is therefore a valid source of a better understanding of everything, including religion. On the other hand, there is a phenomenological world with Haiti on the far horizon and the Ottoman Empire next door, shelled in its own political, economic and cultural "absolutism," to insist on Perry Anderson's term. This phenomenality of the "non-European Other" poses the following inevitable question to transcendental philosophy: was Hegel's presentation of Islam done in a manner typical of the compartmentalizing thought of nineteenth-century Europe?

While there may not be a straightforward answer to this question that will satisfy both the abstract Hegelian and the deterministic Marxian,[23] one thing is clear: Islam is manifest in Hegel's concept of religion not as a *religion*, but as a constituted "absolutism" serving the One. The way in which Islam is explained in Hegel's philosophy is not explored in a contextual or documentary fashion. Instead, it takes place within an already constituted framework of Hellenistic Christianity in which already thought-of human beings behave in different manners towards an already-designed sphere of knowledge. In this particular sphere, Islam functions as a form of "fanaticism" to Hegel. We may say that this reductive view of Islam is roughly analogous to so-called subjective economics of thought, or to be more precise, a utility theory[24] that seeks unity through marginalization of its Others, one in which an understanding of an alien religion from the perspective of an already constituted idealist society is reached without properly inquiring into the way in which this understanding has been constructed in the first place. At the very least, Hegel's analysis of Islam is lacking in philosophical reflection, making Hegel appear to a seasoned and educated reader as a stereotypical representative of his own age: a European man concerned with the way in which an existing mind relates to already-established facts. However, Hegel is not to be excused from ignoring the purely subjective nature of history.

To his credit, Hegel knew more about the history of world religion than most of his contemporaries, but it is not certain to what extent he was indeed versatile in the available literature. Islam and the Arab world represent a palpable gap. Reference to Islam is made only in passing in Parts II and III of *Lectures on the Philosophy of Religion* as an existing adversary to Christianity. There are also sporadic and almost repetitive allusions to Islam in other lectures, such as *Philosophy of World History*, *Philosophy of Art*, and *History of Philosophy*. In all of those scattered references, Hegel paid more attention to a dominant or received impression of Islam without attending to its original texts, subsequent developments, or contemporary living expressions, and without careful documentation of his sources, quoting from memory sometimes:

> Religions have purpose – universal as necessity itself, but at the same time empirical, external, and political in character. Islamic religion, *we are told*, also has a world dominion as its purpose, but of a spiritual rather than a political character.[25]

This "world dominion" in Islam, we soon find out, is motivated by what Hegel sometimes refers to as "nationality," and sometimes the "particularity of religion," but the word he often repeats is "fanaticism," a trait that he believes to be also found in Judaism, albeit conditionally, as I will explain soon. The following quote is an example of what Hegel believes to be a fundamental difference between Islam and Christianity:

> In Islam it is only being a *believer* that matters. This is not obstinacy but *fanaticism*, because although nationality (natural associations), family connections, homeland, etc. remain (limited connections, stable relationships are permitted), the service of the One basically involves the un-limitedness and instability of all subsistence. God's acceptance has occurred once and for all, and what replaces reconciliation or redemption is something that had implicitly *happened*, a choice, an election by grace involving no freedom. We have here a view grounded on power, a blind election, not an election made from the point of freedom.[26]

Two words stand out in this extract: fanaticism and freedom. Let me first define fanaticism, since Hegel has a special use for this term that is not equivalent to the dominant use of the word today. Hegel defines fanaticism as "passion for an abstraction, for an abstract thought, which relates as negating force to the existing object/thought."[27] Fanaticism, in other words, is an obligation to bring other people to the form of worship or religion. Fanatic in Hegel means practical, passionate, particular, zealous, proselytizing. In fact, the opposite of fanaticism is inaction or lethargy. So when Hegel says that "fanaticism" is the goal of Islam, he means that the single purpose of this religion is raised to a universal purpose, and only in its obligation to spread and propagate itself does it become fanatical. But then he also argues that fanaticism is found among the Jews and appears only when their possessions or religion comes under attack, though without the proselytizing impulse that defines Islam:

> Jewish particularity, however, is not polemical because there is no obligation to convert other people to the God of Israel. While others are called upon to glorify the Lord, this is not a goal, as in Islam, which is pursued with fanaticism. Judaism has become fanatical only when attacked, only when its existence has been threatened.[28]

This assertion is a perfect example of Hegel's non-historical and unstudied assessment of both Islam and Judaism, for two reasons. First, there is a clear difference between obligation and encouragement, and when it comes to the latter, no one single religion can be ruled out as non-missionizing. Secondly, it is stated non-equivocally in the Qur'ān that "there is no obligation in religion."[29] While this declarative statement does not stop fanatics from trying to convert others to their religion, the same is true of Judaism. Some Jewish factions did encourage proselytizing well into the second and third centuries if not later, but the dominance of Christianity in the Roman world made such efforts increasingly difficult. While we have less information about active missionizing to pre-Islamic polytheists outside of the Pax Romana, the near universalism of Islam within a generation after Muḥammad had a similar stultifying effect on Judaism as did the Roman adoption of Christianity. Thus, it seems, Jews abandoned missionizing largely because the other, more politically dominant, monotheistic (Abrahamic) religions would simply not allow it.[30] Hegel makes no reference to Christianity, the missing third in the Abrahamic chain, in relationship to fanaticism. On the contrary, Hegel's Christianity is a religion of freedom, whereas Judaism and Islam are religions of commandments as such, where service is not rational for its own sake:

> In any religion, such as Judaism or Islam, where God is comprehended only under the abstract category of the One, this human lack of freedom is the real basis, and humanity's relationship to God takes the form of a heavy yoke of onerous service. True liberation is to be found in Christianity, in the Trinity.[31]

As for the second term, freedom, Hegel bases his theory of world history on this concept. To Hegel, history itself is a development towards absolute freedom: "It is this final goal – freedom – toward which all the world's history has been working. It is this goal to which all the sacrifices have been brought upon the broad altar of the earth in the long flow of time."[32] Let us consider this more carefully. Freedom is based on – in fact *constituted by* – human reason. Hegel's "goal," then, means that freedom comes only after history, that history is the development of human freedom, and that human freedom is man's consciousness of this freedom. This is how Hegel accounts for the master–slave *aufhebung* (dialectic): in order for freedom to be achieved, it must pass through the secular world of bondage and unfreedom. In other words, freedom is not really freedom, but rather the consciousness of it. This consciousness is what brings totality to life.

So far, so good. But if this understanding of freedom as conscious 'understanding' can be told with bias and dematerialization, then Hegel's project of universal freedom poses many questions. Why, one might curiously ask, does Christianity have freedom while Judaism and Islam do not? How do we understand and where do we locate this freedom if it only exists in relationship and as a relationship to the real? Part of understanding this freedom in Christianity and part of Hegel's entire philosophical project, especially in the *History of Religion,* is to prove the existence of freedom in Christianity and Greek religion through its lack in all other world religions. In other words, freedom is defined negatively, which could also mean, to use Hegel's logic against itself, that freedom is not really 'free.'

Here I would like to emphasize a crucial point in Hegel's dialectical thought. Hegel bases his whole logic on the hypothesis that everything which exists can only be itself in relation, and – ultimately – *as* the relation to its Other. Thus Hegel's definition of freedom can also be counterintuitive. If Christianity can be defined by its difference from Islam, how then is Christianity "freedom" when the basic premise of its freedom can only be understood through its difference from other religions? Hegel has a good explanation for this. As previously argued, history to Hegel *is* a dialectical movement in the direction of freedom. This notion somehow allows him to single out Greek and Christian religions as locales for this freedom. Comparing Christianity and Greece to several Oriental religions, primarily Chinese and Indian, Hegel writes:

> In the Eastern religions the first condition is that only the one substance shall, as such, be true, and that the individual neither can attain to any value in as far as he attains himself as against the being in and for itself. In the Greek and Christian religion [sic], on the other hand, the subject knows himself to be free and must be maintained as such; and because the individual this way makes himself independent, it is undoubtedly much more different for Thought to free itself from this individuality and to constitute itself in the independence.[33]

This theory of freedom as a status, one in which history will reach an end, is highly vulnerable. How Hegel was able to equate Greece with Christianity and to connect both to freedom is a complex and convoluted process that took many twists and turns. However, I do not wish to dwell on Hegel's Hellenization of Christianity. Instead, my specific concern is for the validity of Hegel's definition of freedom. The most vexed question is how we come to experience this freedom not just as a physical state of "being free," but also on the level of the mind. Freedom is a receding telos and not an end in itself, part of a coveted form of life that might not exist for us in the manner Hegel conceives of it. Freedom, if we can grasp it, is only there in very limited activities and for a very brief time. "Regardless of what happens," argues Jean-Luc Nancy, "it will be a question of bringing an experience of 'freedom' to light as a theme and putting it at stake as a praxis of thought."[34] In other words, freedom must result from a confrontation with a phenomenological given, or as Nancy puts it, "the testing of something real," the object of thinking and not thinking in itself, whose seizure "will always be illegitimate."[35] There is something dangerous and risky about freedom, and that is why we can easily fall into a guilt trap when we have too much 'freedom.' Even that which in our societies we call enjoyment – sport, fun, recreation, vacation, time-off, unwinding – all such terms have become labels of our consumer culture. Above all, freedom is a subjective experience, one that is reduced to the possibility of staying alive.[36]

The questions we must ask are whether a philosophy of world history is possible without impossible totalization; whether a definition of an essentially subjective experience like freedom is possible without Hegel's Euronormativism that could only see one continuous line between Christian Europe and Ancient Greece; and whether we can construct pacifying gestalts of thought to arrive at the objectivity of the spirit without committing a grave sin against reason by finding meaning where it is quite possible that none exists. This disposition towards Euronormativism, however, is not the most striking in Hegel's work. Rather, it is the brutal calculation with which he dismisses all things Arab or Islamic, or "Oriental," for that reason. Take, for example, his view on Arab philosophy:

> The Arabians, moreover, made a point for the most part of studying the writings of Aristotle very diligently, and of availing themselves more especially both of his metaphysical and logical writings, and also of his *Physics;* they occupied themselves particularly with multiplying commentaries on Aristotle, and developing still further the abstract logical element there present. Many of these commentaries are still extant. Works of this kind are known in the West, and have been even translated into Latin and printed; but much good is not to be got from them.[37]

This evident contempt for the so-called "Arabian" work on Aristotle in which Hegel obviously confuses Arabs with Persians, reveals two facts. First, the denigration of Islamic culture as superfluous and useless in its translations and interpretation of Aristotle; and secondly, the claiming of Aristotle's philosophical heritage as a sole Western intellectual property. Two other important nineteenth-century factors in understanding the deeper implications of the dismissal of Islam in relationship to the Greek tradition in Hegel's philosophy are xenophobia and monopoly of tradition.

A further, equally important component that we can detect in Hegel concerns the geopolitics that Perry Anderson's Montesquieu established and Europe uncritically adopted. The irony is that Eurocentrism and Euronormativism are themselves specifically geopolitical constructs and calculated moves designed to insert the newly established *idea* of Europe (although such geopolitical categorization is neither adequate nor precise in capturing the constitutional complexity of European politics). Yet this philosophically supported geopolitics took place in a cultural context completely different from the one that surrounded the events of September 11. The primary relevance here is not the scholastic environment of nineteenth-century German philosophy or European epistemology in general (a topic frequently discussed by Edward Said and others) but the vicissitudes of European supremacy at the moment of the colonial turn in epistemology.[38]

Hegel and September 11

Why then is a study of Hegel's theory on Islam important now? In order to answer this question, let us examine the ramifications of Hegel's philosophy in the nineteenth and twentieth centuries. Albert Hourani reminds us that "most of the historians and historical thinkers of the nineteenth century were children of Hegel," and that "the general concepts which he represented could be developed in many different ways, with differing emphases."[39] This is why Hegel matters to an understanding of Islam in modern European thought. But what gets elided in this understanding, as usual, is context. Yet precisely in this context the Germanic – or in this case, the *Prussian* – nation, in which Hegel lived and practiced his philosophy of world history, was able to envision for itself an inverted telos, a future in the past, and to find its *spirit,* so to speak, in the older imperial theme of the Holy Roman Empire, and thus its own identification with ancient Rome. This religio-philosophical bond with older empires and Greek philosophy – we have seen how Islam was removed from the frame – also played out in the German classical engagement with Greece and especially with the movement of Greek independence.

Let us consider a variation on this theme in a recent study of Hegel and Islam. Weighing in on Hegel's philosophy of history, Jean-Joseph Goux's "Untimely Islam: September 11th and the Philosophies of History" sets out to explain the historical differences and the different historicities (views of history as progressive, regressive, teleological, circular, or finite) that distinguish Judaism and Christianity from Islam. A specialist in postmodern French philosophy, aesthetic theories, and socio-symbolic interpretation, Goux analyzes the "untimeliness" of Islam in the philosophies of history in this essay. Since my critique of Hegel is not from the inside, that is, not an expository or a "continuist approach" like Goux's, I will address the unexamined context in Goux's analysis of Hegel in the following paragraphs.[40]

Like many scholars attempting to understand the happenings of September 11, Goux undertakes an in-depth critical revision of Islam's position in history, a position informed (he argues) by Christianity's entrance into its third millennium:

> It is important, I think, to take a step back from an event whose media impact, obsessive visual presence in our memories, and short-term political effects run the risk of depriving us of an interpretative framework. It seems to me that what is required to overcome 9/11's obnubilating and obfuscating effect (which is part of terrorism) is the theoretical and speculative distance offered by the philosophies of History.[41]

Goux's argument is resourceful, but as he goes on it seems to be an exercise in Hegelian dialecticism. Drawing on a strong concatenation of European thought on Islam (Turgot, Condorcet, Hegel) and taking the terrorist attacks of September 11 as a springboard for his critical assessment, Goux compares Islam to the West in order to expose "the many violent conflicts that occur all along the 'fault lines' between Islam and the West," which as he emphasizes, "are not merely the expression of another type of historicity that is destined to remain foreign to us," but are also symptoms of "a profound disruption in the traditional and secular relationship to historicity within Islam itself."[42] Such "profound disruption" derives, as Goux continues, from the awkwardness with which Western philosophies of history have treated Islam. Hence the need for Hegel:

> Thinking the Arab-Muslim world in the context of a philosophy of History, assigning it a determinant place in the successive stages of a universal evolution conceived as gradual or progressive, proved to be awkward for thinkers such as Turgot or Condorcet, who, since the Enlightenment, have endeavored to conceive the movement of human societies as a whole. The thinker who confronted this difficulty most lucidly was Hegel. And it was only by a seemingly arbitrary chronological contortion – both highly significant and rich in consequences – that Hegel was able to tackle this problem.[43]

I agree with Goux here. There is no gainsaying that Hegel found a place for Islam within universal history in a way that his predecessors did not or could not. But in order to understand how Hegel "tackle[d] this problem," it is crucial to explore the fields of force that made Hegel's location of Islam necessary at that particular time in European history.

To Goux, Hegel offers a four-part theory of universal history which positions world ideas in light of *Geist* (mind, spirit) according to the logic of internal necessity. In this classification, the "Islam world" falls under Hegel's fourth category. Together with the "Germanic World," Islam belongs to the last stage of *Geist*. The first category/stage, the "Oriental Empire," includes China, Egypt, and Persia; then comes the "Greek World" of ethical freedom, which represents the adolescence of humanity. The third category includes the "Roman World" and "Christianity," both representing a principle of abstract universality:

> As the highest intuition of the One, Islam thus occupies a rather high position in Hegelian History; it belongs to the fourth and final stage of Spirit in the tableau of Universal History. It therefore has nothing to do with the Orient (in the Hegelian sense), which represents the childhood or dawn of History. Islam belongs to the Western Spirit, to the age in which this Spirit arrives at or returns to unity. Yet, this is not its ultimate position, for as we mentioned above, this fourth stage includes a bifurcation, a divergence that unfavorably distinguishes Islam from a Christianity having reached the fully-realized version of itself: Protestantism.[44]

This argument may well be convincing, but it should not be seen as clinching the question of historical differential in the "Christianity–Europe" Hegelian dialectic. In addressing the "bifurcation" in Hegel's fourth stage of human history, Goux explains Islam's devotion to 'Oneness' with its relinquishment of, or indifference to, the secular world. This Hegelian 'indifference' is what distinguishes Islam from Christianity. Christianity, Goux argues, interpreting Hegel, is unique in the sense that its consciousness and subjectivity create a different, more positive relationship to the secular world, one that is interested in lifting it up from its primitivism and barbarism:

> Whence this divergence? Islam remains within the abstraction of spirituality. One must fear and honor God, the One, and adhere to this abstraction. God is an absolute in the face of whom man has no other end, no particularity, nothing individual. This entails an indifferent

> attitude toward the secular world, which is left to its primitivism and its barbarism, and which remains foreign to Spirit and does not reach the consciousness of rational organization… . This is where the divergence with Christianity appears. In Christianity, the consciousness and will of Subjectivity as the divine personality appear in the world as an individual subject. This consciousness then develops itself until it reigns as true Spirit. Thus in Christianity the spiritual goal can be realized in the secular world.[45]

In Goux's analysis, Christianity is a vivid representation of God on earth, although divinity in Hegel is a much more complex category than Goux implies in his essay. According to Goux, it is this representation of human divinity, so to speak – both in its power and vulnerability – that Islam lacks and that makes Christianity *realizable* in the secular world. Using this postulate, Goux goes on to explain what could have otherwise been "a violent offense to chronology, a kind of outrageous anomaly" in Hegel's philosophy of history. Goux argues that Hegel deliberately puts Islam on a deceptively elevated stage, only to reveal the religion's disinterestedness in the secular world. But this argument forgets that Hegel's reference to Islam is epistemologically ill-informed and overlooks the fact that Hegel is a phenomenological dialectical thinker when he approaches the seemingly abstract notion of Islam.

Goux's approach to Islam invites some interesting questions. Why should one believe that there could have been a distortion and anomaly in Hegel's categorization of Islam? Why would Islam's commitment to an abstract de-incarnated "Oneness," its "centeredness" around "the abstraction of spirituality," and its "fear of God" be interpreted as an "indifferent attitude towards the secular world"? What does the 'secular world' mean to Hegel? Moreover, if "indifference" to the 'secular world' does indeed exist in Islam, what does this "indifference" imply and how is it different from the Judeo-Christian perception of the material world? Goux argues that Christianity, or Hegel's understanding of Christianity, breaks away from Islam precisely because of the former's attention to worldliness.

In Hegel, Islam's opposition to "barbarism," though a late-comer among monotheistic religions, still "develops more quickly than Christianity – which needed all of eight centuries before it grew into a worldly form."[46] Likewise, "the principle of the Germanic world became a concrete reality only through the Germanic nations."[47] This means that Islam is not on a different plane from the Germanic world, as Goux claims. In fact, the two examples of the fourth stage of world history explain and complement each other. That fourth stage is not solely Germanic, but *medieval* as well.

Islam's medieval*ness*, Hegel explains, is like old age in nature, but which must not be taken as natural weakness of dotage, since it is the realm of the Spirit. The medieval Germanic stage of world history is "the old age of the Spirit in its complete ripeness, in which Spirit returns to unity with itself, but as Spirit."[48] Hegel defines Islam in this sense as absolute freedom, as "the enlightenment of the oriental world."[49] Moreover, Islam becomes the West (in the Hegelian sense of the West, i.e., consciousness of *Geist* as a free spirit). It is important here to emphasize that the secular world in Hegel is also the world of "brutal barbarism," in which the Spirit finds itself and "builds up as an implicitly organic outward being" to reach "freedom," the one and only goal of world history.[50]

If Islam is not "indifferent" to the secular world, but is indeed freedom from the ecclesiastical authority of the "Church" or the "State," does this leave us with the possibility that Goux misunderstood Hegel, or that Hegel's philosophical views on Islam are far less epistemologically excising than Goux's? Is Islam better off misunderstood by Hegel than by Goux, for after all, Hegel wrote about Islam in a different atmosphere and did not use a terrorist event as a springboard for his critique?[51]

The answer to these questions is *no*. Like many scholars who specialize in Western philosophy, Goux offers a well-meaning attempt to find in the Hegelian idea of world history an answer to Islam's "collision" with the Western world today, arguing that such an answer derives from a philosophical discourse that Goux knows very well and believes is capable of encapsulating the totality of the human experience. Goux's invocation of Hegel's engagement with Islam derives from an urgent need to account for a dangerous collision of two temporalities:

> This collision-effect or untimely upsurge that has often been produced – and even more so today – in the relations between the West and the Arab-Muslim world are rooted in and separated by two very different relationships to narrative and to History. It is thus important in this context to address the two-fold question of Islam in History and History in Islam. This question is, of course, too large to be appropriately

> addressed in an essay. Nonetheless, six years after the events of September 11th, the question deserves at least to be posed. We ought to add that, beyond the terrorist attacks of September 11th, the many violent conflicts that occur all along the "fault lines" are not merely the expression of another type of historicity that is destined to remain foreign to us; that are also perhaps the symptom of a profound disruption in the traditional and secular relationship to historicity within Islam itself.[52]

Like the reasonable writer he tries to be, Goux wishes here to take a moderate position between extremes. But exactly what type of question is a "question of Islam in History and History in Islam?" Does Goux refer to Islam in Hegelian history? World history? Or does he speak about Islam in history in general? And what type of history? Intellectual? Universal? Anthropological? How does a vague question about Islam in history immediately conflict with a vaguer question about "history in Islam?" Does it even follow that Goux's reference to September 11 is an "example" of "untimely Islam," as he proposes? I think not. For to read this exegesis as an instance of ideological discourse – as Goux definitely does – is to attribute a political force to it. Rather than resorting to speculative philosophies of history that are foundationally suspect, let alone empirically impossible to prove, we must ask harder questions about whether or not Hegel's is a single philosophy, a singular structure of thought, or an integrated set of practical knowledge that cannot be understood outside of its particular context. Are we then to understand Islam as a religion that cares only for the vertical (heaven) at the expense of the horizontal (worldly future) and takes the past as an example to follow, abandoning any care for earth – hence September 11? Are we to infer from Goux's so-called 'Hegelian' interpretation that Islam is a religion lacking a worldly or secular telos and therefore heedless of life and its beings? The real burden that philosophy (literally: the love of wisdom) has placed on us is not to invoke a Eurocentric theory of intellectual history and apply it anachronistically to our present – for this, as I hope I have shown in this chapter, would be a mistake superimposed upon an error – but to confront the likelihood that sources within "Western philosophy" may be responsible for producing this divide in the first place.

If on the one hand Hegel's theory on Islam suffers from Europhilia or Prussophilia (blinding and fanatical love for Europe or Prussia) and ethnocentrism (lack of respect for the Other), Goux's theory on the other hand may be accused of essentialism (a view of cultural heritage and identity as an immutable spirit) and an unconscious Euronormative universalism (a belief that Europe sets the norms for the whole world), in addition to a paradoxical combination of ahistoricism (lack of respect for historical and temporal specificities) and historicism (a dangerous particularism that uses history to over-emphasize difference).

This said, Goux's argument is not necessarily culture-specific. It does not state as fact a world that is inhabited by self-contained and uniform cultural identities, each possessing a separate value, although his structuralist analysis of Hegel falls within this "fault line." Nor does it presume that Hegel's philosophy distinctively expresses a "Western" form of historical reason that is impenetrable to the Islamic 'Other.' Herein lies the illusionary synecdoche and the confusion of the part (Hegel/Europe/bin Laden) for the whole (the universe/Islam). The danger in this metonymic 'symbolist' mode of thought that Goux adopts is that even a 'philosophical' reading of September 11 requires a historical context, and one should not rely only on a 'formalist application' of Hegel without a radical contextualization *of* Hegel himself. For doing so simply features an awful "return of the same," but of the "same" changed by the misplaced motives that invited its "return" in the first place.

To give Goux the benefit of the doubt, his analogy is perhaps exercised in good faith and perhaps even from a deeper conviction than a so-called 'universal' theory of intellectual history accepted in his intellectual circle that supposedly has all the answers to today's global problems. This view – that the future is always already accounted for in some sacred past (be it religion or philosophy) – makes some scholars feel comfortable that an all-inclusive theory like Hegel's is capable of explaining Islamic radicalism today. But it is precisely this faith in the unconditional recyclability and infinite applicability of the grand masters of Western philosophy that is alarming. There is no safe anachronistic theory of this sort, and therefore no escape from repeating the same set of misconceptions if we treat derivatives as if they were substance merely because this is the only way we have been taught to think and this is the only language that we think we understand.

4

THE EMERGENCE OF ISLAM AS A HISTORICAL CATEGORY IN BRITISH COLONIAL THOUGHT

> He is the true prototype of the British colonist ... The whole Anglo-Saxon spirit is in Crusoe: the manly independence; the unconscious cruelty; the persistence; the slow yet efficient intelligence; the sexual apathy; the practical, well-balanced religiousness; the calculating taciturnity.
>
> James Joyce, "Daniel Defoe"

In his seminal essay on the Ottoman Empire during the eighteenth century, Albert Hourani takes an ambitious look at the ethno-religious dynamics of the Sultanate in the Fertile Crescent with special reference to Iraq, Syria, Lebanon, Palestine, and Egypt. By the beginning of the eighteenth century, the Balkans, the Fertile Crescent, the North African coast, and Asia Minor had come under the dominion of the Porte. But, as Hourani tells us, this century also witnessed the rise of many dissensions as well as non-conformist political and religious movements, especially in Lebanon, Armenia, and Najd, making this period a time of major shifts in the balance of power within the Ottoman Empire:

> Change was striking not only at the balance of political forces, but the social and intellectual structure on which it rested. Like all forms of government, the Ottoman system rested on a certain distribution of social power and a system of received ideas. Three principles were

> implicit in its structure: first, the political supremacy of Moslems over Christians; secondly, the existence of an Islamic orthodoxy of which the Sultan was defender; and thirdly, the primacy of religion over ethnic or other loyalties. In the eighteenth century all three pillars were shaken.[1]

Those inward forces that Hourani adeptly highlights, including the rise of Ibn Taymiyya-inspired Wahhābism and Ghazālī-oriented Ihyā'ism, in addition to numerous Christian intellectual movements in Lebanon and Armenia,[2] were not working in isolation from external influences. Towards the end of the seventeenth century and throughout the eighteenth, the hierarchy of power between Western Europe and Turkey shifted, irrevocably changing the relationship between Islam and the West. Fueled with the rhetoric of intellectual, cultural, and religious difference, this shift became dramatically more pronounced in the nineteenth century as the increasing pressure of a scientifically and militarily empowered Europe dictated the rules of world supremacy and shattered the myth of coherence in *Dār al-Islām* once and for all.

As I explained in the previous chapter, cultural developments in Western Europe involved the interaction and circulation of ideas among writers and intellectuals who were aware of the shift in the balance of power between the Ottoman Empire and Western Europe and conscious of the general mood of their times. Hegelianism is a good example of this phenomenon. Though the ideology was initiated by one thinker, Hegelian thought at large reflected the mood of the middle-class general public as well as the more specialized Young Hegelian thinkers like David Strauss, Bruno Bauer, Ludwig Feuerbach, and others. The cultural side of Hegelianism was inspired by European scientific progress and a rising spirit of liberalism that made the Ottoman Empire with its Islamic theology look medieval and archaic by comparison. Similarly, what we call the change in the public spirit of Europe at the turn of the century reflected not only cultural ideas stemming from a 'civilizational' difference between Islam and the West, but also a general impulse to defend Christian dogma now attacked by many intellectual currents from within, including Darwin's "positivistic determinism" and the so-called Hegelian higher critics, in addition to the external threat of the Ottoman Empire.

For the sake of specificity, the geographical contours of this chapter are limited to Britain, although there were important political developments in other places in Western Europe that led to the demise of the Porte and the 'scramble for Africa.' The emphasis on Britain is useful for consideration of its colonization of significant parts of the Arab-Muslim world, especially Egypt.

While writings about the Arab-Muslim world in eighteenth-century England were produced largely by academics and learned travelers, I would be mistaken to center my analysis entirely upon a critique of the thought of certain known scholars whose ideas, at one period in history, may or may not have influenced the political decisions of their rulers. I therefore take into consideration other discursive productions of eighteenth-century Britain, especially philological, epistolary, and novelistic writings. I also consider the fact that many philological studies and travel narratives of the eighteenth and nineteenth centuries were formulated with a *sovereign or national interest* in mind. John Richardson's *Dictionary, Arabic, Persian, and English* for example, is "most humbly dedicated to the King ... by his most dutiful servant and most faithful subject." Similarly, Lady Lucie Duff Gordon's *Letters from Egypt* address the Queen of England on many occasions.

But since cultural history is not only a habit of mind but also draws upon a much greater variety of influences, I focus in this chapter mainly on investigating the mechanics of cultural productions that allowed this kind of 'interest' to thrive and become symptomatic of a broader historical understanding and positioning of the Arab-Muslim world in nineteenth-century England. I argue that even before the emergence of anti-Islamic bias in the works of J.C. McCoan, or Mary Shelley, the eighteenth century served as a clear predecessor to an imminent condition of coloniality. This condition, evident in works like Daniel Defoe's *Robinson Crusoe* (1719) and in national reactions to major catastrophic events like the smallpox epidemic, indicates that many writers' and travelers' accounts of the non-European world stemmed not only from a general position of antipathy and confrontation, but also from an *inherited* cultural and religious bias. My goal is to identify one strand of British culture as part of an imperialist discourse that is partially anti-Arab and anti-Islamic in its epistemic varieties, which must not be confused with colonial practices or reactions of the colonized, which are the topic of the next chapter.

Figure 4.1 "Robinson Crusoe and Man Friday," by Carl Offterdinger (1829–89)

Articulating Difference: Cultural Hegemony and Colonial Disgust

Although the connection between coloniality and Defoe's *Robinson Crusoe* has been made by many writers and intellectuals, including James Joyce,[3] Edward Said,[4] Peter Hulme,[5] and Derek Walcott,[6] the present emphasis on this text is because, in retrospect, this tale of adventure and self-sufficiency would come to metonymize British colonial brutality at its most extreme, as I illustrate with reference to Egypt in the next chapter. It is worth noting that though the rise of the English novel is a sign of literary modernity (according to Ian Watt),[7] this very genre is a product of an unconscious colonial epistemology and testifies to a dominant mode of thought that informed the discourse of imperialism two hundred years before Britain embarked on its colonial projects in the Arab world.

In the Preface to *Robinson Crusoe*, Defoe insists that his narrative is a "true account," seeking to make his narrative believable by asserting that it was dictated by 'reality' or had the ability to 'report' such a reality. Of course, Defoe's novel was not generally believed to be a true account, but its 'veracity' has always been understood as a generic convention. But since his claims to authenticity stem from a manner of thinking that gives literature the status of history, Defoe's statement is worthy of consideration. Not only is Crusoe a master of his own new world, but he also happens to master writing, the very condition for entering into a conquering capitalist society according to poststructuralist writers like Michel de Certeau.[8] As Crusoe tells us, "I drew up the state of my affairs in writing, not so much to leave them to any that were to come after me, for I was likely to have but few heirs, as to deliver my thoughts from daily poring upon them, and afflicting my mind."[9]

The novel's first lines tell us about the vaulting ambition of Crusoe, his "rambling thoughts," and his desire to explore the unknown. As the narrator reports, "There was something fatal in his nature. He had conceived the idea, he must go to sea."[10] The misfortunes of his two brothers, the tears of his relatives, the advice of his friends, the protest of his reason, and the remorse of his conscience are all powerless in their attempts to restrain him. Crusoe arguably represents the West's unswerving desire for expansion. Crusoe works all day and all night; he is a carpenter, an oarsman, a porter, a hunter, a tiller of the ground, a milkman, a basket-maker, a grinder, baker, and a book-keeper. But his work is planned and rational. He sets to work only after deliberate calculation and reflection. When he seeks a spot for his tent, he enumerates the four conditions of the place he requires. But this is not all. Step by step, Defoe's Crusoe must recreate and re-master the inventions and acquisitions of human industry, like the pioneers of Australia and America. By imaginatively re-subjecting the West to the test of human intellect against nature and the savage, Defoe exalts his hero as a conqueror and master of the island: "I was lord of the whole Manor; or if I pleas'd, I might call myself King, or emperor over the whole Country which I have Possession of. There were no Rivals. I had no Competitor, none to dispute Sovereignty or Command with me."[11]

Crusoe's island is a haven of modernity: it isolates a place of one's own, and reproduces all the surrounding objects in the form of a bricolage by a dominant subject capable of transforming the 'natural' into the 'civilized.' The desire to write is an exercise of mental freedom. But this freedom also marks an assertion of power over time and space, which is embodied in Crusoe's decision to write his diary. As a new space of mastery, writing becomes the epitome of 'modern' civilization, as well as the dream of the present Englishman to create a new universe different from the past.

On the island, Crusoe acquires a community habit, even though he is his own community. On the day he sees "the print of a naked man's foot on the shore," he stands, "like one thunderstruck," and flees "like a hare to cover."[12] A foreigner represents a violation of his community and a threat to his system. But this leads us to another question. If we accept the hypothesis that the novel is an exercise of individual will (another variation on the theme of modernity), why are Friday and the cannibals he represents necessary at all? Why is Friday's conversion to Christianity even relevant, and what can we learn about the connection between Friday's name and Crusoe's, with its etymological reference to crucifixion? Is the reason for including a cannibal in the novel motivated by a desire to add an exotic flavor to the narrative, or could there be a better argument for Friday's relevance to the plot, not to speak of the particular region in the world where the events take place?

I am not trying to repeat an argument already made by other critics, notably Peter Hulme, that Defoe's novel is a 'mimetic' allegory of colonialism, or that it is concerned with the more epistemic task of reasserting the beginnings of colonial encounters in order to proclaim Europe's supremacy over its (Caribbean) colonies.[13] Regardless of whether or not Defoe's novel is a celebration of emergent capitalism as Karl Marx sees it[14] or an ideological remapping of European colonization, it succeeds in showing us that the formation of the modern (European) Self – what has at least since the Enlightenment become known as the "subject" – is necessarily formed in opposition to what is Other to this Self. If Defoe's novel coincides with a moment in European thought when an understanding of history was based on the idea of legitimation, it is scarcely surprising that the narrative's events take place on a 'foreign' island. The geographical location of this island would of course serve as new ground for the modern discovery of the subject.

In this respect, Crusoe's island with its "barbaric cannibals" is not significantly different from Lord Cromer's Egypt with its "barbaric Muslims" that I will discuss at greater length in the next chapter.[15] Although written almost two hundred years prior to the British occupation of Egypt, Defoe's account of Crusoe's encounter with Friday calls to mind Lord Cromer's language about the Egyptians in *Modern Egypt* (1907). This two-volume memoir is written in a manner that seeks to convince its readers that England created the idea of civilization. This book consistently depicts Islam as a barbaric religion and Egyptians and Sudanese as irrevocably Other, less than human, or at least naturally subordinate to Europeans – much like the character of Friday on Crusoe's Island.[16] In his book, mainly written to justify the role of Britain in Egypt, Cromer depicts Muslim Egyptians not only as socially different from Christians but also as lower in status. His definition of Islam takes an essentialist outlook of a primordial religion resistant to change, as if he were oblivious of the way that essentialist views of religion had long been under sustained intellectual attack by eminent critics like Wilfrid Blunt (1840–1922).[17] This marvelous historicization of the Englishman's role in the European and non-European worlds is of course best understood in light of major shifts in economic and political power in the British Empire during the 1860s. The so-called 'non-interventionist' policy of England in the colonies was only used as a placating phrase to deflect or appease opposition to colonial expansion among the English public. Decades after England had settled in Egypt, its official colonial tone of radical civilizational essentialism still prevailed.

This geopolitical 'impression' of human civilization, namely that one cannot be civilized without being Christian, white, and educated in the European system, created a deeply rooted antipathy towards Islam. This imaginary Euronormativism would eventually transform aggressive European colonialism into a legitimate project and perpetuate such agendas for more than two centuries. After 24 years of ruling Egypt as the British commissioner, Cromer replicated Crusoe's scenario with Friday, describing a different belief system (Islam in this case) as a hopeless and incorrigible religion, believing that the high moral values of Christianity would allow the British Empire to avoid the pitfalls that brought the Roman Empire to ruin.[18] A closer look at both narratives reveals that the subjection of the Other to the so-called 'civilizing' Self derives from a complex process of self-formation and self-idealization ingrained since the rise of modernity in the notion of the (European) subject which, if it had to have an Other, required this Other to be by definition inferior to the Self. This Other is inevitably submissive and remains in the 'natural' course of a would-be-independent, that is, an infant crawling along the path of civilization. In a fatherless universe, which is an important trope in colonial modernity, the mastery of writing establishes and distinguishes a new power as a source from which imperialist discourses derive their strength and control history, that is, the privilege of making, fabricating, and writing beginnings.

Like Defoe's novel, Cromer's narrative takes on the form of a memoir, becoming completely immersed in Britain as its central character, and forcing us to see everything through the eyes of Cromer himself. In his eyes, Islam debases and relegates women to a "marked" secondarity: "Unfortunately the great Arabian reformer of the seventh century was driven by the necessities of his position to do more than found a religion. He endeavoured to found a social system. The reasons why Islam as a social system has been a complete failure are manifold. First and foremost Islam keeps women in a position of marked inferiority."[19] It is writing that makes both Crusoe and Cromer masters, and it is the lack of it that makes Friday and the Egyptians their servants.

Like Crusoe on the island, Cromer in Egypt becomes the subject who writes about the country and its 'governable' Orientals. In another article, he writes that "in their present state of political immaturity the peoples of the East "were singularly incapable of judging what … was best in their own interests. Questions should be decided for them and not by them."[20] In other words, Friday and the Egyptians are dependents of the likes of Cromer and Crusoe, in education, in language, and in naming, as submission is the most basic condition of those who have just been elevated from the realm of barbarism to that of the human and of civilization. In the imaginative world of *Robison Crusoe* and *Modern Egypt*, Englishness is a curious amalgamation of Christianity, whiteness, and mental superiority.

There is, undeniably, a remarkable difference between an eighteenth-century work of fiction and a twentieth-century book recounting the experience of someone who came to symbolize "the pro-consular tradition in British imperialism."[21] But through a scrupulous examination of what Crusoe himself describes as "a very strange encounter,"[22] and "a new Scene of my life,"[23] I wish to emphasize the point that that "scene" and that "encounter" with the Other (which does not make Crusoe question for once that *he* in fact is the Other) are not just the result of the fictive underpinnings of an eighteenth-century novelistic mind, but are deeply tied to the expansionist ambitions of the British Empire-to-be. The composition and achievement of this British imperialist Self *requires* a master–slave moment, and the locus of this experience in Defoe's *Robinson Crusoe* could not have been chosen more appropriately.

In this very context, one can argue that European modernity has never been completely secular. Missionary campaigns in colonized Africa were

Figure 4.2 Anti-imperialist and anti-missionary cartoon: "The New African Mission" (1875)

inextricably linked to a so-called modern humanitarian project. Crusoe himself, whose name, as I noted earlier, etymologically invokes the cross, embarks on a journey of Christian salvation and reconciliation, crowned with the physical and spiritual saving of a barbarous cannibal. However, Friday's conversion to Christianity does not in the least affect the master–slave hierarchy that Crusoe establishes and maintains throughout. Unity in faith, it appears, is not enough to establish social and political equity.

Likewise, the Prince of Abyssinia in Samuel Johnson's novel *Rasselas* (1759), who is apparently envious of 'life in Europe,' poses the following question to his court advisor Imlac: "By what means are the Europeans thus powerful? Or why, since they can so easily visit Asia and Africa for trade or conquest, cannot the Asiaticks and Africans invade their coasts, plant colonies in their ports, and give laws to their natural princes? The same wind that carries them back would bring us thither."[24] In response to Rasselas's query, Imlac acknowledges the power of the Europeans, which he attributes mainly to a higher degree of wisdom and knowledge granted the European man by the mysterious work of the Divine: "They are more powerful, Sir, than we, answered Imlac, because they are wiser; knowledge will always predominate over ignorance, as man governs the other animals. But why their knowledge is more than ours, I know not what reason can be given, but the unsearchable will of the Supreme Being."[25] It is as if the rest of the world, including the part of it that is actually the cradle of Christianity, is not to be equal to the English or the European, not just because it is non-Christian, but also because of its supposed mental and racial inferiority.

Vicious Plague-ridden Muslim Bodies

Imperialist imaginings of the Other not just as cannibal or infidel but also as 'disease carrier' dominated eighteenth-century British ideology's fierce distinction between Islam and Christianity, the first conceived of as a spiritually empty superstitious belief, and the latter as the only 'true' religion. Typically enough, in his 1790 treatise, Sir Robert Walker, physician and Fellow of the Royal College of Surgeons, made the argument that Arabia was responsible for the spread of the smallpox epidemic in Britain and Europe: "We are indebted to the Arabians for the first accounts of small-pox, among whom the disease appears to have been common, and who were the means of spreading its infection through the different kingdoms of Europe."[26]

This and many other medical accounts appearing at the outbreak of smallpox in eighteenth-century England show us how anti-Islam and anti-Arab sentiments were tied to a pervasive fear of the Ottoman Other. This is the moment when Islam and the Arab world were upgraded from a cultural or racial group to a historical category in Europe's positivistic schema of intellectual history. This is also the moment when the anti-Arab British 'hero' was no longer an individual or an army but an entire field of knowledge, like medicine.

It is interesting how by the early nineteenth century smallpox inoculation, which originated and was practiced in the Arab world and Turkey, became a European medical 'invention,' while the disease itself was connected with the birth of Prophet Muḥammad. "As England emerges into a colonialist modernity," the literary critic Felicity Nussbaum writes, "its wish to amputate from national memory a past associated with the ancient and the Arabic reaches crisis force and is strongly evident in the discussion of smallpox and inoculation."[27] Nussbaum's observation is supported by volumes of medical treatises on the smallpox outbreak that appeared in eighteenth-century Britain and continued throughout the nineteenth.[28] A notable anti-Islamic polemicist of the early nineteenth century is James Plumptre, who took every chance he had to connect the smallpox plague with Islam. An active priest and playwright, Plumptre writes in his 1805 *Sermons* that "the Arabian Pestilence," a phrase he uses to refer to smallpox, "had its rise in Arabia, at the very time of the Imposter Mahomet, and was spread by the Saracen invaders whithersoever they carried their arms and doctrines."[29]

Lady Mary Wortley Montagu (1689–1762) in a much different tone composed her account of the inoculation in the early eighteenth century. A close reading of Lady Montagu's letters reveals that the lines between health and disease, or normalcy and the abnormal, were only constructed to protect Britain against its so-called enemies in an age of imperialism. Lady Montagu refutes the allegations against the Muslim world on the heated topic of inoculation, not only by exposing the medicinal errors of the Members of the Royal College of Physicians, but also by sending her son to receive inoculation in Turkey.[30] Afflicted by the death of her brother Lord Kingston of smallpox, she traveled to Turkey in order to get her son "engrafted."[31] In the process, Lady Montagu learned a great deal about the bias of her own culture against Turkey and Islam:

> Every year thousands undergo this Operation, and the French Ambassador says pleasantly that they take the Smallpox here [in Turkey] by way of diversion as they take the Waters in other Countrys [sic]. There is no example of anyone that has dy'd in it, and you may believe I am very well satisfy'd of the safety of the Experiment since I intend to try it on my dear little Son. I am Patriot enough to take pains to bring this useful invention into fashion in England, and I should not fail to write to some of our Doctors very particularly about it if I knew any one of'em that I thought had Virtue enough to destroy such a considerable branch of their Revenue for the good of Mankind.[32]

It is evident here that Lady Montagu writes against the grain. The defiant medical discourse of the Royal College of Physicians which committed murder in the name of medicine and national arrogance[33] was not separated from the general *épistémè* that regarded Islam as a culturally inferior category.

Indeed, Lady Montagu was not the only one to notice this phenomenon. In his "Dissertation on the Languages, Literatures, and Manners of Eastern Nations," which accompanies his *Dictionary, Arabic, Persian, and English* (1777), John Richardson draws attention to this Self versus Other discourse and vehemently condemns what he perceives as predominant political predispositions and biases against the Arab-Muslim world in the British Empire. In his study, Richardson provides an excellent example of how philological scholarship of alien cultures should be conducted. In his work, he sets out to expose the ignorance and biases in his contemporaries' accounts of Islam by citing the example of the story of Lysimachus and the Greek historian:

> The story of Lysimachus and one Greek historian, may indeed, with justice, be applied to many others. This prince, in the partition of Alexander's empire, became King of Thrace: he had been one of the most active of that conqueror's commanders; and was present at every event which deserved the attention of history. A Grecian had written an account of the Persian conquest; and he wished to read it before the King. The monarch listened with equal attention and wonder: "All this is very fine," says he, when the historian had finished, "but where was I when those things were performed?"[34]

This parable speaks for itself. Richardson is simply confirming the obvious fact that the telling of history is not necessarily the history that happened and that no eighteenth-century historian simply 'happens' upon Islam or the Arabs for the sake of mere intellectual curiosity. In his work, Richardson calls for an accurate and unbiased view of history that aims "to improve the great system of social life." Richardson does this by employing a methodology of studying Arab and Islamic studies that is fact-based and relies on specialization rather than polemics. Fighting a cause similar to Edward Said's but almost two centuries earlier, Richardson takes aim at "modern compilers of ancient history" who willfully "conceal their ignorance of the languages and literatures of the East" under one general and unsupported assertion that they are "wild, uninteresting, and obscure," or what modern scholarship refers to as "Orientalism." Richardson's anti-mainstream view of history is a result not only of acquired first-hand knowledge but also of an ethical insight that what is distant and alien is not necessarily subhuman or barbarian.

According to Richardson, most eighteenth-century scholars encountered Islam as the founding religion of Europe's arch enemy, the Ottoman Empire, the language of non-Christian political and nationalistic discourses (a perpetual source of misunderstanding in the Christian West), and the culture that enveloped all the curiosities and secret fantasies of a bewildering Orient, especially after the translation of *Les mille et une nuits* by Antoine Galland between 1704 and 1717 and its translation into English as *The Arabian Nights* between 1706 and 1708.[35] Richardson's account takes issue with the kind of knowledge generated when England's interest in the Arab-Muslim world is hemmed in by two simultaneous forces: European Enlightenment urgencies for "civilizing" other cultures, and a growing historical reassessment of a familiar Christian "self" versus an unfamiliar Islamic "Other."

Islam and the Residing Nineteenth-Century Orientalist

Historiographical European accounts of Islam, which assumed a scholarly status in the eighteenth century and flourished in the nineteenth, can best be understood in the framework of major changes in historical thought and the rise of systematic scholarship about distant cultures. Since not every historian is a John Richardson, the fact remains that for the most part, English interest in Islam and the Arab world conformed to a nationalist fashioning of the British self in opposition to its Other. The result is that very little of what goes on in the philological or scientific assessment has much to say to scholars interested in the nationalist discourses.[36] But since there is never interpretation or knowledge where there is no interest, and since there is no scholarship without precedence or motivation, what exactly are the interests of a nineteenth-century European scholar or traveler, like Edward Lane, for example, in reading and decoding Islam? A simple answer could be that he is transmitting to his own people knowledge about another culture unknown to them. Still, how is one to overcome the difficulties of living in another culture and yet manage to decode it as easily as if he were decoding a Shakespearean sonnet? This is tricky, especially when knowledge of the Arab world and Islam is subject to imprecision and hasty interpretation even today. What exactly is at stake, then, in a scholarly effort seeking to overcome distances and insurmountable cultural barriers in order to make knowledge of the Arab and Islamic world accessible to the English reader?

This is not to say that knowledge of another culture is not possible or useful, but in order to ascertain the objectivity of this knowledge and save it from lapsing into stereotype and myth, a few conditions other than the misleading proto-scientific 'positivistic' methods of research need to be met – conditions that most English and European scholars of Arabic, Islam, and the Middle East of the time lacked. First, a conveyer of historical knowledge must be answerable to and in healthy contact with the alien culture s/he historicizes. It is unfortunate that most of what the West knew about the non-Western world was delivered in the frameworks of xenophobia and imperialism. There can rarely be healthy assimilation and conveyance of knowledge under political domination.

The second condition is based on the first: the need for non-political anthropological and social knowledge, that is, knowledge of the social world, the lived linguistic expression, and the daily realities of the culture in question as opposed to geographical, philological, or historical knowledge conveyed through the lens of a dominant *épistémè* of binary oppositions, as de Certeau has shown us in the case of de Léry's *Histoire*. This knowledge is crucial for matters of interpretation and judgment, and this is where one's awareness of one's own culture is juxtaposed to one's understanding of another.

Taking Edward William Lane's classic work *An Account of the Manners and Customs of the Modern Egyptians* (1836) as a case in point,[37] we find that Lane's 'scholarly' understanding of Egypt and Islam does not appear to differ fundamentally from work done on Arab and Muslim cultures in the eighteenth century.[38] Such works do not get completed overnight. Special training is necessary to reach functional proficiency in Arabic in order to live among and communicate with Egyptians (using Classical and Modern Standard Arabic, in addition to colloquial Egyptian Arabic). The result could be a best-seller or an ever-widening gap between assertions based on personal experience in an alien culture and the far more dominant assertions of one's home culture.

Views differ on Lane's *Account*. While the historian H.S. Deighton sees it as a political text, Edward Said regards it as a variation on Orientalism. Deighton sees Lane's *Account* as an important public text, the first political book of its kind written during Europe's 'scramble for Africa' to speak about the Egyptian peasants, describe their religious rituals, address them as the real natives of Egypt, and detail their daily afflictions under the Ottoman regime known as *sukhra* or forced labor:

> In part, Lane's attitude to the native people of Egypt was a direct result of Palmerston's determination to resist the French project for digging the Suez Canal. Frustrated in the attempt to secure, by diplomatic means, the repeal of the *ferman*, which gave de Lesseps the necessary authority to go ahead with his project, successive British governments switched their attacks to its likely social effect on Egypt itself. The Canal, it was argued, would not benefit Egypt at all, and would do incalculable harm to the native Egyptians, both during its construction by the ruthless use of forced labour, and afterwards by increasing and making permanent the European community in the country, which was represented as being for the most part rapacious, unscrupulous and, from the point of view of Egyptian interests, thoroughly undesirable.[39]

To Deighton, then, Lane's work reflects an existing political discourse in England, one in which the populace's attitude towards Egyptians had little to do with the Egyptians themselves or with their cultural practices, but with the colonial war over Egypt being fought against France. The usual formula occurs: the so-called humanitarian intervention becomes an easy pretext for asserting power. Britain's description of its intervention in Egypt's politics as an attempt to stop France from inflicting what Deighton describes as "intolerable harm to native Egyptians" is part of a larger pattern where every major colonial intervention has been justified as humanitarian and as a "civilizing mission."

Said, however, takes a different approach to Lane and sees him as an ideal example for his case against European Orientalists. In fact, there is a special category for Lane's work in Said's theory of Orientalism. Said regards Lane as one of three types of "residing" nineteenth-century Orientalists. To Said, Lane is "the writer who intends to use his residence for the specific task of providing professional Orientalism with scientific material, who considers his residence a form of scientific observation."[40] Said accuses Lane of having a double identity, of being what in our modern terms would be called a secret agent. While one part of Lane's identity, argues Said, immerses itself with

Egyptians and "floats easily in the unsuspected Muslim sea," the other skillfully hides its historiographical agenda and submerges itself as it relentlessly seeks to transform Egyptian Muslims into a stereotypical European text:

> What [Lane] says about the Orient is therefore to be understood as description obtained in a one-way exchange: as *they* spoke and behaved, *he* observed and wrote down. His power is to have existed among them as a native speaker, as it were, and also a secret writer. And what he wrote was intended as useful knowledge not for them, but for Europe and its various disseminating institutions. For that's one thing that Lane's prose never lets us forget: that ego, the first pronoun moving through Egyptian customs, rituals, festivals, infancy, adulthood, and burial rites, is in reality both an Oriental masquerade and an Orientalist device for capturing and conveying valuable, otherwise inaccessible information.[41]

While it is possible that Lane was engaged in an act of historiographical reduction of Egypt, it is still hard to agree with Said's theory that the former was a malicious manipulator and a cunning conspirer, for one important reason: there is no evidence, textual or otherwise, to incriminate Lane and there is nothing wrong with a scholar conveying his own impressions of the culture he immersed himself in for many years. This is a personal account that neither Said nor anyone living beyond Lane's time can simply dismiss as conniving. Said's categories are not founded on any credible sociological grounding, making one wonder why the 'Orient' is above criticism and why precisely three types of "residing Orientalist" existed.

There is, however, a clear anti-Ottoman political context to Lane's work, whose dramatic depiction of life in ancient Egypt did not distract him from addressing the country's contemporary Islam, ushering his readers through 'fascinating' religious rituals and cultural practices.[42] In his book, Lane pulled no punches in showing the barbarism and inhumanity of the Turks in Egypt. Dwelling on the negative connotations of the word *fallāḥ* (peasant; pl. *fallāḥīn*), Lane writes, "the Turks always apply this term to the Egyptians in general in an abusive sense as meaning the 'boors' or the 'clowns.'"[43] Lane, however, fails to see the contradiction between his critique of the Turks and his own position on the Egyptian *fallāḥīn*. "The felláheen [sic] of Egypt," he continues, "cannot be justly represented in a very favourable light with regard to their domestic and social condition and manners. In the worst point of view, they resemble their bedawee [sic: i.e. Bedouin] ancestors, without possessing many of the virtues of the inhabitants of the desert."[44]

If we take this statement as a sign of the discourse that produced it, then the reserved and somewhat belittling tone of Lane's narrative reveals how England's apparent sympathy towards the Egyptian *fallāḥīn* was not simply a fashionable sentiment in nineteenth-century England but a politically charged document of imperialism, exercised more in the spirit of chivalrous and 'charitable' Britishness towards wretched victims than in egalitarian feelings for Egyptians. In a similar account, the British author and traveler James Augustus St. John referred to the Egyptian *fallāḥīn* in a like tone.[45]

This persistent reference to the wretched and slave-like condition of Egypt's peasants is not without imperialist motivations. In the decades preceding the British occupation of Egypt, political correspondence between England and France underscored the question of the Egyptian *fallāḥīn*. In 1855, the British ambassador in Paris wrote to the French government warning against the use of forced labor, which seemed the only way possible to carry out the project of digging the Suez Canal.[46] The British warning resulted in the promulgation of a policy prohibiting the use of corvée, said to have diligently been monitored by the British officials in Egypt.[47] Eventually, England was able to end the forced labor of 60,000 *fallāḥīn* on the Canal.[48] Years later, it became clear that forced labor prohibition was only a practice of interventionist English politics to undermine French enterprises in Egypt. As soon as England occupied Egypt in 1882, its standards were completely reversed as it undertook large-scale projects that relied on forced labor, including the construction of the Alexandria–Suez railway, Britain's preferred alternative to the Canal.[49]

Justified by a humane call to protect abused peasants, eliminate slavery, and civilize the country, England's mission in Egypt had an enormous agenda for economic gain. On reading Samuel W. Baker's travel narrative on Egypt, *Spectator* Editor-in-Chief Meredith Townsend commented:

> With 5000 Arabs thoroughly disciplined, a man like Mr. Baker would ensure order from Khartoum to the lake and that must one day be the first step towards the utilization of the vast regions which now yield only elephant tusks to Europe and females to the harems of Egypt, Turkey and Africa.[50]

According to Townsend, a well-established colonial government was needed for Britain's full economic control over the Nile Valley. Written less than two decades before England occupied Egypt, and without regard for the business-like nature of the occupational project, Townsend's comment anticipates such a colonial scheme and reflects the attitude already inherent in the English public sphere toward exploiting Egyptian and Sudanese resources. Townsend's comment also serves as a reminder that England's occupation of Egypt was not a sudden or unexpected event as some historians have argued.[51]

As we have seen in Lane's account, England's interest in Egypt expressed itself not only in crude 'business' terms but in moral terms as well. Lady Lucie Duff Gordon's *Letters from Egypt* (1862–69) is a good example of this nationalist tendency.[52] In her letters, Lady Duff Gordon speaks about Egypt's historical importance and relates it to the biblical past. Like Lane's *Account*, Lady Duff Gordon's *Letters* is written with a rhetoric of compassion and a desire to draw attention to the significance of Egypt's 'Judeo-Christian' history. Her reference to Egypt's impoverished inhabitants is calculated to provoke British sympathy for the cause of the Egyptian peasants. The wide circulation and favorable reception of her letters, especially among Unitarians, led a reviewer to argue that "[T]he Asiatic can never be understood by those who hate him and the woman who thinks every Arab graceful and dignified will understand him far better than one who is only impressed by his … squalor."[53]

Written from the perspective of a British traveler who identifies with the persecution of Egyptians under the Ottomans, *Letters from Egypt* provides a scathing criticism of Khedive Ismail (1863–79) who is known to have granted unprecedented privileges to Europeans in Egypt in his frenetic attempt to expand the country's economic resources. One reference is remarkably clear throughout Lady Duff Gordon's letters: heavy taxes and labor under corvée were imposed fiercely in Egypt in the 1860s; Ismail's regime was so abusive of Egyptian peasants that they revolted against him. Lady Duff Gordon's letters portray this miserable condition with unfailing lucidity and empathy towards her Egyptian hosts.[54]

Benefiting from an existing religious discourse and a rising middle class morality, Lady Duff Gordon's travelogue includes three recurrent leitmotifs. First, it triggers a kind of sympathy among Unitarian members of the nineteenth-century British community by comparing Egypt's biblical past to the present miserable conditions of its inhabitants. Secondly, it creates a 'global' spirit of imperial authority and moral responsibility expressed by the British middle class; and finally, it underscores the horror of Ottoman atrocities in Egypt. These leitmotifs are undoubtedly produced by an Orientalist *épistémè*. But what is new about them is that unlike Lane's account, they are not the scholarly work of a premeditated 'Orientalist' mind. They are rather the writings of a female bourgeoise British subject advised to move to Egypt for medical reasons. Nonetheless, the letters still urge England to intervene to save Egypt from its ruthless Turks. Duff Gordon saw Egypt as "one vast 'plantation' where the master works his slaves without even feeding them."[55]

Inadvertently or not, her letters added a Christian element to England's prospective colonial mission in Egypt, while still emphasizing the more urgent problem that faced the country: "I wish they could see the domineering of the Greeks and Maltese as Christians… . There are plenty of other divisions besides that of Christian and Muslim. Here in Egypt it is clear enough: it is Arab versus Turk."[56] She "felt the 'foot of the Turk' heavy indeed"[57] and ascribed much of Egypt's dilemma to the abuses of the Ottoman Empire: "The Sultan is worn out, and the Muslims here know it, and say it would be the best day for the Arabs if he were driven out; that after all a Turk never was the true … Commander of the Faithful."[58] Moreover, she played the role of the wise and faithful ambassadress in her letters, briefing the Queen as well as the British community of native support should Britain decide to "invade" Egypt:

> Two great Sheykhs of Bishareen and Abab'deh came here and picked me up out walking alone. We went and sat in a field, and they begged me to communicate to the Queen of England that they would join her troops if she would invade Egypt. One laid my hand on his hand and said 'Thou hast 3,000 men in thy hand.' The other rules 10,000. They say there are 30,000 Arabs (bedaween) ready to join the English, for they fear that the Viceroy will try to work and rob them like the fellaheen, and if so they will fight to the last, or else go off into Syria. I was rather frightened – for them, I mean, and told them that our Queen could do nothing till 600 Sheykhs and 400 Ameers had talked in public – all whose talk was printed and read at Stambool and Cairo, and that they must not think of such a thing from our Queen, but if things became bad, it would be better for them to go off into Syria.[59]

Lady Duff Gordon thus saw herself as the voice of Egypt and as a faithful eye-witness reporter to the Empire. While we do not know to what extent her letters had an effect on Britain's policy in Egypt, there is no doubt that her account was more grist that came to the mill of pre-existing animosity towards the Ottoman Empire, serving both as a reminder of Britain's 'moral' responsibility and a pretext for colonizing Egypt in 1882.

Immediately after Britain occupied Egypt, reference to this global spirit of moral responsibility was reaffirmed. In the *Preface* to the second edition of J.C. McCoan's *Egypt* (1882, republished as *Egypt As It Is*), the publisher has this to say about Britain's intervention in Egypt:

> On the whole, that intervention has been wisely directed, and been the means of delivering the people from grinding oppressions, and laying the foundations of a better civilization. But human nature in Egypt is the same that it is elsewhere. The followers of Mohamet [sic] do not like to be under the rule of Christians, and the instinct of nationality among them is strong. The native populations revolt at seeing the Khedive under the sway of foreigners, who receive large salaries for administering the government according to European and Christian methods... . What will be the outcome, immediate or remote, of the conflict upon which England has entered, it would be idle to predict. That the Suez Canal will be protected for the world's use, in any event, no doubt needs to be entertained... . Let us hope that, as a consequence of those changes, or in spite of them, the course of civilization and Christianity in the East may be promoted.
>
> August 1, 1882.[60]

Prefacing McCoan's already widely circulated book so that it would promote a war of "civilization and Christianity" against backwardness and Islam, this statement confirms the Christian-capitalist undertones of England's 'civilizing mission.' Like Lady Duff Gordon's letters, McCoan's account carries an Orientalist epistemology, though with a different emphasis. The book's re-publication and massive circulation testifies to the existence of a militant colonial current of Christendom in nineteenth-century England. This current embraces the mythical and imagined notion of a modern British morality with a historic mission of restoring Christianity and civilization to Egypt and thus, by implication, liberating it from barbarism and Islam. It is obvious from this note that what kept the 'idea' of the British Empire intact was a sense of 'high culture' considered necessary no matter how it was achieved. Not only does the publisher relate Christianity to the Enlightenment in a crude dehistoricized fashion, but he also manages to collapse them both into a secular mission manifested in imperialist 'high culture.' Because of that concept of colonial modernity, notions like geopolitical tenacity and pluralist cultural exclusivism did not perish or disappear from Britain. To many, including McCoan, the nineteenth-century English logo of colonialism read as follows: "If you are not Christian, you are not civilized." The irony is that this ecclesiastical coloniality somehow identifies itself as English or European at large, which would also make McCoan's text read: "If you are not English or European, you are not Christian or civilized." In other words, secular modernity has become Britain's new Christianity. With this transformation, a new concept of history different from medieval Christian history is constructed in Britain, not of "God," or of "man," but of God's Christian Englishman.

Within this framework, it is not difficult to guess how and why the 'scramble for Africa' brought with it the desire to relate Europe to rational thinking and to find a legitimate genealogy tracing the history of thinking and the birth of the "idea" back to Ancient Greece. Centralizing Greece as the geophilosophical locus of Europe became the task of nineteenth-century Orientalism. What is excluded from this history, as Said has painfully reminded us, is not just the "non-Christian," but the non-European, the non-thinking, the non-West, and the non-civilized.[61]

Islam and Monstrosity

I began this chapter with a critique of the nationalist *épistémè* in British colonial thought in the eighteenth and nineteenth centuries. I then traced aspects of this coloniality in various literary, philological, and historiographical narratives by investigating its formative pillars. I now conclude with a well-known nineteenth-century literary text whose construction relies principally on the critique of humanity versus monstrosity: Mary Shelley's *Frankenstein* (1817).

In this early nineteenth-century novel, Frankenstein's famous imaginative monster studies the account of creation in the Bible in order to argue with his maker, Victor, and to convince him to create a partner for him, akin to the biblical story of Adam and Eve. There is more irony to this story than meets the eye.[62] When the so-called monster runs away from Victor's lab and takes shelter in a country cottage to avoid human contact after he realizes his own ugliness, he begins his educational journey into humanity by listening to French lessons given to an Arab woman by the name of Safie, a name which means in Arabic "pure" or "clear," and, whether intentionally or not, implies the process of cleansing and purification that Safie is to undergo. Safie is presented in the novel as a woman who has been rescued from the barbarity of the Arab Islamic world and is now receiving her first lessons of humanization.[63] But this humanization is presented as Westernization. It is as if Safie herself, and by proxy her entire background and tradition, were in a monster-stage, at the very starting point along the path of true human civilization:

> Safie related, that her mother was a Christian Arab, seized and made a slave by the Turks; recommended by her beauty, she had won the heart of the father of Safie, who married her. The young girl spoke in high and enthusiastic terms of her mother, who, born in freedom, spurned the bondage to which she was now reduced. She instructed her daughter in the tenets of her religion, and taught her to aspire to higher powers of intellect and independence of spirit, forbidden to the female followers of Mahomet. This lady died. But her lessons were indelibly impressed on the mind of Safie, who sickened at the prospect of again returning to Asia, and being immured within the walls of a harem, allowed only to occupy herself with infantile amusements, ill suited to the temper of her soul, now accustomed to grand ideas and a noble emulation for virtue. The prospect of marrying a Christian, and remaining in a country where women were allowed to take a rank in society, was enchanting to her.[64]

As seen in this passage, Safie's father, the only Muslim/Turk in Shelley's novel, is reduced to a lusty, evil, treacherous opportunist willing to lie and break his promises to a noble Christian, Felix, a gallant and chivalrous young man ready to sacrifice his own life to save the lives of the Muslim Turk and his daughter. The unnamed father serves as a foil and a destroyer of a pure romantic love affair between the valiant Felix and Safie, who wish to marry. Safie is represented as resentful of her father's Islam. She is an adherent of her mother's Christianity, which according to the narrator is superior to Islam as it preaches virtue, freedom, and grand ideas. In short, British Christianity, or

Mary Shelley's nineteenth century's romanticized vision of it, is everything that Arabian Islam is not. If we add this to the education that Safie (and the monster in hiding) must receive, then the message is clear: the only path to civilization is one that involves Christianity, French lessons, Goethe's *Werther*, and John Milton's *Paradise Lost*. Shelley's Safie and the monster are foreign samples in a lab of the grand project of modernity. They must master the knowledge of *Western* man to count as civilized humans.[65]

It is not an excuse that this novella was written by an 18-year-old who must have imbibed the cultural bias of her own society without much criticism. What we learn is that epistemic assumptions of hegemony and superiority are not new in colonial discourses. Many postcolonial writers, including Fanon and Said, addressed such issues in their respective critiques of colonial reason. Both Fanon and Said have provided insightful critiques of European colonialism in Arab-Muslim countries like Algeria and Egypt. Fanon has rightly argued that "the colonial world is a world cut in two."[66] In this "two-ness," the colonized are denied a space in European modernity, not only geographically, or in terms of social equity, but most importantly in terms of intellectual thought. For centuries, the Arab-Muslim world has been perceived as incapable of complex philosophical thinking – a privilege reserved for the West – and therefore far removed from the intelligent principles and values of European civilization. According to this line of thought, which is not entirely different from what we currently see reflected in American and European media, Muslims are seen as disrespectful of the value of human life, irrational, unable to be reasoned with, and able to act only in terms of aggression, barbarism, and violence. Here again, Fanon is helpful. "All values," he writes, "are irrevocably poisoned and diseased as soon as they are allowed in contact with the colonized race."[67] This disease has attacked the Muslim Other and made it an object of modern European discourse, produced and labeled in the West, then exported back to the Arab world to trigger a never-ending clash of the most flagrant kind between the West and Islam.[68]

In the end, British colonial thought became the "embarrassment" of its own modernity, not only in economic and political terms, but in terms of identity and culture. Imperialist discourse permeated eighteenth and nineteenth-century Britain and provided the raw material for its colonial adventures in Africa and Asia. Like all European forms of colonialism, the dialectic of European colonial legacy, the harm it did to 'Other' and 'Self,' has led to a negative construction of the Arab-Muslim world.

5

DISCIPLINING ISLAM

Colonial Egypt, a Case Study

Egypt served my turn.
You'll never plumb the Oriental mind,
And if you did, it isn't worth the toil.

Rudyard Kipling, "One Viceroy Resigns: Lord Dufferin to Lord Lansdowne"

There has never been a document of culture which was not at one and the same time a document of barbarism.

Walter Benjamin, "Theses on the Philosophy of History"

The opportunity to represent and historicize Islam accurately across wide spans of space and time was limited due to the predominance of one-sided narratives of colonial history. For England and France and their crony empires, this issue of bias stretches back at least as far as early modernity, perpetuated by the problematic disparity between popular representations of colonial history and the realities it excluded. Are we, therefore, trapped in a largely colonial historiography of Islam? What narratives of Islam and its relation to the colonial West, mostly silenced to date at least within mainstream North American and European versions of history, might still be told? In order to answer these questions, one must first address such specific Eurocentric assessments of Islam which now tend to describe it – to use a more fashionable term given the political limitations on the category of 'religion' – as "globalized" Islam.

In this chapter I argue that the inherent contradiction between the liberal ideals imported from Europe and the denial of fundamental rights and privileges in the colonies are a main reason for the rise of postcolonial tension in the Arab-Muslim world today. The ravages of colonialism have been transformed into the nationalist rhetoric that the Arab-Muslim world lives by today, ideology that binds communities together and becomes almost a religion. This 'religion' is predicated on remembering the brutal perpetrations of colonial Europe. Every time those memories are invoked (in museums, TV series, or Friday sermons), a sense of resentment and indignation is rekindled. To the Arab-Muslim world, colonialism did not perish; it metamorphosed as cultural memory and like a dominant gene it still makes its imprints on every new generation despite the postnationalist attempts towards globalization.

The texts I deal with here embody such colonial tensions between Islam and the West. To the extent that colonial Europe's influence on Islam is hemmed by a number of complex issues, including the conflict between modernity and traditional culture in addition to the conflict-ridden process of the emergence of versions of modernity and nationalism in the postcolonial Arab-Muslim world, it must follow that these narratives will offer an alternative history. Many postcolonial critics, including Homi Bhabha, Gayatri Spivak, and Ranajit Guha, suggest that this in fact is the case with colonialism in general, simply because the larger problem with colonial historiography is that only the West controlled the keys of history and allowed no room for the non-Western.[1] Said has previously argued that Islam, both in its Ottoman and Western colonial stages, came to be viewed as "encroachments upon Christian Europe" to the point that "what remained current about Islam was some necessarily diminished version of those great dangerous forces that it symbolized for Europe."[2] The task of rescuing the writing of modern Arab-Islamic historiography from the domination of the 'grand narratives' of modernity and restoring it to history is far from over.

France: After the "Rude Awakening": Napoléon's "*L'Orient*" (1789–1801)

> L'Organisation de l'Orient est, en somme, le fait capital de la période moderne. (The organization of the Orient is, in sum, the principal fact of the modern period)[3]

In an essay on the Egyptian novelist Naguib Mahfouz, J.M. Coetzee links the emergence of narrative in Egypt to the country's first contact with

Europe at the end of the eighteenth century. He regards this contact as the most defining moment of Egyptian modernity:

> When Napoleon Bonaparte invaded Egypt in 1798, the slumbers of the Arab Near East were rudely awakened. Egypt, followed by the rest of the region, was forced to reorient itself away from Turkey and toward Europe. A body of secular European ideas – those that had inspired the French Revolution – broke through the barriers that had separated Islam from the West.[4]

Coetzee's essay may lead one to question Coetzee's assumption that during the one hundred and thirty years between Bonaparte's invasion and Mahfouz's novels, Egypt's cultural and intellectual life was uniform and unproblematic. Still, one should not regard Coetzee's argument as overreaching with respect to a complex tradition, especially if this tradition is not only foreign to him culturally and historically, but also linguistically, a fact that Coetzee himself modestly acknowledges. The emphasis on continuity and totalization we find in Coetzee is the result of a benign critical intention predicated on the need to find some past point of departure that makes the present more meaningful.

In fact, I find Coetzee's trope to be a useful organizing principle precisely because it captures the double-edge: the rudeness of colonial violence to a predominantly Muslim society along with that society's awakened interest in science and technology. After all, broadly speaking, Coetzee is not incorrect. The "rude awakening" that he describes constitutes one of many threads of a well-executed imperialist project aimed at expanding European dominion through colonies in Africa. The cultural and intellectual currents, and modes of thoughts and behavior that were fashioned through them, were a reaction to this colonial modernity and still have a considerable impact on the Arab-Muslim world today. They can indeed be traced back to the Napoleonic Campaign.

While Egypt had been the African center of this European myth long before Bonaparte's invasion, its first "rude awakening" actually happened not during but in the aftermath of the French occupation (1798–1801). In the few decades that followed Bonaparte's three-year invasion, Egypt absorbed a range of Western ideas, concepts, and institutions considered by Europe to be inseparable from modernization. Some even argue that much of Egypt's cultural turmoil and unrest today derives from the irreconcilable fundamental difference between Arab Islamic conservatism and liberal secularism imparted by European colonialism since Bonaparte.[5] To extend Coetzee's argument even further, the French invasion must have triggered important questions among many Egyptians that scholars would try to answer over the next century. Al-Jabartī and al-Ṭahṭāwī, for instance, represent the first nineteenth-century scholarly generation that attempted to consider the Egyptian 'self' in relationship to the French 'Other.' Among the questions that both scholars pose is whether a predominantly Muslim country like Egypt can become modern without having to internalize French modernity in its genealogical sense, that is, without losing itself to Western ideals and values and without having to live through the Enlightenment that produced France's secularist and scientific knowledge in the first place.

To the extent that "the barriers that had separated (Ottoman) Islam from (a secular) West," were indeed broken by Bonaparte's three-year campaign, one should not overlook the imperialistic *raison d'être* of that campaign and its impact on Europe. Egypt had vital military and economic advantages for France.[6] At that time, Egypt had strategic access to land and sea routes to Africa, the Arabian Peninsula, and India. The potential wealth of Egypt's soil, especially in the Delta, coupled with a rich and partially discovered Pharaonic history that had long engaged Europe's exotic curiosity, were all factors vital to France's decision to occupy Egypt.

The fate of the Islamic Empire under the 'sick man of Europe' was reaching a point of decline while Egypt was usurped and looted by its Mameluke rulers.[7] In short, the time was ripe for France to 'cultivate' Egypt. But whether this cultivation is called modernization, organization or liquidation, the looming demise of the Ottoman Empire was certainly a principal fact in the nineteenth century, and the French invasion of Egypt was a notable confirmation of that demise. The historian J. Christopher Herold sees the campaign as an inevitable result of Egypt's appeal to France:

> As far as Egypt was concerned, nearly all the memoranda advocated its acquisition and described it in the most glowing colours. The climate was salubrious; the potential productivity of the country was unlimited; the population was submissive; new crops, such as indigo and sugar cane, could be raised; a canal from Suez to the Mediterranean could be constructed; thousands of enterprising Frenchmen could

> settle there to cultivate the land and to trade in its goods; militarily, the operation presented no difficulty; rumors about endemic plague and trachoma were exaggerated if not false; and so forth.[8]

Herold's account reveals the thorough and well-planned colonial project that modern France had conceived for Egypt and the Egyptians. It shows how Egypt, while still a central part of the Ottoman Empire, had already been imagined into a French future. In a sense, Egypt became the unwitting prey of an economically and militarily ambitious imperialism. The French Campaign in Egypt points to the emergence of a new type of occupational thinking in Western Europe where life in the land of the pre-modern or non-modern Other was no longer simply an object of epistemology; the act of studying the Other had transformed itself into an act of "acquisition," to use Herold's words.

In France's colonial project, Egypt was no longer what it represented for its people or for the Ottoman Empire, but what it "could become" for France. The death-defying leap from theory to praxis once again failed: France's colonial project in Egypt did not last more than three years, when in August of 1801, its troops were withdrawn from Egypt in accordance with the agreement signed by General Belliard with British and Turkish commanders on June 27 of the same year.[9] When Napoleon received his crushing defeat in Waterloo in 1814, the balance of power in modern Europe tipped towards England. Henceforth, France's ambitions in Africa were redefined and indeed supervised by England. When the Suez Canal project was finally put into effect by the French engineer Ferdinand de Lesseps 68 years later, it was clear that England, not France, had contrived its own colonial plans for Egypt.

The French Campaign was responsible, however, for another "rude awakening." The 'expedition' (a problematic term usually used as a euphemism to conceal the military nature of the French occupation and give it the veneer of an innocent exploratory mission) was not exclusively military. Nor was Bonaparte, only 29 years old at the time, a traditional army leader. A politician, a legislator, and above all, a patron of the sciences, Bonaparte had diverse interests in Egypt that displayed themselves in various fields. As the commanding general of the French Campaign, he aimed to establish a modern infrastructure in Egypt and liberate a country that deserved, he claimed, better treatment from its leaders, the Mamelukes, who again

Figure 5.1 Ferdinand de Lesseps in Alexandria (1865)

according to Bonaparte, desecrated the land and abused its inhabitants. In reality, however, part of Bonaparte's expansionist program was to expand the French Republic by adding to his country's patrimony a significant part of civilization still undiscovered at that time. Thus, in addition to the army, 500 French *savants* traveled on board the *Orient*, with 19 civil engineers and 16 cartographers, under the leadership of Gaspard Monge, France's most renowned scientist at the time.[10]

If the Napoleonic Campaign was the first occasion in modern history when Islam clashed with the West, it is crucial to mention that the confrontation with France took place on many levels: military, scientific, linguistic, cultural, and political. It was not just the defeat of sword-carrying, mounted *mamālīk* that alerted the Egyptians to their own vulnerability and that of their leaders. Just as crucial was the sudden introduction of different ways of life, different behavior, different systems of management and research, and new technological instruments, all of which left a tremendous impact on every aspect of the nation's life, leading eventually to its *nahḍa* (awakening/renaissance) in the nineteenth century. But before that *nahḍa*, in fact in order for it to emerge, a significant phase of self-assessment had to take place.

The French as Other: Al-Jabartī's Muslim Gaze

While there are indeed compelling reasons to consider 1798 a year of Egyptian awakening, it is a mistake to attribute the rise of modern Egyptian thought to the Napoleonic Campaign alone.[11] During Napoleon's years in Egypt, a time of collective indignation against the French colonizer, liberalism was still a growing concept in Europe. Although Bonaparte's campaign did bring seeds of cultural and political liberalism to Egypt, it took almost a century for Egypt's political consciousness to produce liberalism in the modern sense. One of the campaign's most lasting effects was to show that new sources of power, new ways of thinking, and new methods of production and management could make Egypt a much better place to reside in. When the French Campaign ended in 1801, Egyptians were still far from conceiving their own project of modernity, but they had been pushed towards a different way of thinking because of that French Other. Whether rejecting or assimilating French colonization, a kind of 'thinking otherwise' evolved that would later serve as a baseline for intellectual and literary modernity.

Historiographically, we see a kernel of modern thought in the Egyptian critique of the sociopolitical implications of the French Campaign. Thanks to the encounter with France, an Egyptian historian, 'Abd al-Raḥmān al-Jabartī, lays bare the false pretense of his Mameluke rulers who failed to act like "true Muslims" while commending the courage and discipline of the French, who did. This contradiction between eschatological theory and practice (something that al-Jabartī's intellectual successor, Rifā'a al-Ṭahṭāwī, would not fail to underscore) invites critical self-evaluation and rigorous critique not just of Self versus Other but also of 'actual' versus 'ideal.' A kind of Egyptian Enlightenment would soon emerge and express itself in many aspects of modern Egyptian life, with emphasis on the desire to reconsider and reevaluate the country's glorified religious tradition.

Seeing the French vis-à-vis the Ottomans and the Mamelukes provided 'Abd al-Raḥmān al-Jabartī (1754–1825/6) with an opportunity to assess the primary impact of the West upon Islam, making him the first Egyptian Muslim to write about the clash of cultures between the East and the West in modern history. In three volumes, al-Jabartī writes a history of the French Campaign from within and provides an account of "someone," as Said puts it adeptly, "who paid the price, was figuratively captured and vanquished."[12] I will not endeavor, as did Said, to compare al-Jabartī's chronicle with the

French Campaign's *Description de l'Egypte,* for I believe that these are two completely different kinds of writing. I do, however, agree that the proto-scientific spirit with which *Le Description* was written is no guarantee for its objectivity. It is also important to emphasize that al-Jabartī was not in fact *ignored* by Napoleon, as Said believes he was, since the former's book was not written during the French occupation. In fact, al-Jabartī started *'Ajā'ib al-Āthār fī al-Tarājim wa-l-Akhbār* [Wondrous chronicles of biographies and accounts] in 1805, four years after the French army had evacuated Egypt, and did not finish it until shortly before his death in 1825/26.

Al-Jabartī's text is important because it offers a better understanding of the dynamics of confrontation between Islam and the secular West at the outset of the nineteenth century. His chronicle becomes an example of how fascination with the modern is counterpoised with Islamic conservatism. In fact the very title of his work, *'Ajā'ib* (wonders), is already an Islamic judgment on the French experience in Egypt. In the Islamic tradition, the term *'ajā'ib* refers to unfamiliar, irrational, and new matters that faithful Muslims must approach with caution, unless they come from God. The term was also used in the same manner in *Alf Layla wa Layla* [A thousand and one nights] as well as by Ibn Baṭṭūṭa, the fourteenth–century traveler and scholar, in his book *Tuḥfat al-Nuẓār fī gharā'ib al-amṣār wa 'ajā'b al-Asfār* [A gift for the voyeurs who contemplate the marvels of cities and the wonders of travelling], which is often simply referred to as *al-Riḥla* [The journey].The lexicographer al-Aṣfhānī defines the use of the noun *'ajab* in Arabic as "the condition of man's exposure to something unkown," and adds that "*'ajab* or *ta'jjub* cannot be ascribed to Allāh because he is all-knowing."[13] The Arabic root *'a-j-b,* from which the term derives, has a specifically negative connotation in Islam, especially in the Qur'ān and the Ḥadīth. In this sense, both *'ajība* (wonder) and the related term *bid'a* (something new, strange) imply charlatanism or superficial admiration. When al-Jabartī uses the word *'ajā'ib* to describe the content of his narrative, he also labels it as lexicon of danger, one that should rally Muslims around their faith in the very act of reading the text. It is as if he were saying 'what you are about to read is new, strange, and will fascinate you, but it should only it make you a better Muslim and hold on to your faith more strongly,' thus invoking a restoration of faith in divinity despite the inexplicability and unfamiliarity of the new objects witnessed. This is because *'ajā'ib* by virtue of their extraordinary phenomenalism have the power to shake one's faith.

It appears that in writing the first Islamic narrative of the French Expedition, al-Jabartī was drawn mainly by the disciplined thought that governed the French throughout their occupation of Egypt. This interest is seen in comparison to the noticeable condition of decline that existed in Egypt, politically, militarily, and administratively. Ironically enough, the book is an excellent record of the Frenchmen's acts of bravery and gallantry in comparison to the Muslim Mamelukes:

> Then came Saturday morning. By then [the French] had reached Umm Dinār. There were many people and the event was enormous. Untold and indescribable numbers of people from Būlāq and its surroundings, east and west, gathered for that day… . The Ghuzz, soldiers and Mamelukes also amassed at both banks, but their will was weakened, their hearts detracted, their opinions divided. They were envious of one another, worried about their own lives and well-being, sunk in their ignorance and conceit, overconfident in their tattered clothes and self-importance, concerned about the decrease in their numbers, thoughtless of the consequences, disrespecting of their enemy, and corrupt both in their thinking and their standpoints. They were the complete opposite of the other group, the French, who actually acted as if they were sincere followers of the Islamic nation (*umma)* in the early years of Islam, seeing themselves as true fighters, showing no fear of the numbers of their enemy and revealing no discouragement by the death of their fellow French fighters.[14]

As one can see from al-Jabartī's critique, the Mamelukes suffered from a naïve underestimate of the power of their enemy and of their own, coupled with a clear sense of overweening pride. "The piquancy of the situation," notes the eminent historian Arnold Toynbee, "lay in the fact that the French had descended in Egypt before – in the twelfth and thirteenth centuries – at a time when they had been the inferiors of the Orientals in general civilization, not excluding the art of war." Toynbee describes the medieval French Knight as a "clumsier and less expert version of the Mameluke" and as one who had "been badly beaten and had abandoned the attempt to conquer Egypt as a total failure." But that was 550 years before. It took the French soldier more than half a millennium to "metamorphose from the Frank of 1250 into the Westerner of 1789." During those five centuries, however, the

Mamelukes did not know this. Consequently, when they received news that Bonaparte had decided to invade Egypt by way of Alexandria, the Mamelukes proposed to deal with him as their ancestors had dealt with Saint-Louis. They rode out confidently to trample his army under their horses' hoofs, only to encounter not men (as they conceived of human capacity in 1798) but creatures armed with all the incomprehensible and irresistible powers of what Toynbee refers to as "Mr. Wells's 'Martians'." Egypt became a battleground on which French supermen and Egyptian cavemen engaged one another.[15]

> In a socio-political assessment of the war, al-Jabartī writes that the French enjoyed a different level of freedom than the Egyptians. Although al-Jabartī cites extreme instances of this freedom he commends the French for acting according to the dictates of reason and rationality. Although al-Jabartī admires many characteristics in the French occupier, including their devotion to science and the arts, and to social, political, and legal systems, he could not forgive their cultural permissiveness that violated his Islamic tradition. According to the historian André Raymond, "the Frenchmen's lust for Egyptian women turned into a kind of obsession that consumed a great deal of their energy and money."[16]

This "obsession" played a major part in souring the French–Egyptian relation, especially when the French soldiers were saturated with more than eight decades of Orientalist fantasies of sexually uninhibited Egyptian/Arabian women since Antoine Galland's introduction of *Les Mille et une nuits, contes arabes traduits en français* ("Thousand and one nights, Arab stories translated into French") to French readers. Galland's work is the first European translation of *A Thousand and One Nights* (1704–17).[17] According to al-Jabartī, the French army expected a Scheherazade or a Cleopatra at every corner. Despite their high hopes for the so-called Egyptian dream, "the resources afforded by the Mameluke's harems, did not prove as copious as the [French] army had expected."[18] Al-Jabartī's chronicle records numerous examples of French behavior he finds completely inappropriate and immoral:

> Their women wear no veils or decent clothing. They do not even seem to care about revealing their private parts. When someone had

> to respond to the call of nature, he would do so anywhere, even in full sight of people. And when he is finished, he would leave without cleaning himself, unless he happened to be a well-cultured man; then he may wipe himself with a piece of paper with writing on it if available, and otherwise he would just go about unclean. Their men sleep with any women they like and vice versa, and sometimes a woman would go to the barber's and ask him to shave her private parts, offering to pay him if he liked.[19]

As can be seen from this quotation, most of the problematic behavior al-Jabartī reports about the men and women of the French Campaign pertain to their interaction with Muslim Egyptians and to their public demeanor, especially when it comes to male and female dress codes and ethics. Al-Jabartī's dismay over the loss of traditional gender barriers is clearly pronounced. Much of his concern stems from the fear that French women's behavior in Egypt would influence Muslim Egyptian women and cause them to be unveiled:

> Among the [the new negative influences] are the lack of decency and shame when it comes the manners of their [French women] dressings. When the French occupied Egypt, some soldiers brought their women with them. Their faces were unveiled, they would wear colorful dresses, hold colored handkerchiefs, and cover their shoulders with adorned and dyed kashmir pieces. [The French women] would ride horses and donkeys with violence, while laughing, giggling, and flirting with the grooms and low-class public. They soon attracted the minds and hearts of the impulsive and unchaste women who mingled with them.[20]

Thus al-Jabartī, despite his seeming broadmindedness and acceptance of some aspects of French modernity, still shows reservation when it comes to modesty and propriety, especially the threat of changing gender roles and social behavior. This degree of conservatism against French women's manners and dress codes puts al-Jabartī at risk of being labeled with one-dimensionality. André Raymond, for instance, disagrees with al-Jabartī on the degree and the extent of French (im)morality in Egypt, although he still finds the occupation to be pernicious and uncaring when it comes to the so-called civilization mission:

> It is without a doubt excessive to suggest, as did al-Jabarti [sic], that the French occupation was a project deliberately intent on demoralizing Egypt by debasing the status of Islam, encouraging loose morality, and destroying its social structure. Yet, one could not say that in practice, the occupation was really supportive of Egypt's achievement of a high level of civilization, a declared objective of the French.[21]

What Raymond describes as "excessive" in al-Jabartī's account opens the door for reflection on the relationality of moral judgment in general. It is important to remember that by virtue of his training, al-Jabartī can only resort to the sharī'a and to formative principles of right and wrong based on Islam as it was practiced in Egypt when he evaluates the behavior and manners of the French in Egypt. What is still astonishingly novel in the long and closed-off tradition of Arab-Islamic historiography, perhaps since the time of Ibn Khaldūn, is al-Jabartī''s unprecedented success in overcoming the limits of his inherited discipline and in recording, despite some obvious reservations, many of the French occupiers' merits, especially in matters of science and combat.

Reading al-Jabartī's *'Ajā'ib* leaves us with no doubt that in the eyes of a Muslim man, the French remain a foreign Other, one whose social behavior is shocking to a predominantly conservative Self. Still, a close reading reveals that this Other is far from an object of xenophobia. Al-Jabartī repeatedly hails the French as "more Muslim" and more gallant in their combat than the Mamelukes themselves. Despite his limited vision of the entire colonial event, al-Jabartī enjoys a sense of historical objectivity which allows him to see the occupying Other as an enemy with a high sense of discipline and order, a desire for justice, and a devotion to knowledge and scientific research. Admittedly, al-Jabartī's argumentative logic often appears provincial, and his sole criterion for judgment is Islamic morality. Yet in al-Jabartī's writing we see what was in a way the most significant contribution of the French occupation. It was only the clash with colonial France that opened a window for critical thinking in modern Islamic historiography, allowing al-Jabartī to report the tyranny and the greed of his country's leaders, lay bare the myth of their invincibility, and expose their anarchic dispositions and vicious exploitations of the Egyptian *fallāḥīn* (peasants).[22]

We also see al-Jabartī's commitment to recording the experience of French occupation without the use of monolithic or polemical thinking in other telling ways. The scope of new ideas that the French brought was far-reaching, as evidenced by al-Jabartī's description of an experiment that he and a group of friends witnessed in a French lab:

> Among the strange things I have seen in this place is the sight of one of their scientists holding a vial containing what appears to be water. He then poured some of it in a cup and mixed it with some other liquid from another vial. All of a sudden, the water rose while colored smoke began to soar out of the cup until it finally evaporated and the water in the cup was dry and turned into a yellow stone. He took the stone out of the cup, so we could all feel it with our own hands and see it with our own eyes. Then he did the same thing with another kind of water, and turned it into a red (*yāqūt*) stone. And then he took a very small portion of white dust, placed it on a table and hit it gently with a hammer. It made a terrifying noise that resembles the dying of "al-Qarabana."[23] It scared us all and they laughed at us. They have strange devices and chemical combinations with effects that far exceed our minds.[24]

The salient aspect of this account is a fascination whose source al-Jabartī accords a certain level of respect – in fact an unequivocal acknowledgment of mental superiority or precedence – for a new and different way of thinking capable of manipulating science to an amazing degree that both fascinates and bewilders the Egyptians. This does not simply mean that Egypt was at a different social and scientific level from Europe, but that the result of the Napoleonic invasion must have been shocking and disturbing as well. Based on al-Jabartī's narrative, there is therefore a significant benefit to the French presence: the importation of a new kind of knowledge. This knowledge compelled the Egyptians to face themselves and evaluate their historical position. Al-Jabartī's chronicle records this epistemological gain with as much precision as could be expected from a highly educated scholar of his time. He vividly describes his daily comings and goings in occupied Cairo, notably his visits to the Egyptian Scientific Society, which the French established in Cairo.

Indeed, there are moments in the narrative when it almost seems that no invasion has taken place and that Islam and secular Europe have successfully come together in Egypt. In an almost nostalgic spirit, al-Jabartī recounts how he spent his time reading and visiting the Museum of Natural History annexed to the Society; how he studied the paintings of French artists like Denon, Dutertre, Redoutè, and Rigo; and how he observed the chemistry and physics laboratories brought by the French, trying to learn how electricity was generated. In his *'Ajā'ib*, al-Jabartī was careful to document the names of every researcher and scientist he encountered. These include natural scientists like Berthollet, Conté, Dolomieu, Geoffroy Saint-Hilaire, and Desgenettes; surgeons like Dubois and Larrey; astronomers like Nouet; mathematicians like Monge; entomologists like Savigny; chemists like Decotiles; botanists like Delille; and engineers like Champy. Al-Jabartī sometimes visited the Society alone, sometimes with fellow Egyptian scholars like al-Shaykh al-Sadāt and al-Shaykh Ḥasan al-'Aṭṭār, and sometimes with his friend Ismā'īl al-Khashshāb, an Egyptian poet. The latter's fascination with the French and with their scientific modernity was so high that he composed a poem in praise of Rigo, the expedition's official painter.[25]

But in the end, no amount of transferred knowledge can mitigate the cruel fact of colonialism. As Raymond says, "*il n'y a pas d'occupation heureuse*" (there is no happy occupation). This statement sums up the fact that French modernity could not justify its invasion of Egypt. As part of his short-lived campaign, though, Bonaparte did what he could to convince Muslim Egyptians of his *mission civilisatrice*. He tried to affirm the non-Christian nature of his campaign by citing his abhorrence of the Pope and of the Knights of Malta. He even used the Arabic language to make sure that the Egyptians would understand that he was not a crusader and had in fact destroyed the papal chair of Malta and Greece en route to Egypt. "Napoleon tried everywhere," writes Said, "to prove that he was fighting *for* Islam, everything he said was translated into Koranic Arabic, just as the French army was urged by its command always to remember the Islamic sensibility."[26] In his messages to the Egyptians, he did all he could to win the Egyptians' hearts:

> Dear Egyptians, they may tell you that I only came to this part [of the world] with the aim of eliminating your religion. This is a lie, so do not believe it, and tell those liars thatI am here only to save your rights and to free you from the tyrants, and that I worship God Almighty and respect his prophet Muḥammad and the glorious Qur'an more than the Mamelukes themselves.[27]

Egyptians, who had more than one occasion to see the French as invaders acting in contradiction to religious principles, were extremely suspicious and distrustful of such rhetoric. Acting as a good old-fashioned colonialist, Bonaparte could only be received with vehement aggression on the part of a people who saw him as a destroyer of their land and religions. It was not exactly "from the first moment that the *armée d'Egypte* appeared on the Egyptian horizon," as Said argues, that "every effort was made to convince the Muslims that 'nous sommes les vrais musulmans,' as Bonaparte's proclamation of July 2, 1798, put it to the people of Alexandria."[28] The French colonizers' first action was an immediate manifestation of power in the public killing of Muḥammad Kurayyim, the governor of Alexandria, who refused to surrender the city and fought a lost battle against the French army. Kurayyim was soon shot by the French army in a public square in Cairo on September 6, 1798. The murder of Kurayyim sparked the Cairo Revolution against Napoleon and his army.[29]

The Egyptian writer 'Abd al-Muḥsin Ṭāhā Badr attributes this hostility to the Egyptians' lack of preparedness and to their suspicions that Napoleon was a cold-blooded, apathetic occupier:

> It was not only the Egyptians' aggressive attitude that weakened the effects of the French Campaign, but its effects were also weakened by the Egyptians' lack of cultural readiness and lack of ability to understand the behaviors of the French which appeared extremely abnormal to the Egyptians. The Egyptians' provocation over such manners manifested itself in the simplest of all activities performed by the French, such as cleaning the streets and providing lamp-posts in front of houses. It is not strange that al-Jabartī himself would sound provoked, shocked, and appalled when recounting the behavior of French women, their un-veiledness, their interference in matters of government, and their influence on some Egyptian women who emulated them.[30]

These, and many other *'ajā'ib,* or 'novel' products in commodities and services, were in fact too modern and too suspicious to be immediately accepted and practiced by Muslim Egyptians at large.[31] In this context it is important to emphasize that al-Jabartī's text is not a record of a "confrontation between Christendom and Islam,"[32] as some may argue – though al-Jabartī maintained his quintessentially Islamic outlook throughout – but rather reflects a love-hate relationship, or perhaps a fusion of fascination, contempt, and fear of the foreign occupier. Al-Jabartī is typical of intellectuals who do not know how to respond to cultures outside their own domain. But he is intelligent enough to see that the French soldiers never cared to intervene in the religious rituals of the Egyptians, that the French army was not attired in white gowns with red crosses to obliterate Islam, and that it had more dedication to science and knowledge than theology. In fact, when France invaded Egypt, the life of typical Egyptian *fallāḥīn* was comprised of back-breaking toil in the fields from sunrise to sunset. The idea that colonization by a foreign power was a necessary price to pay in return for a better life bewildered them. It appeared to the *fallāḥīn* that Bonaparte wanted to destroy their familiar settings and replace them with new administrative systems modeled on France. Therefore, the *fallāḥīn* could only comprehend the French presence in terms of good versus evil. Whether Napoleon was believed by the Egyptians or not, thanks to al-Jabartī's *'Ajā'ib* (Wonders), one can see how this expansionist Bonapartism brought forth part of an "other" world with its advanced science and technology and exposed it to the full view of all Egyptians, something never heard or seen before in the Arab-Muslim world, and something that would change the course of Islam's sociopolitical and cultural history for generations to come.

The British Empire and the Ruses of Denshawai

With the English occupation, Egypt's colonial history repeats itself and comes full circle in less than half a century. The Ottomans' use and abuse of native Egyptian peasants justified the 1798 Napoleonic Campaign. Now, according to England, France proposed to abuse native Egyptians in digging the Canal. In this cynical game of imperialism, France played the role of the enemy that Istanbul had played some fifty years before. France's abusive Canal project in turn provided the moral pretext for Britain's intervention. Like France before it, England fashioned its so-called 'humane mission' in Egypt into the noble act of saving the country's native inhabitants from the grip of pashas and 'foreigners.'

In what follows, I re-open the question of the 'humane mission' with a case study of the (in)famous massacre that took place in Egypt during the early days of English colonialism, namely the Denshawai affair of 1906. I examine some texts that thematize the affair and its appropriation in colonial and postcolonial narratives. I aim to investigate how cumulative historiographies of the Denshawai affair, in newspaper reports and editorials, poems, songs, speeches, and sermons, reflect the manner in which various classes

(Ottoman, Muslim, Coptic, non-Coptic Christian, and secular political elites as well as peasants) contributed to a nationalistic rubric for the first time in the history of modern Egypt. The texts I focus on here include vol. 137 of the 1906 Parliamentary Papers of the House of Commons; Hāfiz Ibrāhīm's *The Denshawai Event* (1906); Ahmad Shawqī's *Denshawai's Anniversary* (1907); Mahmūd Ṭāhir Ḥaqqī's *The Virgin of Denshawai* (1906); and Bernard Shaw's 'Preface for Politicians' in *John Bull's Other Island* (1907).[33]

Central to my argument is the proposition that historical 'authenticity' does not lie in faithful or scientifically approved methods of writing history. In many ways, all the texts just mentioned offer a history. But the nuances that surface in the very act of representing Denshawai become more important than the superficial sequences of causality that characterize common writings recounting any event. Although the Denshawai affair is more than simply an occasion to elaborate on colonial encounters between Islam and the West, I would like to apply the abstract assumptions of many of these theories to a re-reading of this particular portion of Egypt's history which is also an important, yet less studied event in Britain's colonial history.

The Denshawai affair involved a clash between English officers and peasants. A number of English officers went pigeon-shooting in Denshawai, an Egyptian village in the mid-Delta region, and ended up setting fire to a threshing floor. In the subsequent confusion, one of the English officers was killed. Lord Cromer, the British Commissioner at the time, decided to teach the Egyptian peasants a lesson. A tribunal was held in Shibīn al-Kumm, a district close to Denshawai, where the incident is said to have taken place. Four men were sentenced to death and 50 to flogging and imprisonment. The condemned were hanged and whipped in front of their families in their own village.[34]

Some brief remarks on the nature of British colonialism will help put the event in its cultural and historical context. A highly sophisticated machinery that functioned differently in different nations, the British Empire provided a complex system of government. This complexity is best exemplified by Hannah Arendt's study of the trajectory of modern British and other European colonialisms and their connection to global conquest and expansionism. With respect to Africa more particularly, Arendt traces two main political tools of imperialistic government: scientific racism, and scientific bureaucracy.[35] The latter applies to predominantly Muslim countries like Algeria, Egypt, and the Sudan; the former to certain subjects whose looks

Figure 5.2 Photographs of the executions at Denshawai. Above: the hanging of Zahrān, one of the four *fallāḥīn* sentenced to death. Below: village guards and dignitaries observing the executions.

and manners were viewed as shocking, frightful, non-human, and strikingly dissimilar to Europeans.

Arendt does not really state that these distinct Western justifications for colonialism yielded different kinds of colonialism or different colonial enterprises. Nor does she explain how colonial administrations are different. But one could infer that racism and bureaucracy play a significant role in the assimilation of local elite and/or in the assumptions of whether or not the natives are capable of 'civilization.' Arendt's attribution of bureaucratic efficiency to England's civilizing agenda in Egypt and other Muslim countries suggests a link between a secular form of government and the discourse of modernity more generally.

Cromer and the Logic of Victorian Colonialism

In imperialistic discourse, the link between administration and modernity points to the transition from barbarism to so-called 'enlightenment.' As an apparatus of government, bureaucracy becomes the demarcation line dividing European humanity from Arab-Muslim subhumanity. This dichotomy is summed up most emphatically, both with absolute conviction and vigor, in the writings of Lord Cromer. His two-volume work on Egypt published in 1908, at the end of over 20 years of service as British commissioner, is the most interesting witness to Arendt's category of scientificity, namely, European colonialism's use of modern bureaucracy to justify colonial aggression:

> Looking to the special intricacies of the Egyptian system of government, to the license of the local press, to the ignorance and credulity of the mass of the Egyptian population, to the absence of Egyptian statesmen capable of controlling the Egyptian society and of guiding the very complicated machine of government, it appears to me impossible to blind oneself to the fact that the Egypt of today is very different from the Egypt of the pre-occupation days. A return to personal rule of the oriental type would create a revolution… . It may be that at some future period the Egyptians may be rendered capable of governing themselves without the presence of a foreign army in their midst, and without foreign guidance in civil and military Affairs; but that period is far distant… . It is a contradiction in terms to describe a country as self-governing when all its most important laws are passed, not by any of its inhabitants or by any institutions existing within its own confines, but by the governments and legislative institutions of sixteen foreign powers.[36]

Cromer repeatedly emphasizes the significant change in government his rule had brought about and its difference from an 'oriental' or 'Islamic' type of rule. This change of governments is part and parcel of the civilizing mission. Cromer's outlook on Egyptian government reveals an obvious fact: modern British colonization presents itself as a 'civilizing project.' The first requirement of this project is the establishment of a centrally organized political system which replaces people's primary and traditional loyalty to family, religion, or even communal associations with their loyalty to a civilized modern state.

Figure 5.3 Lord Cromer

It is easy in this respect to see Cromer as a product of the Eurocentric '*épistémè*' when it comes to the question of civilization. Cromer, who spent 24 years in Egypt, not only accepted the Orientalist stereotype of the 'ignorance and credulity of all Egyptians,' but promoted it by seeking to transform Egypt into 'governable forms' that might in the very long run be capable of achieving 'eventual autonomy.' With knowledge of at least four languages, including Arabic, and with a remarkable versatility that shows itself in every Latin insertion in his two-volume text, Cromer makes one wonder how he could have ignored, or at least used so triumphantly and so reductively, a word like 'civilization' with its rich historical implications that extend far beyond two centuries of British expansionism. And yet Cromer as an individual is not to blame. Imperialism subjugates not only the colonized, but the people who serve it as well. In his farewell speech on May 4, 1907, delivered at the Opera House in Cairo, Cromer echoes the same intellectual hubris that characterized both his government and his anti-Islamic discourse on Egypt:

> Can any sane man believe that a country which has for centuries past been exposed to the worst forms of misgovernment at the hands of

> its rulers, from Pharaohs to Pashas, and in which, but ten years ago, only 9.5 per cent of the men and 3 per cent of the women could read and write, is capable of suddenly springing into a position which will enable it to exercise full right of autonomy?[37]

Though Cromer emphasizes the low literacy rates and the bad leadership that preceded his rule of Egypt, his rhetoric still belongs to a belief system that views non-Europeans as subordinate and peripheral. It is no wonder that his provocative discourse provoked cultural resistance. The April 12, 1907 issue of the newspaper *al-Liwā'* includes an article by Muṣṭafā Kāmil, the leader of the Egyptian nationalists at the time, denouncing Cromer's unforgivable practices in Egypt. Kāmil describes him as a destroyer of peace, a hater of Islam, and above all, a careless imperialist who seeks the welfare of his empire at the expense of the destitution and effacement of all Egyptians:

> What shall we remember of the policy of Lord Cromer in Egypt? We shall remember that he is the one who struck the Khedivial throne with an iron hand. We shall remember that he invaded the Sudan using our own people and our own wealth and then deprived us of all sovereignty there. We shall remember that he deprived the Egyptian government and the National Ministry of its proper power. We shall remember that he denied the poor the right to education and fought against the use of Arabic language. We shall remember that he accused Egyptians of imbecility and infantile thinking, and pronounced to the world the superiority of the Englishman over the Egyptian. We shall remember that he ridiculed Islam and strove to abolish national sentiments and prevent the nation from having a representative voice.[38]

Kāmil contends that Cromer's long-term project to produce an Egypt modeled on the British example is at best utopic and unrealistic in a country whose people are looked down upon and treated as subhuman. Cromer's 'modern' project, which consists of changing Egypt from "a personal rule of the oriental type" to a system in which "the Egyptians may be rendered capable of governing themselves without the presence of a foreign army," reveals itself to be nothing but a project of imperialistic expansion. On more than one occasion in his book, Cromer refers to the degree of modernity

Figure 5.4 British troops at the Giza Pyramids after the bombardment of Alexandria in 1882

that Egypt has achieved since its introduction to Western civilization at the hands of England. He writes:

> No one can fully realize the extent of the change that has come over Egypt since the British occupation took place unless he is in some degree familiar with the system under which the country was governed in the days of Ismail Pasha. The contrast between now and then is indeed, remarkable. A new spirit has been instilled into the population of Egypt. Even the peasant has learnt to scan his rights. Even the Pasha has learned that others besides himself have rights which must be respected. The Courbash [whip] may hang on the walls of the Moudirieh [Police Station], but the Moudir [head of Police Department] no longer dares to employ it on the back of fellaheen. All these things have been accomplished by a small body of Englishmen who devoted their energies to the work of Egyptian regeneration.[39]

Cromer's language celebrates British chivalry and makes of the Egyptian people an object of colonial knowledge. The reference to the rights of the Egyptians and the redemption of the *fallāḥīn* (peasants) from elitist abuses is a valid one, so one must conclude that humanity is not denied to the

Egyptians after all. It is nevertheless assumed that one should credit Britain for regenerating Egypt and for the administration of new human and liberal values. The administrative system introduced by Britain, especially the legal system in the Denshawai case, played an important role in institutionalizing the European paradigm and in doing away with existing norms.[40]

Denshawai and Islamic Nationalism

One can distinguish two dominant veins of historical narratives competing to represent those early encounters between Egypt and Britain. The first, as we have seen, is the British version of the colonial mission and its language of legitimation in Cromer's work *Modern Egypt* and in the Parliamentary Papers. The second is the bourgeois nationalist elitism of Egypt, which credits itself with serving the cause of the Egyptian people and leading them from colonial domination to freedom through national and international campaigns: Muṣṭafā Kāmil and Mahmūd al-Ṭāhir Ḥaqqī belong to this group, though to a different degree. What started in 1882 (the actual date of British control over Egypt after the defeat of 'Urābī at the Battle of al-Tall al-Kabīr) as an essentially civilizing task seeking to make a modern state of Egypt quickly gave rise to a multidimensional nationalism among the Egyptian intelligentsia. The critiques engendered by this nationalism addressed both modernity and the complex issues associated with the vexed question of who could speak for whom.

Before the Denshawai affair, there was a widespread belief in Britain that colonial Egypt was a richer, more progressive nation and that the *fallāḥīn* were happier under British rule. Newspapers and books launched campaigns of imperial propaganda. *The Times* of London established a correspondence network in Egypt as early as 1882.[41] Economically, Egypt was a plantation colony, with cheap native labor and wealthy British merchants granted monopoly in cotton and produce. Foreign companies took over the economy and exploited already existing native industries.[42]

The tone of the pre-Denshawai local press was still resistant, but mild. Thus, Muṣṭafā Kāmil's newspaper, *al-Liwā'*, would publish articles speaking of the failure to teach Islamic history at schools and of the English desire to nip in the bud any patriotic feelings or celebration of exemplary Islamic figures and events. *Al-Mu'ayyad*, another local newspaper, criticized the practice of offering jobs to British and foreign subjects and denying them to Egyptians.[43] Egyptian nationalists gained the impression that English education was deliberately tailored to produce submissive, secular Egyptians. But with readership of the local press limited to the educated middle class and the elite, the nationalist program of Muṣṭafā Kāmil's newspaper was almost defunct. The paper relied on minor, almost ineffective issues like seeking to denounce Cromer's social favoritism, or attacking the colonial education policy that imposed English as the language of primary schools and the medium of instruction in secondary schools at the expense of Arabic and the study of the Qur'ān. All this was part of a good cause but not quite sufficient to rally public and international opinion against Britain, even if Cromer's educational policy was seen as a means of erasing the Arabic language and the essential personality of the nation.

But history tells us that what happened in Denshawai was not new or unforeseeable. The Egyptian *fallāḥīn*'s revolt against the British army began as early as the beginning of the British occupation. Other similar events include the Pyramids quail-hunting affair in March, 1887, the Qaṣr al-Muntazah (Muntazah Palace) attack on a British officer in Alexandria in June, 1900, and the foxi-hunting affair of 'Ayn Shams in July, 1901.[44] From the time of Muḥammad 'Alī up to the British expedition, and as far back as the three-year French occupation of Egypt (1799–1803), many incidents of *fallāḥīn* resistance have been recorded. Even the 1882 'Urābī Revolution is considered by many to be a *fallāḥīn* revolt.

Many British officers were attacked by natives before Denshawai. Take for example the incident known as the Pyramids quail-hunting affair. On March 27, 1887, two British officers were severely wounded in a fight with the *fallāḥīn* that ended in the killing of an Egyptian *fallāḥ* near the Pyramids area. In the trial, three sheikhs (Muslim preachers) were fined and imprisoned, while six others received between 20 and 50 lashes. The sentence was carried out in a public place before the village of the accused, at the same time of the day that the incident was believed to have taken place. This incident later came to be known as 'Little Denshawai.'

A number of factors led to the media frenzy over the Denshawai affair. The first was the law. The foreignness of the legal system under which the sentences were carried out shocked all Egyptians. In Denshawai, modern British law played a constitutive role in defining the Egyptians as colonial subjects and in legitimating a dominant redistribution of power that reduced Egyptians to minority status. So at a time when elitist nationalism lacked the means to revitalize its cause, the Denshawai affair acted as a timely catalyst.[45] It quickly supplied the raw material to strengthen the weak nationalist movement and helped Muṣṭafā Kāmil and the Khedive put aside personal enmity after a break in their relationship in 1904. The opposition that the Denshawai affair provoked took the form of a wide-scale nationalist movement, journalistic as well as literary. It stemmed from a communal trauma and was able to monopolize public indignation in order to reach all Egyptians after long being confined only to metropolitan Cairo.

In the aftermath of Denshawai, literature joined journalism as a significant element of anti-colonial print culture. Since the time of al-Ṭahṭāwī, modern Egyptian literature has been preoccupied with sociohistorical concerns, particularly in the representation of what Edward Said calls "repressed or resistant history."[46] In a similar fashion, the literature on Denshawai represents not so much the event of Denshawai as it does a moment of recognition, of understanding, and above all, of an emerging consciousness that Egypt exists and is aware of its subjugation to a ruthless imperialism.

The multiplication of the colonial Self (England) through the space of the Other (Egypt) is responsible for the emergence of an 'anti-colonial modernity' whose genesis is comparable to the same phenomena that (in)formed modern European nationalism: resisting the subjugation of one people's religion, language, customs, ideas, and laws by another. What happened in Denshawai in 1906 had made it obvious to the Egyptian elite – and through them to the public – that the colonial government had failed in the eyes of the locals and that a new, modern Egyptian state was poised to emerge. The Denshawai affair became the content of the form in a meta-narrative promoted by the nationalists in the struggle for independence.

Egyptian Literature and the Poetics of Denshawai

Nationalist literature has been described by some critics as typical of the so-called Third World where writers do not separate the private from the public, and where literary writing has a necessary political dimension that represents a national allegory. "The story of the private individual destiny," writes Fredric Jameson, "is always an allegory of the embattled situation of the public third-world culture and society."[47] Though reductive on many levels, this view of Third World texts as always allegorical does find support in this respect. Ḥafiz Ibrāhīm (d. 1912) and Ahmad Shawqī (d. 1932) could be seen to have produced a rhetoric linked to the spirit of nationalism *à la*

Jameson, even though the language of poetry is usually more connotative than the language of narrative, lacking elaborate details and sequential logic.

Shawqī and Ḥāfiẓ were the two most prominent Egyptian poets at the time of the Denshawai affair. Both wrote poems about it. Ibrāhīm's was written in the immediate aftermath in 1906 and it aimed to denounce the cruelty of British rule. Shawqī's was written on the first anniversary in 1907 with the intention of demanding pardon for the prisoners. The two poems testify to the intricate relationship between modern Egyptian literature, the inception of nationalism, and the constructions of collective identity.[48] Certainly, the pressure of the event was reason enough to inspire both poets, but it also highlights the role of literature in registering what is known and what is socially shared.[49]

Classified by many Arab critics as neo-classicists, Ibrāhīm and Shawqī, like many other poets and literary figures of the time, followed the example of Maḥmūd Sāmī al-Barūdī not only by radically celebrating traumatic events like Denshawai, but also by extolling ancient traditions that writers might treat in thematic rather than formal terms, and by invoking in particular the glories of Egypt's Islamic and Pharaonic past. While seeming to position Egyptian literature within a modern context, literary figures such al-Barūdī, Ibrāhīm, and Shawqī in fact actively engaged in an attempt to defy British literary canons, a project directly related to colonial education.[50] The poetic works of al-Bārūdī, Shawqī, and Ibrāhīm teem with verses that glorify Islam, revere Christianity, and tell Egyptians that they are, above all, members of their own community and that they cannot be truly strong without working together through the media of their shared language and their shared religious traditions.[51]

Due to the orality and musicality of poetry, which allows it to spread even among the unlettered, the Denshawai poems by Ibrāhīm and Shawqī enabled many Egyptians to rid themselves of the unqualified acceptance of British superiority to begin to question the assumptions and practices of the colonial mentality. Although the two poems emphasize literature's didactic and 'realistic' function, specifically by attempting to socialize Egyptians in new ways of self-conception and new terms of symbolizing and enacting social cohesion, in both form and style they remain sensitive to the aesthetics of poetry. For instance, both poems analyze the ways in which the Egyptians as colonial subjects have been rendered obscure to themselves, or relegated to the margin, or even deformed through a kind of power capable of twisting the penal system for colonial purposes. But all this is accomplished within the framework of the formal complexity of Arabic prosody. The results might be lines that are sympathetic and haunting yet still poetically balanced, as in Shawqī's:

> O Denshawai, peace be upon your hills | Days have taken away the happiness of your land
> Witnesses of your sentence have left the scene | It is futile to bring them back again
> Months have passed for those in their graves | And a year has elapsed for those in fetters
> What has befallen the widows | And what does the morning of the orphan look like?
> Twenty homes were deserted | And after bliss are now dark and desolate.
> I wish I knew,[52] were there pigeons in the barns | Or were the barns tainted with doom?
> Oh Nero, if you lived in the time of Cromer | You would learn how sentences are executed
> Wail, you pigeons of Denshawai and terrify | The sleepless people of the Nile valley
> In pains, reliving the horrors of the day that | Made the earth tremble under their feet.[53]

The response may also take the form of an ironic and defeatist reaction that is nonetheless charged with cadence and poetic metaphor, as in the case of Ibrāhīm. In Ibrāhīm's poem, Denshawai is not so much a portrayal of the atrocities of British rule in Egypt as the reflective voice of the Egyptians, which Ibrāhīm invokes by the use of "we" rather than the "I" of his personae:

> You, who are ruling us | Have you forgotten our loyalty and meekness?
> Reduce your army and sleep peacefully | Resume your hunt and rove the lands
> And if you feel like hunting a pigeon | On top of those hills, go ahead and shoot the people
> We and the pigeons are the alike | The yokes have not left our necks[54]
> Dignify your killings if you choose not to pardon | Were you seeking

justice or retribution?
I wish I knew, is this the investigation Court | Or has Nero's age come back?[55]

In any event, both cases remain a response to a traumatic event caused by colonization, a response in which literature becomes the site of a project aimed at breaking down the power of a merciless colonizer before any reconstruction can take place. Even an exclusively non-referential phrase like *alā layta shiʿrī* (Oh I wish I knew), which might appear completely dehistoricized inasmuch as it is a formula from the pre-Islamic period, seems to ask us to adopt a certain attitude (an unbearable state of chagrin being implied). Non-historical phrases in Shawqī and Ibrāhīm are still powerfully contextual operators. Shawqī's poem begins with the traditional Islamic veneration of the dead *ʿalā-rubākī salām*, thus reminding all Egyptians that the unavenged are their fellow Muslim brothers. This echo of the figure of *al-aṭlāl* (ruins) is a trope found in the *qaṣīda* (ode), the quintessentially classic Arabic poem.[56] Although Shawqī's empty houses could be merely formulaic or in actuality refer extratextually to the houses of the dead peasants, they also clearly refer to the poetic convention that Shawqī chose as a form for his elegy. The same could be said of the tradition of *al-marāthī* (elegiac poetry), which both Shawqī and Ibrāhīm are invoking in their poems.

The two poems end with a series of questions. Ibrāhīm wonders, "How would the strong seek vengeance from the weak who have already surrendered to him?" Shawqī asks, "I wish I knew, were there pigeons in the barns | or were the barns tainted with death and doom?" The two poems pose these questions through their sad and angry dialogical tones that assume a cognizant audience already part of a discourse in place. This discourse is structured around a silence that enables the two poems to take place. In other words, the two poems cannot be separated from the historical event they represent. But the silence here is also textual silence, or a silence assumed to be textual, resembling the gap [*le creux*] that Pierre Macherey locates in the text as it unfolds, "its vacuum where nothing is said, and which no system of representation could ever fulfill."[57] In describing Denshawai, the silences in Ibrāhīm's and Shawqī's poems become that very history of Denshawai.

If the Egyptian literature of the first decade of the twentieth century is anti-colonial in spirit, then too cultural production, and not just the literary, will become more easily a pan-Islamic one, although still a pro-nationalist project, in which customs, social practices, and national heroes are all elevated to the status of saints. The concluding lines in Ibrāhīm's poem show this shift through a scathing comparison of the cowardly Cairians with the gallantry of the executed *fallāḥīn*. The lines are a powerful and impatient call for activism:

> They were flogged, and if they had a choice | They would cling to the robes of unafraid
> They were executed, and if it were up to them | They would welcome execution
> Vying for death while its cup | passes around their lips with a bitter taste
> Two deaths, one imminent and glaring | Like a pouncing tiger, the other far and lurking
> If you are ever asked about the *Kināna*,[58] | Say it is a nation of jokey people[59]

Amidst the indignation surrounding Denshawai, violence and revolt become high moral values. It is not surprising that four years later crimes would still be committed in the name of Denshawai: in 1910, Ibrāhīm al-Wardānī, a Christian nationalist, assassinated the Egyptian Coptic collaborator, Butrus Ghālī, who had served as chairman of the court in the Denshawai tribunal. Moments after the assassination, al-Wardani walked to the police station, surrendered and confessed that he had killed Ghālī in retaliation for the Denshawai victims.

Denshawai and the Emergence of the Arabic Novel

Some critics agree that the Arabic novel emerged in 1906, the year in which Mahmūd Ṭāhir Ḥaqqī's *'Adhrā' Denshawai* [The virgin of Denshawai] was published. However, other critics qualify this achievement of Haqqi's and describe his work as the first 'political' novel in Arabic literature, not the first full-fledged novel, which is believed to have appeared eight years later with the publication of Muḥammad Husayn Heikal's *Zaynab* in 1914. At any rate, *'Adhrā' Denshawai* emerged amidst significant intellectual, political, and social changes that had a sweeping influence on Egypt at the turn of the century.

Like Ibrāhīm's and Shawqī's poems, Ḥaqqī's "The Virgin of Denshawai" emerged amidst the same intellectual, political, and social changes that took place in Egypt at the turn of the century. The novel depicts the historical event of Denshawai with few changes to the reported facts. Some characters, e.g., Sitt al-Dār, are merely allegorical. However, the character of al-Hilbāwī is a historical person and his representation in the novel suggests that he was as much a prime target of the author's investigations as were the British. While it is not easy to understand the real motives behind the author's containing both clear-cut historical referents (such as al-Hilbāwī) and generic allegorical references (such as Sitt al-Dār) in the novel, Haqqī successfully represents the predicament of the *fallāḥīn* by employing both types of characters and portraying their conflicting emotions of hatred and fear of the British. Read from a sociological perspective, Ḥaqqī's novel offers a history of Egypt's rural life at the turn of the century. The romantic image of an almost idyllic Muslim community is not without its allusions to impoverishment and human rights violations inflicted by Britain. As represented in the novel, the *fallāḥīn* are so cut off from the affairs of their country that they know nothing of their own government and have almost no way to affect the decisions that control their destiny.

In Ḥaqqī's novel, the Muslim *fallāḥīn* of Denshawai are usually referred to as the "damned, stung by fate," and controlled by forces beyond their understanding. Faced by the recklessness of some British officers who were shooting their pigeons and destroying their stocks in pursuit of vain, aristocratic sporting, the *fallāḥīn* first resign themselves to their lot. They accept the practices of those who are alien. But when the shooting starts a fire in one of the barns and kills Mabrūka, wife of Muḥammad 'Abd al-Nabbī, the *fallāḥīn* become enraged, attack the officers, and confiscate their weapons. At this point, the officers run away, but one of them (Captain Paul) has a sunstroke and collapses. One of the *fallāḥīn*, Sayyid Aḥmad Sa'īd, approaches Captain Paul and tries to give him some water to drink, but he dies just as his fellow officers arrive at the scene. The officers conclude that Sayyid has killed him, so they kill Sayyid. In the 'show trial' that follows, 52 of the *fallāḥīn* are condemned.

Though unequivocally based on the Denshawai event, Ḥaqqī's text begins with a disclaimer that "this novel is more literary than historical."[60] Ḥaqqī is reported to have been fired from his post as secretary to 'Abd al-Ḥalīm Pāsha 'Āṣim (Minister of *Awqāf*, government supervision of estates in mortmain) due to his publication of the novel. Ḥaqqī felt compelled to deliver his disclaimer because writing about this particular topic was a dangerous undertaking for many reasons:

> First, there are many stories about this incident, and they differ in terms of what caused it, how it happened, the methods of investigation that followed, the punishments enforced, and carrying out of sentences. So the whole subject is precarious, and any misrepresented word might cause me unnecessary trouble, therefore I took extreme caution in my writing, and always used euphemism to refrain from commentary on many of the events so as not end up joining the line of the Denshawai accused or to be the last one punished because of this incident.[61]

Ḥaqqī's disclaimer complicates the relationship between text/author and the colonial event. The circumstances that cause Ḥaqqī to write a disclaimer reflect his awareness of the repercussions of his own writings on the public. Ḥaqqī stresses the fictivity of his text, but this very insistence creates a different kind of historicity, namely the experience of silence and censorship. Even if Ḥaqqī's statement does not portray fear, and even if he himself was forced to write the disclaimer in order to publish his work and at the same time keep his job, his disclaimer still reflects a sense of worry. By insisting on the profoundly human, Ḥaqqī's novel changes one's perspectives on what really matters in a colonial event. Major names and incidents from the 'historical' Denshawai are absent in the novel, and, if mentioned, they are often relegated to the margins of the plot. Marginal incidents, however, become crucial if not central. 'Insignificant' happenings – those that are usually unimportant to non-fictional historical narratives – such as the description of the beauty of nature, the amicable conversations among men after the evening prayers, and the charming sight of a woman carrying a basket over her head or engaged in everyday life activities, are given prominence. These examples of 'local color' and native customs have a direct connection to national consciousness. They also imply that the novel is a critical comment on what is omitted in the methodical writing of history. In writing a kind of history that mainstream historians would never write, Ḥaqqī seems to be calling for the need to create a national identity that the British were seeking to obliterate. Ḥaqqī appears to present himself as a patriot depicting the brutal conditions under which Egyptians lived during the British occupation of English occupation. In this way, Ḥaqqī's novel offers a decolonization of history by dismantling colonial historiography. The representation of particular events in the novel is not only a judgment of the social content of these events but also a presentation of a different approach to history, recalling what Lukács refers to as "the whole question of whether one regards history as subjective or objective."[62] In the novel, Ḥaqqī learns to grant agency and authority to the Egyptian peasants. A good example is in "The Special Court," the novel's eighth chapter:

> After the court clerk had sat down upon reading the regulations of the Court of Justice, he cast an eye towards the journalists and newspaper correspondents. Only then did Ibrāhīm Pasha al-Hilbāwī rise and ask the court to send one of the court ushers to go and buy two liters of cologne to sprinkle it on the floor of the courtroom in order to dispel the smell emanating from the accused villagers.
>
> "Which brand do you prefer?" asked one of the members.
>
> "Atkinson," answered al-Hilbāwī in a smooth accent. No sooner had he uttered the word than the audience burst out laughing. Some of the accused thought 'Atkinson' was a legal term for 'pardon.'[63]

The prosecutor's pompous request for cologne creates an atmosphere somewhere between black comedy and mock epic. His smooth pronunciation of the foreign word 'Atkinson,' which the accused villagers completely misinterpret, exposes the wide discrepancy between a corrupted wealthy class and an honorable poor one. The word 'Atkinson' trivializes the whole situation and makes the seriousness of the court of justice appear ludicrous and absurd, even as the lives of 52 villagers is at stake. Ḥaqqī's use of different dialects of Arabic in this court scene, in addition to the air of realism that envelops the whole novel, expresses an acute consciousness of the social gaps and class conflicts within the occupied Egyptian community. Al-Hilbāwī's language in the courtroom echoes Cromer's description of the Egyptians in *Modern Egypt*. Both smack of the same hubris and superiority. On sitting down after reading the regulations, the court clerk too "casts a look" at the only class he belongs to, the professional class of "journalists and newspaper correspondents." In this divided world, the *fallāḥīn* speak a different language. The bringing together of conflicting dialects calls for a common language to be understood by all Egyptians. The linguistic misunderstanding in the courtroom could only signify chaos and incompatibility.

The courtroom scene becomes a microcosm of Egypt, with its different sociolinguistic varieties and registers, different classes, and divided interests. The linguistic confusion also reveals social hierarchies and foreshadows the unjust sentences about to be pronounced. The relationship between language and the nation is of great significance. The message is scarcely obscure: in order for Egypt to become a nation, it needs to speak a common language. If, as this passage sardonically implies, the language of the community is what links a nation together, this language is insufficient without a model. A good start for establishing this model is through literature, i.e., through the very language of Ḥaqqī's text, which is simultaneously critical and normalizing. This irony makes Ḥaqqī's novel both a detached literary experiment enclosed within its own self-referentiality (since it includes absolutely fictional characters) and a dialogue with imperial power, demystifying its linguistic code and its al-Hilbāwī-like apprentices. If anything, Ḥaqqī's novel exemplifies a crucial time in Egyptian history when the Arabic language mocked the logic of signification of the colonial language of British rule.

Ḥaqqī's artistic additions to the farcical justice of the courtroom scene enable him to free himself from some of the restrictions of normal historical writing. He can be episodic and fragmentary, add or delete events altogether. This is not merely freedom from the constraints of the history of Denshawai but also freedom to choose and to foreground, and thus to offer an understanding that holds the immediacy of direct perception.

Although, strictly speaking, his is a literary creation that does not make any claims to historical 'accuracy,' Ḥaqqī's novel still offers a structured unconscious with the powerful suggestion that history is nothing but a created text. The literary construction of a historical event does not *prove* the constructed nature of historical writing, but it does put it into question. "We experience the 'fictionalization' of history," argues Hayden White, "as an explanation for the same reason we experience great fiction as an illumination of a world that we inhabit along with the author. In both we recognize the forms by which consciousness both constitutes and colonizes the world it seeks to inhabit comfortably."[64] In other words, if history is constructed, it can be reconstructed, and if histories are told in a certain way, they can retold in a different one, so that those who have been colonized can write back and 're-emplot' their history, to change the meaning of events and their significance for the economy of the whole set of events that make up life.[65]

Ḥaqqī's work could be read as an extended metaphor of poems of the likes of Ibrāhīm and Shawqī. Britain had already given its version of the Denshawai affair and had already passed the sentences and archived them. Modern Egyptian fiction could only negotiate – after the fact – the dramatic reconstitution of that event. In London's official version of the "Attack on the British Officers of Denshawai" contained in the Parliamentary Papers, "the officers had been invited to shoot by a local landowner [when] the villagers at once assumed a hostile attitude.... The attack was probably premeditated, and the small fire which broke out on a threshing-floor [not on a granary, as previously stated] and which was at once extinguished, was probably a pre-concerted signal, and not the chief cause of the excitement."[66]

Read with such a colonial context in mind, the novel risks not being literature at all, and is almost transformed into a historical commentary on the Egyptian struggle against British colonialism. Ḥaqqī's attempt to rewrite history oddly mirrors the drama set in vol. 137 of the 1906 Parliamentary Papers of the House of Commons. One has to admit that Ḥaqqī's heroization of the Egyptian peasants and Britain's heroization of the English officers reflect biased narratives. The Parliamentary Papers' case, although apparently even-handed and pertaining to seemingly judiciary procedures, is no less ideological than Ḥaqqī's. Ḥaqqī's choices of character and theme, and the way he represents his material, reveal his own sense of identity and his empathy with the calamity of his fellow Egyptians. On the other hand, although the version offered by the Parliamentary Papers claims to be a true history, it remains a dramatization of a historical event. Contrasts between Islam and the West, England and Egypt, order and decadence stand at the center of these Papers. In the novel, however, Ḥaqqī seeks not only to correct or re-appropriate a traumatic event, but also to use the world of fiction as a weapon in the war against the colonizer.

With these Egyptian representations of Denshawai, we find ourselves at a point in time when literature serves a substantially political end. The reception and interpretation of a literary text is no longer the center of a self-contained exercise called literary criticism, but the product of a specific cultural milieu. Literature in this particular sense is divorced from the creative production of a mimetic object and consciously derives its substance from the historical, not just to record an event, but also because literature always proposes things that cannot be proposed outside of it. These texts are no longer merely self-referential, but constitute an alternative narrative of history, a concept that has been convincingly laid down by Fredric Jameson, whose theory of the 'political unconscious' stems from an understanding of history as a dialectic that forms a "judgment on us and on the moment of history in which we live," as he pointed out in his early work on Marxism.[67]

The Denshawai event marks a moment in Egyptian history when literature supports emerging nationalism. But the nationalism of Denshawai failed. It lacked the wisdom of carefully studied strategic thinking and organized resistance. It was 'rhetoric' without 'grammar,' to use a linguistic metaphor; it opened a space for a public redisplay of the bodies of the Denshawai victims and a public exposure of English atrocities in the colonies, but it could not mobilize the momentum of all Egyptians to take immediate full-scale action against the occupation.

In this failed national movement the famous *Khuṭab* (speeches) of Muṣṭafā Kāmil almost erased the *fallāḥīn*. Absent from Kāmil's narrative are the actual accounts or testimonials of the *fallāḥīn* who witnessed the event. Instead, he finds satisfaction in promulgating the news that education of the Egyptians under the English would only teach the Egyptians the superiority of English culture over their own. The political narrative of Denshawai used by Muṣṭafā Kāmil, like its literary counterpart, fabricates a single subject out of many Egyptian subjects whose identities needed to be constructed only to serve the unified ego of bourgeois individualism. In rallying the Egyptians against the British, Muṣṭafā Kāmil is said to have collaborated with the Khedive and to have acted on his behalf as Britain deprived the latter of his pre-occupation privileges. Shawqī, for his part, famous among Egyptians as *Shāʿir al-Qaṣr* (the Poet of the Palace), did not respond immediately to the massacre of Denshawai, but composed his poem a year later, in an attempt to petition amnesty for the prisoners. Kāmil's endeavor to bring together the Egyptian nation was essential to Egypt's heroic, albeit nominal, independence from British colonialism in 1922.

A Shamrock Denshawai?

At the time of the Denshawai affair, Ireland was under the yoke of British imperial power. Like their Egyptian counterparts, Irish nationalists used Denshawai, a little village no one outside of Egypt would have heard of or cared about, to denounce the British Empire. George Bernard Shaw led this movement. With Shaw, Denshawai became a mere *isti'āra* (both 'allegory' and 'borrowing' in Arabic) for the flagrant atrocities that English militarism had already perpetrated in Ireland. Denshawai was important for Ireland because it could help rally world opinion against the abuses of the Empire. Speaking from and for another country, Shaw might be expected to have had an agenda different from that of the Egyptian writers who addressed Denshawai. Catholic Ireland was not Muslim Egypt, and Shaw was a Fabian, after all, who believed in gaining equal rights for men and women. But since all is grist that comes to the mill of colonialism, both Egypt and Ireland were indeed victims of the same pernicious power. Shaw writes from a dominant nationalistic spirit similar to that of Ibrāhīm, Shawqī, and Ḥaqqī. It is a spirit that seeks to assign an origin to the nation and to celebrate that origin in a moment of shared suffering. Shaw dedicated an exhaustive Preface to *John Bull's Other Island*, almost a hundred pages in length, to the Denshawai affair, based, as he says, on "the story from the two parliamentary papers in which our officials have done their utmost to whitewash the tribunals and the pigeon-shooting party, and to blackwash the villagers."[68]

Since Shaw's knowledge of the Denshawai affair is based entirely on his reading of the two 1906 articles of the Parliamentary Papers plus a few English and French newspapers, one cannot say that his version of Denshawai is a faithful portrait. However, what we are concerned with here is *why* he took the interest that he did in Denshawai and why he represented it the way he did. Certainly, Shaw's Preface differs in form as well as content from both history and literature. Shaw provides 'real details' aimed to bring credibility to his argument and to take away the indeterminacy of purely literary compositions. Even though it is presented with historical reference and political speech, Shaw's account is not history, for it is dramatized. After reading his Preface, one finds that in spite of Shaw's concern for historical accuracy, he allows himself to create and invent, here and there, some significant details and peculiar angles of vision, especially in the Scaffold Scene, that give a pretense of immediacy to Denshawai itself. This is not to say that Shaw's tendency to dramatize means that his account of Denshawai is 'merely' fictive. Perhaps it is a kind of writing intended to vulgarize history and devaluate its authority.

In *Time and Narrative*, Paul Ricoeur argues that "history aims at knowledge, an organized vision, established upon chains of causal or teleological relationships on the basis of meanings and values."[69] Based on this argument, the restoration of the past or the reference to a specific historical event must serve a present purpose that has to be actively constructed. This is exactly what Shaw does with Denshawai. He declares that his main purpose in re-staging the event "is to show the results to be expected if one's respect for the law is shaken." His message is clear: "No Englishman who is content to leave Abdel-el-Nebi and his twenty-year-old neighbor in penal servitude for life, and to plume himself on the power to do it, can pretend to be fit to govern either my country or his own."[70] It is the whole system of governance and administration that bothers Shaw and motivates his narrative. His narrative treats the Denshawai affair as an important piece of criminal evidence in a large colonial investigation scene.

But it also seems that Shaw transforms Denshawai from a historical event to a dramatic episode, moving from a description of the bloody details of public executions to a call for immediate global action against the British Empire. Shaw's explanation of the events leading up to the execution is informed by a metaphor of theatricality that constitutes his condemnation of the penal practices of the Army of Occupation in Egypt. The public executions and the floggings of the *fallāḥīn* in particular become his raw material. The scaffold becomes a stage for punishment. On this stage, the major object is not the enactment but the reception of punishment in a state of pure terror. As in Ḥaqqī's novel, Shaw's ironic tone does not all mitigate the hideousness of the scaffold scene:

> Hanging, however, is the least sensational form of public execution: it lacks those elements of blood and torture for which the military and bureaucratic imagination lusts. So, as they had room for only one man on the gallows, and had to leave him hanging half an hour to make sure work and give his family plenty of time to watch him swinging (slowly turning round and round on himself, as the local papers described it), thus having two hours to kill as well as four men, they kept the entertainment going by flogging eight men with fifty lashes each: eleven more than the utmost permitted by the law of Moses in times which our Army of Occupation no doubt considers barbarous.[71]

The principal instrument of terror used by colonial England, and intensified by Shaw, is 'spectacular' violence. The torture inflicted upon the condemned *fallāḥīn* is not just an expression of lawless English rage. It also aims to take as its true object the minds of those watching. According to Shaw's sarcastic re-staging of the Denshawai scene, in this theater of violence the English army of the occupation becomes a sort of a playwright that uses the scaffold as its stage, the condemned and the executioners as its actors, and the families watching as the audience. In short, the occupying army creates a theater of terror in Denshawai, a barbaric and savage display. This is the key point in Shaw's critique.

In the staging of a 'drama' that is supposed to be didactic, the English occupying army complicates the drama's mimetic function. In what might be called the 'revenge tragedy' of hanging four *fallāḥīn* in the same spot where an English officer had died, how, one may ask, should the audience respond to react to this scene? As a climax? As a dénouement, the falling action of the last scene in the last act? Or as the complication of the action? If the mimetic function of this drama is to produce a certain reception, there is no place for purging the emotions of pity and fear, although there is definitely a building up of emotions like hatred and indignation. This is no purgation or Aristotelian catharsis. It is not even a drama in any artistic sense. People are actually dying and undergoing punishment. The scene is unquestionably dramatic, but it is more immediate and present than a theatrical representation would be.

Although not stated in Shaw's critique, the message of the occupier is clear: learn from the examples of these hanged and flogged bodies that have committed the crime of transgression against the collective body of the English army. The audience is to read this text of colonial violence for its moral, legal, as well political significance. Shaw exposes the logic of the British Empire. England wants the world to know that Denshawai is a theater of justice, that the body of the English army has been assaulted, and that a public execution comes as a logical result to establish order and reassert power. Shaw, however, turns this logic of 'justice' against itself by showing how the Denshawai drama is a kind of brutalization intended to terrorize potentially rebellious Egyptians. What was actually performed publicly was less a hanging and flogging of the guilty than a manifestation of a political allegory on the restoration of power.

Since the audience is the targeted subject of the Denshawai scaffold scene, the desire of the playwright/English army for a dramatic effect fails. The true subjects of punishment have not been subdued. On the contrary, Shaw's text reveals that the *fallāḥīn*'s resistance has been reinforced by the very procedure it sought to suppress. Shaw's Foucauldian irony is that the entire English penal system that is supposed to maintain order has become the 'danger' that needs to be resisted and annihilated. In Shaw's version, the *fallāḥīn*'s reaction was immediate. "Just think of it," argues Shaw forcibly, "in a population nearly ten millions, one [English] irrigation inspector is stoned. The Denshawai executions are then carried out to make the law respected. The result is that [a few days after the Denshawai affray] three natives knock a soldier off his donkey and rob him."[72]

The barbarity of public execution marked not only the beginning of the end of the English occupation in Egypt, but also the appearance of a different body arising from the ruins of the Denshawai tragedy.[73] The unity born of colonial penal injustice and resistance to this injustice thus becomes another historical event that would fashion Egypt's attitude towards England and Europe and continues to do so today. The Denshawai affair has become not only a teachable example of colonial abuses, but a painful memory of Western violence in the colonies.

Memories of Colonial Violence in a Nationalist Age

In postcolonial Egypt, the Denshawai affair became a record of national memory. In *postnationalist* Egypt, the Denshawai affair became a record of colonial barbarism. Of all these various representations, Ahdaf Soueif's novel, *The Map of Love* (1999) offers a terse yet cogent recollection of the affair, where it is used as a background to reflect the sympathies of the Muslim Egyptian aristocratic class with the lot of the hanged *fallāḥīn*. Inasmuch as the postcolonial battle is no longer against the presence of the English colonizer, it is worth asking what Soueif's narrative is trying to convey. While postcolonial literature tends to justify or reconsider a historical situation, it also reflects a certain need. The reconstruction of history, which is also a sort of revisionism, is born out of a present indignation with particular historical threads. What is it, one may ask, that Soueif's Anglophone text offers in this contemporary glance back at the Denshawai scene?

Soueif's novel raises the question of identity formation and cultural reformulation. Written in the language of the former colonizer, Soueif's text is much like the apologetic narrative that permeates postcolonial literature. Soueif's rewriting of Denshawai becomes a question of colonial memory and not of history. Both are essential elements of Arab-Muslim nationalist thought. When Arab nationalism seeks a tradition to defend and celebrate, it usually imagines a more ancient past redeemed through sacred and literary themes. After 93 years, Soueif's text opens up a literary space that questions memory and forgetting. Narrating a love story that begins during the occupation, Soueif refuses to ignore the victims of England's colonial brutality. Nevertheless, the fictional pashas of her novel appear to draw attention to the perspective of Turkish-Muslim aristocracy so that Ottoman Islam, too, might have a role in the redemption of the moment of colonial aggression. It is from this small window that Soueif's novel reconstructs Denshawai as a history of Ottoman imperial redemption.

However, the narrative runs the risk of contributing to the creation of myth. The novel's attempt at historical redemption is based on the false assumption that the English occupation shattered the Islamic past of Egypt. This rhetoric of invasion creates the illusion of a lost moment of theological harmony and unity in the Egyptian society under Ottoman hegemony, which in fact did not necessarily exist. With its reminiscences and exaggerated emphasis on the kindness and gentleness of a pre-occupation ruling aristocracy, Soueif's novel creates an imagined continuity that gets ruptured by imperialistic intervention. The story of aristocrats in love, which Soueif traces back to the turn of the century, omits any reference to the long-established *sukhra* system (the whipping and enslavement of the *fallāḥīn* as serfs) that Muslim aristocrats had created. Soueif's aristocrats are depicted as sympathetic, ethical, and critical of the English "barbarity," although they themselves are guilty of much barbarism:

> 28 June 1906
> In the *salamlek* Ahmad Hilmi's hands cover his face. His shoulders shake and a muffled choking sound rises from behind his hands. Sharif Pasha al-Baroudi puts a hand on his shoulder. Husni Bey al-Ghamrawi sits forward, his elbows on his knees, staring at the floor. Isma'il Basha Sabri holds his prayer beads still in his hands. The three men sit in silence. Above, behind the *mashrabiyya*, Layla and Anna kneel side by side on the hard banquette. They make no effort to wipe away the tears that fall silently down their faces.
>
> 'I am sorry.' Ahmad Hilmi wipes his face and straightens his shoulders. 'It was barbaric,' he says. 'Barbaric. The gallows set up in the village, the "bride" next to them, the people herded in to watch. They hang one man, leave him dangling there in front of his family

> and his people, and tie another to the "bride" and whip him. And again. And again ...'
>
> There is silence
>
> 'And they call themselves civilized,' he says
>
> The men do not speak.
>
> 'Yusuf Saleem,' he says, 'twenty-two years old. He stood on the platform, turned towards the villagers and shouted, "May Allah curse the oppressors!" Then, they hanged him.[74]

This passage raises an unavoidable question. Why does Soueif's text forget, or omit, the abuses of the Pashas? Which class is Soueif's novel redeeming, the aristocrats or the *fallāḥīn*? The violent scene of execution has been portrayed directly and graphically by Ibrāhīm, Shawqī, Ḥaqqī, and Shaw. Soueif reduces the scene to an off-screen conversation in the *salamlek*[75] of an aristocratic family, as though the 'uncivilized' spectacle of execution is so emotionally charged that it opens up the wound in a dramatic fashion.

What remains strikingly original about Soueif's version of Denshawai is the timing of her invocation of such a traumatic moment in colonial history. In 1999, long after nearly all the eyewitnesses of the Denshawai event are dead, the novel becomes a reminder, albeit an eclectic one, that postcolonial Britain may have forgotten the violence of what happened. The implication might be that England has forgotten the violence of Denshawai, and, furthermore, that it has now reached a triumph of culture that reverses barbarism. The novel then becomes an act of postcolonial memory, a belated revenge narrative and a reminder of a kind of failure. But for Soueif, this is no longer a narrative about the failure of England's modernizing and civilizing mission in the colonies. Rather, forgetting one's own history is a failure here. Soueif's novel compels England to face its own history, to remember the massacre of Denshawai, and to stop acting like a modern and civilized country whose celebration of the success of its culture is predicated on forgetting. After almost a century, Soueif's novel revisits the scene of Denshawai and belabors the distinction between culture and barbarism, and, most of all, between colonial history and postcolonial memory.

In the end, one can read colonial history as a way of reinscribing the demarcation between opposing forces. Cromer glorifies British colonialism, not once referring to the Denshawai affair in his two-volume work; Shawqī and Ibrāhīm, as well as Shaw, use Denshawai to stress the barbaric dimension of British rule; Ḥaqqī's text continues the tradition of Shawqī and Ibrāhīm, as does Soueif's novel. Each text shows the extent to which the colonial event is constructed by this method of radical contextualization. But Nietzsche, whose ambivalent views on Islam have been the subject of many recent studies,[76] tells us that history as a process of totality disappears and instead we have "chaos" to be ordered as one likes. Paul Veyne, on the other hand, contends that "history is what we make of it," even more radically, that "history does not exist." Not only is Denshawai written in these histories, but, also, and more importantly, Denshawai itself has become a "textual event."[77]

EPILOGUE

Historicizing the Enemy, Globalizing Islam, Giving Violence a New Name

> It is merely in the night of our ignorance that all alien shapes take on the same hue.
>
> Perry Anderson, *Lineages of the Absolutist State*

Historicizing the Enemy

I began this book with the attempt to restore Islam to a code of knowledge by considering a protracted modern history of encounters with the West and the corresponding personal sensibilities as well public discourses that emerged from those encounters, especially in the field of intellectual history. The conflict with Islam today, for which both Western Europe and America are fully militarized, will not be resolved simply by an interdisciplinary contextualization of the various forces that both created and perpetuated it, just as an understanding of the sensibility of the Arab-Muslim world requires more than political pacification and campaign promises, and definitely more than the passionate attempts at guarding the values of the so-called global world against the 'fanaticism' of Islam and its adherents.

My concluding thoughts depend not so much on exposing post-September 11 Islamophobia as on emphasizing that this Islamophobia is the lingering effect of a crooked history of oppression that not only legitimized colonial and imperial domination in the last century, but also managed to reproduce itself in the postcolonial and sustain its underlying xenophobic codes up to the present day. Against the continuity thesis of this pernicious dogma, one cannot but return to history. I am not arguing that history repeats itself, for this is another *ignis fatuus* that many cyclical historians like to chase. To me, history matters not only because it positions the present geopolitical understanding of Islam in relation to important contexts of colonialism, decolonization, and globalization, but also because it has become a discourse of conquest.

As a critique of colonialism and violence finally took place in the heart of Europe towards the end of World War I, leading to the Versailles Treaty of 1919, problematic categories of humanism, freedom, democracy, civilization, and equality came into question. The Treaty itself was convened in the spirit of such ideals. Not only did Europe take its own values for granted in the Versailles Treaty, seeking to apply them to its colonized subjects, but it ironically failed to uphold these same ideals. The Versailles Treaty was therefore a major disappointment to colonized subjects and to anti-colonial movements in general within Europe and abroad.[1] Not one single occupied Arab country would gain its full independence from European colonialism before 1950: Libya (Italy) in 1951, Sudan (Britain), Tunisia (France), and Morocco (France) in 1956, Iraq (Britain) in 1958, Kuwait (Britain) in 1961, Algeria (France) in 1962, South Yemen (Britain) in 1967.

As we have seen in the example of the Denshawai affair, colonial violence remained present in public, not only in Egypt but throughout the Arab world, until the second half of the twentieth century. Long after gibbeting and public hanging in chains were abolished in England (in 1832 and 1834 respectively), both were still practiced in the colonies. It is difficult to ignore the remarkable similarity between France's torture of Algerian natives and labeling of them as terrorists and America's torture of Iraqis in Abu Ghraib.[2] This is not just a manifestation of Western power but a continuation of the logic of industrial modernity responsible for producing the technology and the machinery that equipped colonialism. Without the dichotomous logic of this modernity, which split the world into powerful and powerless states, and without its insidious metamorphosis into one superpower, there would have been no colonialism.

I am not arguing that European and American intervention in the Middle East justifies terrorism, or that Western bias against the Arab world is *responsible* for the emergence of Islamic fundamentalism or the horrifying events of September 11. Nothing justifies crude, unprovoked violence. We should have no tolerance for disrespect of human life, and there is no excuse for the cold-blooded killing of innocent civilians. But we must not forget that the West had an important role to play in nourishing the soils where the belligerent ideologies of terrorists germinated and thrived.[3]

With the fall of communism, America has replaced the threatening Russian Other with the ominous Islamic Other in a remarkably short span of time.[4] Confronting this Islamic Other in all its difference and menace, and all its internal and external danger, has certainly been one of the main challenges for United States security even pre-dating September 11, not only because of the terrorist activities of groups like al-Qaeda, but also because the United States has made enemies by imposing its political will on many national and international decisions made in the last 50 years, from Sukarno in Indonesia to Nasser in Egypt, from oil economy to outer space, and from the UN to NATO.

This interventionist policy has prompted some writers to address the coming into being of the United States as the Empire of a new Eurocentric system of social and economic control.[5] But just as postmodernity today is not restricted to EuroAmerica or a defined geographical space, Eurocentrism too must be understood in transnational and global terms. As Arif Dirlik puts it, "a radical critique of Eurocentrism must rest on a radical critique of the whole project of modernity understood in terms of the life-world that is cultural and material at once."[6] For this reason, the current operating assumptions of the world compel us to persist in critiquing Eurocentrism in its post-national, post-theological, and postmodern manifestations. A serious critique of Eurocentrism must confront contemporary world issues and examine notions like terrorism, globalization and cosmopolitanism in order to assess their relationship to power in its vicious circularity, both as a product of culture and as culture-producing. The transformations of the global economy, the economic, political, and military dependency of the new nation-states of the Middle East on Europe and America, and the hybridity of post-national and post-theological cultures are all telling examples of this power's capacity to manifest itself in various forms. But first, we need to ask direct questions: how do we reach operative definitions of terms like 'globalization' or 'cosmopolitanism,' and where do we situate Islam in relationship to them? Even more explicitly, what are the characteristic 'international' features of globalization and what belief system(s), if any, does it include or exclude; what sort of culture(s) does globalization incorporate, and what political postulates does it embrace both in Europe and America?

As many scholars have pointed out, there are major differences between Islam in Europe and in the USA, which render different the experience of an immigrant in the two contexts, especially with regard to the socioeconomic status of Muslim immigrants.[7] Those differences are essentially political in nature. The USA's tradition of pluralism in a strong civil society produces a citizenry different in many ways from Europe where the intertwining of such factors as class, race, and religion has deepened the segregation of Muslim communities.[8] However, in both places, the Muslim immigrant is relegated to second-class citizenship, especially after September 11. This relegation, though in part socioeconomic, is the very ideology of Islamophobia, that is, an imaginary relationship towards the real, especially after the September 11 events. In the aftermath of those attacks, a series of terrorist attacks was triggered in Europe ranging from the Madrid bombing (2004), to the assassination of the Dutch filmmaker van Gogh in the same year, to the London explosions of 2005, to *les émeutes de banlieues* (French civil riot) in 2005, and followed by the Danish cartoon controversy of 2006. All those events have given Islam an unavoidable visibility on the world map and provided the means for Islam to be viewed as a threat to global order and stability in both Europe and the USA.

The Islamophobia ideology, like all ideologies, derives from empirical events that are interpreted in such a manner that reaches beyond the historical specificity of their occurrence. The danger that lies in such ideology-charged perception of Muslims as a menace to the security and liberal welfare of the world is that it turns into a concept that no longer needs the historical event or its causal links to justify itself. In other words, the Islamophobia ideology is a sentence uttered before a crime is even committed, an order that cancels the need for critical historical consciousness. Today, this ideology, which is itself a renewed manifestation of deeply rooted Islamophobia in the West, enables the rising denigration and unquestionable depiction, almost standardization, of Islam as a peril in world history, expanding across geographical boundaries without the need to explain, examine, or contextualize the content or nature of this peril. This is a tragic situation: the referent 'Islam' is treated as a fight between antagonists and apologists rather than as a vigorous discussion among qualified specialists.

Globalizing Islam

A major challenge in writing about globalization and Islam today is the baffling plethora of references on the topic which come from a vast number of academic disciplines (political science, sociology, anthropology, economics, and the humanities) as well as media and fiction. As I elucidate below, it has been my observation that these disciplines engage with topics like "Islam in a global world," "globalized Islam," or "Islam and globalization" from disparate perspectives, generally showing a severe lack of interdisciplinarity and distorting the core meaning of the 'global' and its specific relationship to the 'Islamic.' The unfortunate result of this divide is that our current understanding of 'Islam and the global' or 'Islam as global' is limited to the specific disciplinary contexts and political frameworks that employ the term and whose modes of operation are in need of careful examination.

For this reason, I choose to consider the 'Islam debate' in relation to globalization as a postnationalist phenomenon, by which I mean the understanding of globalization as a categorical certainty referring to a 'borderless' transnational world order in which an organizational force arranges and harmonizes our practices and policies. From this narrower perspective, one can roughly divide responses to the question of globalization and Islam into two rival camps.[9]

The first camp sees Islam as a global force. This 'globalist' camp endorses the idea that Islam is becoming or seeking to become an *umma* (nation) in a new world order that defines and controls the ways societies interact with each other. The second camp resists the 'globalization of Islam' formula altogether, doubting the motives behind the desire to establish 'universal grounds' for the global world. This 'anti-globalist' group questions the very idea of 'globalization' and perceives it as the product of a capitalist Euro-American agenda targeting Islam and framing it as an enemy of global advancement in order to legitimate its establishment of particular 'universal grounds' for the global world. This group also takes an interest in historicizing 'globalization' and defining it as a recently emerging set of discursive claims about the world seeking aggressively to reorder that world in terms of itself.[10]

To them, one may add the sociologists and political scientists of Islam as a 'globalized' phenomenon, with particular reference to Muslim migrations and their impact on movements such as nationalism, Islamicism, and neofundamentalism. Edward Said, for instance, puts a question mark on 'globalization,' warning against refraining from practicing "humanistic critique" and opening the field of history to radical interrogations. Although there is more to 'globalization,' as Said argues, than just "a system by which a small financial elite expand[s] its power over the whole globe, inflating commodity and service prices (usually in the non-Western world) to the higher economic ones,"[11] this warning should not be taken lightly, especially when we remember that at the apex of Western colonialism, European idealist philosophy was flourishing. Nor should it slip from our cultural memory that in its moment of intellectual glory, especially in the Hegelian and Heideggerian phases, European philosophy acted with complicity towards slavery, racial discrimination, and colonialism. The bastion of human wisdom and the alleged inheritor of Greek humanism and freedom, so to speak, stood mute before the age of imperialism; it did not fight hegemony or condemn the European self-conception of superiority, but went on to define pure and practical reason (Kant), phenomenalize the "spirit" and dialecticize power relations (Hegel), or ponder "the will to power" (Nietzsche) and the ontological question of *Dasein* (Heidegger).

Before we examine the imbrications of globalization and Islam more closely, it is important to recall the circumstances leading to the 'emergence' of Islam as a 'global force' in Western political discourses. In the aftermath of World War II, the Arab world faced numerous challenges. First, there was the arduous struggle for decolonization and the dramatic transformations each country underwent. Secondly, there was the rise and fall of Nasserite pan-Arabism, the Algerian war, and the bellicose years of the Arab–Israeli conflict beginning in 1948 and persisting to the present day, what is known as the 1967 *naksa* (setback), followed by *ḥarb al-Istinzāf* (the War of Attrition, 1976–70). Then came the 1973 October War (a.k.a. the Yom Kippur War, or the Ramadan War), the oil boom, the rise of Gulf Islam, the persistence of autocracy, and the radical downturn in economic conditions. All this, in combination with employment opportunities in postwar Europe, led millions of Arab Muslims (Arab Jewish and Christian migrations had started decades before) to immigrate to Europe and North America between 1950 and 1990. While those migrations noticeably increased the Muslim population in the West, they ultimately led to a change in the nature and position of Islam in the West. As I elucidate in what follows, this change did not go unnoticed by a European public keenly aware of the new presence of Islam on its soil.

But as we address this awareness, it is worth noting that not all proponents of the globalization thesis see Islam in negative terms. For example, in his recent book *Globalized Islam,* Olivier Roy offers a genealogically extensive analysis of Muslim migrations to Europe. Roy argues correctly that Muslims usually choose to come to stable labor-oriented markets of Europe from their economically challenged and politically suppressive postcolonial Third World. Roy defines "global Muslims" as "either Muslims who settled permanently in non-Muslim countries (mainly in the West), or Muslims who try to distance themselves from a given Muslim culture and stress their belonging to a universal *ummah* [sic] whether in a purely quietist way or through global action."[12] He sees globalization as the category that led to a confusing objectification of Islam: "Globalisation has blurred the connection between a religion, a pristine culture, a specific society and a territory. The local authority of religion has disappeared, specifically, but not solely, through the experience of being Muslim in the West."[13]

The disappearance of Islam's local authority, according to Roy, is due mainly to Muslim migrations to Western Europe and the USA. The structural salience of organized Islam and the prominently felt "Islamic" presence of Muslim immigrants in Europe have led to the rise of "re-Islamisation," or "Islamic revivalism," Roy's terms for Muslims' desire and quest for a pure, de-cultured form of Islam.[14] Because of this de-culturing revivalism, globalization renders Islam a service by freeing it from the embedded cultures and inherited impurities that tainted Islam's core thesis throughout the ages. To Roy, globalization thus works to "dissociate Islam from any given culture and provide a model that could work beyond any culture."[15] Roy even goes further in his argument to state that globalization *produced* fundamentalism "because it acknowledges without nostalgia the loss of pristine cultures, and sees as positive the opportunity to build a universal religious identity, delinked from any specific culture."[16]

Roy's argument fails to situate Islam in relation to the larger context of intra-European migrations post-World War II and postcolonial changes in European identity. But even when he tends to correlate the West with reason and Islam with a search for a lost *umma* (nation), his argument that the notion of diaspora is becoming obsolete and that Muslims in Europe *respect the laws* of their host countries is quite compelling: "The relationship between Western Muslims and Muslim countries is no longer diasporic. Syrians and Yemenis in the United States feel above all that they are Arab-Americans. The link is no longer one between a diaspora and a host country, but between immigrants and a new set of identities, most of them provided by the host countries."[17]

Roy also prefers to generalize rather than specify when referring to movements like 'fundamentalism' and 'neofundamentalism,' which can sometimes be confusing. For instance, he acknowledges the spiritual side of neofundamentalism as *da'wā* (proselytizing and preaching) at the expense of the political: "For neofundamentalists the aim of action is salvation, not revolution."[18] This could be misleading since neofundamentalism, a category under which Roy places al-Qaeda as well as Tablighi Jama'a,[19] undoubtedly has a "jihadist" agenda in the context in which Roy employs the term. Despite his explanatory note, Roy still uses the term 'jihad' reductively and ahistorically, especially in his reference to the genesis of al-Qaeda's rage.[20] In fact, a linguistically and historically informed analysis of jihad would have significantly bolstered Roy's otherwise forceful argument. I am not just referring to the multiple meanings of 'jihad' in the Qur'ān, the ḥadīth, or Islamic historiography, but more importantly to the ways the term has been hijacked, both by Muslim extremists' efforts to manipulate and inculcate uneducated Muslims and by Western media's and Islamophobics' charged way of framing the global danger of Islam and legitimation of the so-called "war on terror."[21] At the conclusion of his study, Roy returns to this issue rather indirectly, when he makes the salient argument that "the globalization of Islam should be dealt with *while remembering that terrorism is a marginal symptom* that tells a lot, as does any symptom, and obliges everybody (above all Muslims) to go beyond wishful thinking, misgiving, and passivity."[22] This seminal point is a reminder that the 'Islam debate' in the West is more a debate on *the West* than it is on Islam. Roy's work is an invitation for reassessment. Terrorism is an existing threat to global security, but we must think critically about the ways in which this threat is understood and handled.[23] An essentialist and culturalist 'globalization of Islam' is an index of fossilized Islamophobia that can only be treated if we start by acknowledging its persistence.

Islamophobia and Globalization

As alluded to earlier in this book, Islamophobia began as fiction and in fiction. A phobia, as Freud tells us, is a kind of anxiety where we form "a relation to external danger but in which we must judge the fear exaggerated out of all proportion."[24] On the individual level, phobias are psychological disorders which Freud finds "puzzling" and occurring mostly among "small children."[25] On the societal level, phobias are a contagion prompted by social rather than infantile anxiety. Social anxieties happen when a public discourse (like art, fiction, audio-visual media), which is usually considered the main source of knowledge on an unfamiliar topic or concept, transmits fear that is shared collectively without any credible rational basis or verification of that external danger. This prompts us to ask the following questions: what are people afraid of in Islam? How did terrorism become so strongly associated with Islam? In this context, a point that has been made before must be made again: there is a correlation between political interest and social phobias.

Noam Chomsky cogently puts this relationship into perspective when he warns that "all over the place, from the popular culture to the propaganda system, there is constant pressure to make people feel that they are helpless, that the only role they can have is to ratify decisions and to consume."[26] The novelist William Gibson makes a similar point regarding the constructed relationship between terrorism and media: "[T]here is always a point at which the terrorist ceases to manipulate the media gestalt. A point at which the violence may well escalate, but beyond which the terrorist has become symptomatic of the media gestalt itself. Terrorism as we ordinarily understand it is innately media-related."[27] The "helplessness" of news consumers which Chomsky emphasizes and the media monopoly of terrorism which Gibson highlights, both reflect a deplorable state of dependency among the populace. This dependency results from innocent assumptions of the credibility of and uncritical reliability on media sources. Media coverage does not consist of mere reporting of news or events, but of impressions influenced by partisan corporational interests and political biases.

A representative example of the globalist camp's 'phobic' imagination of Arab Muslims in Europe as a menacing global presence can be found in the British author Anthony Burgess's novella, *1985*, which begins with the following lines: "It was the week before Christmas, Monday midday, mild and muggy, and the muezzins of West London were yodeling about there being no God but Allah: *'La ilaha illa'lah. La ilaha illa'lah.'*"[28] In this cacotopic work, Islam looms large. Muslim Arabs are establishing themselves in metropolitan Europe while mosques are being built in the center of London. Although written in 1978, the image of Islam that Burgess portrays is eerily relevant to the recent events in Switzerland involving the banning of minarets. Burgess's novel is mainly a critique of the expanding power of trade unions and syndicalism in Britain. Yet it reveals the West's obsession with Islam as a threat and points to a predominant monolithic imagining of 'Islam' as a nation.

In the imagined world of Burgess's 1985, trade unions have become the *bête noire* of postmodernity, so powerful that they are in full control of society, while at the same time a silent danger is slowly materializing. This danger is the ascendancy of Islam to cultural and political power in Europe. Burgess envisions London, the colonial capital of the twentieth century, as teeming with mosques and rich Arab Muslims as a result of large-scale immigration from the Middle East to Europe. In this nightmarish dystopia, global Islam has become the galvanizing force of a new world order, one in which Arab oil money has bought up the morally and intellectually bankrupt West. Interestingly enough, Burgess pits Christianity and Islam against each other in an inevitable conflict where one force must dominate the other. In the novella, Burgess foretells that the collapse of Christianity and the decline of self-confidence and self-belief in the West will leave a spiritual and cultural vacuum. Looking into the near future, Burgess argues that the power of Islam is poised to fill this emptiness with a meaning of its own:

> Where would Tucland be without the Arabs? The oil at a price even more exorbitant, flowed in from Islam and kept Tucland's industries going. And Islam was not only the hot desert but also the cold ocean… . The Arabs were in Britain to stay. They owned Al-Dorchester, Al-Klaridges, Al-Browns, various Al-Hiltons and Al-Idayinns, with soft drinks in the bars and no bacon for breakfast. They owned things that people did not even know they owned, including distilleries and breweries. And, in Great Smith Street, soon would stand the symbol of their strength – the Masjid-ul-Haram or Great Mosque of London."[29]

Burgess's implication is that as materialistic syndicalism destroys itself from within, it will leave the West powerless against the rising power of Islam. Bev Jones, Burgess's protagonist, randomly waves at a car as his bus is late. Finally a green Spivak stops for him and he has the following conversation with its gaunt driver:

> 'What's your trade'? asked Bev, 'or, of course, profession?'
>
> 'I'm with Bevis the Builders,' said the man. 'We specialize in the erection of mosques. I have built mosques all over the world. I built that one off the Vila della Conciliazione in Rome… . At present, I am engaged in the Great Smith Street contract.'
>
> 'Ah,' said Bev. 'The Masjid-ul-Haram.'
>
> 'You speak Arabic?'
>
> 'La. Ma hiya jinsiyatuk?'
>
> The man chuckled. 'First you say no, then you ask me where I'm from. Call me Islamic, no more. Islam is a country, just as your Tucland is a country. Ideas and beliefs make countries. The big difference between Islam and the materialistic syndicalist states is the difference between God and a bottle of beer.'[30]

This ideational 'country of Islam' constitutes through Muslim immigration and control of resources an insidious agenda of supremacy and indoctrination, where the wealth amassed by oil allows the Arabs to control the West's energy supplies. In this brilliantly depicted dystopia, Burgess expresses his own disgust with the material and moral lapse of his contemporary England as a conduit to critique the present condition of Britain and direct attention to an imminent threat. The idea is that if England were to suffer the most horrifying of nightmares, this nightmare would not be its transformation into a piggish "big brother" totalitarian state, as Orwell had it in *Nineteen Eighty-Four*, but worse still, it would be an Islamic take-over. The threat is not only that 'the Muslims are coming,' but that the European order as it used to be will cease to exist. Burgess makes it clear in his novella that his profound sense of unease comes from the fear that the world he now inhabits is slowly but surely erasing the very core of his identity as an Englishman in Europe:

> At dawn on Christmas Eve there was no bread, for the bakers locked the doors on their flour stocks and went on strike;"[31] … So they sat together that evening chewing dates and cracking walnuts… . and they saw *White Christmas* with Saint Bing and Rosemary Clooney, and when *Arab Hour* came on they switched over to a new musical version of Charles Dickens's *A Christmas Carol*.[32]

Written in part as a response to George Orwell's *Nineteen Eighty-Four*, where the world is lost to a conflict between vast totalitarian empires, Burgess's less known work carries a warning against a world lost to reverse Islamic colonization of Europe. Like a *Spanish Tragedy à la* Thomas Kyd, there is an inherent subtext of European guilt and Muslim revenge underlying Burgess's work. But what is intriguing about this fictive representation of Islam as an uncontrollable dominant force in Europe is that it strikes a chord with current research on the 'problem' of Muslim immigration in the West and its impact on globalization. In European capitalist societies, the new global transformations have rekindled xenophobia, cultural bigotry, and old ideological preconceptions, particularly in response to mass labor migrations from the Arab world into metropolitan Europe. These costs of globalization have become the fuel of "culture talk" in Europe.

In a more recent development of these dramatic consequences of globalization, the *Financial Times* columnist Christopher Caldwell addresses the question of immigration and European identity in a lengthy study targeting the 'global menace' of Islam in Europe. Caldwell's depiction of Islam as a threat to Europe dwarfs Burgess's *1985* by comparison.[33] According to Caldwell, Europe has now become a "continent of migrants." Those immigrants include a substantial body of Muslims, who are posing what Caldwell bluntly describes as "the most acute problems" because of their belief. Caldwell connects the rise of Muslim immigration to Europe with major changes in European landscape and culture. Caldwell, who unsurprisingly embraces Samuel Huntington's concept of the "clash of civilizations,"[34] forcefully argues that Islam has increasingly challenged habitual patterns of European life and is currently threatening to transform Europe into a continent different from itself.[35] The demographic explosion of immigrants, argues Caldwell, has made Europe a continent with more immigrants than natives for the first time in its modern history. According to Caldwell, the explosive population growth of Muslims immigrants in particular puts Europe in a difficult cultural situation as it staggers to retain its identity. In other words, Europe's identity is now at stake due to the emergence of a strong Muslim population: "The Islam professed by roughly half of Europe's new arrivals sits uneasily with European traditions of secularism. In the struggle between the two, it would be arrogant to assume secularism has the stronger hand. The spiritual tawdriness Islamic immigrants perceive in the modern West is not imaginary. It may be Europe's biggest liability in preserving its culture."[36] According to Caldwell, Europe completely misjudged the cultural implications of non-assimilationist Muslim migrants, overrated its reliability on foreign labor, and continued its flexible immigration policies while unaware of the danger lying down the road: "It is certain that Europe will emerge changed from its confrontation with Islam. It is far less certain that Islam will prove assimilable. Europe finds itself in a contest with Islam for the allegiance of its newcomers. For now, Islam is the stronger party in that contest."[37]

In his critique, Caldwell emphasizes the negative side-effects of Muslim immigrations to Europe: the 2004 and 2005 bombings in Madrid and London, the 2005 civil unrest in France, the increasing number of Muslim inmates in European prisons, plus many other vices that range from honor killings to the virginity-restorative "hymen repair operations."[38] But Caldwell forgets that a vast number of Muslim immigrants are more secular in their leanings and hold key positions in governments as well as in respected fields like medicine and public service. While the majority of Muslim migrants seek to maintain traditions and cultural practices of the places they migrated from, Caldwell cannot simply reduce them to a vicious category of criminals in order to make his point. The taxonomic typicality with which Caldwell treats all Muslims in Europe is at best naive and renders his argument reductive and doubtful. He treats Muslims as if they all come from a self-contained civilization and share an identical version of Islam.

It is true, as we have seen from the recent events in France, Italy, Denmark, and Switzerland, that Islam has a more prominent visibility in Europe than ever before. This visibility should not be misinterpreted as an "Islam Revolution," to invoke Caldwell's phobic title. It is rather evidence that Europe's Muslims are eager to practice their religion where they live and raise their children. According to the French historian Claude Langlois, Islam has become "France's second most important religion."[39] This new reality, Langlois maintains, means that the increasing number of Muslims in France (four million at the time of his study) demands that Islam be acknowledged and not looked at as an alien, inferior religion. This means that Islam can no longer be treated with the same outdated colonial distaste, and, more importantly, that European Muslims "will no longer tolerate being treated as second-class citizens."[40]

Langlois's observation is an important prehistory that helps put Caldwell's study into context. Caldwell's writing seems provoked by the greater visibility of mosques in Europe. This reveals a new sense of vulnerability, for the construction of more mosques with minarets will end Catholicism's long-standing monopoly over Europe's religious architecture. In other words, Caldwell's implication is that Europe is either Catholic or secular. There is no and there will be no middle ground:

> When Archbishop (later Cardinal) Lustiger of Paris spoke at a rally organized by the Parent-Teacher Association of parochial schools in the Paris area on April 24, 1982, he had this to say about the history of religious education in France: "All things considered, we can pride ourselves on the fact that our culture has been able to accommodate the three religions that Emperor Napoleon I recognized: Catholicism, the Protestant Church, and Judaism. But what a difficult problem we face now with the unforeseen arrival of large numbers of French-speaking children of Islamic background!"[41]

This "difficult problem" of French-speaking Islam which Cardinal Lustiger pronouncedly addresses is a tragic reminder that Islam in Europe now is doubly rejected as a foreign religion that oddly lies between the Scylla and Charybdis of Judeo-Christianity and secularism. This is why the processes of educational secularization in France and the architectural trimmings of minarets in Switzerland are current symptoms of Europe's post-theological 'theological' discomfort with Islam. If the political potency of Christian authority has become history in Europe and is now replaced by parliaments and prime ministers, then must Islam seem awkward as well as backward?

What we learn from Cardinal Lustiger's address is that Europe still relies on a discourse of Christian history and ethnic identities which led to the establishment of stereotypes, among them sentiments like "Arabs are a problem," and "Islam is a threat." In an age of supposed secularism, Caldwell's study, much like Burgess's fiction and Cardinal Lustiger's odd and ahistorical marriage of Christianity and Judaism, tells another important story: Europe did not integrate its immigrants' children, which explains much of the present day Islamophobia. The French still call the Arabs in France '*Beurs*' (a racial and stereotyping term that refers to Maghrebis and their offspring), the Germans call them '*schlitzohrig*' (cunning), '*scheinheilig*' (hypocritical), '*gewaltbereit*' (ready to be violent or extremist), '*intolerant*' (intolerant, especially towards women). Excluded, European Muslims find themselves forced to return to an imaginary home of Islam in search of a shelter and a cure for their lacerated sensibilities caught between cold inhospitable lands and remote disconnected origins.

One would expect that Caldwell's invoking of a 'common European identity' should rely on the claim to a unique, monolithic, and coherent European history. This is exactly what is problematic in Caldwell's argument, and this is the myth that the Swiss literary critic Adolf Muschg expertly dispels as follows:

> What holds Europe together and what divides it are at heart the same thing: common memories and habits, acquired step by step through the process of distancing itself from fatal habits. Europe is what Europe is becoming. It is neither the Occident nor the cradle of civilization; it does not have a monopoly on science, enlightenment, and modernity. It shouldn't attempt to ground its identity in any other way than through its own experiences: any claims for exclusivity can only lead into the same delusion and pretension through which Europe of the nineteenth century believed itself to represent the rest of the world, and entitled to dominate it.[42]

Caldwell therefore is haunted by what he perceives as the threatening diversity of Europe. One sad lesson Caldwell's book teaches us is that a willful repression of certain aspects of European history is needed in order to keep the myth of Europe alive. For in addition to the arrival of Muslim immigrants from post-colonies, major transformations in European demographics were caused by intra-European changes in the flow of labor and capital within the larger context of the globalization process. Therefore, in historicizing Muslim immigrations to Europe, it is incorrect to rely on common ideological assumptions that the population of Europe has been ethnically homogeneous. The activism of non-Muslim minority communities in Europe and long-standing pre-colonial, colonial, and postcolonial intercontinental migrations within Europe has been instrumental in reshaping Europe's demographics. These population displacements were the result of diverse causes.[43] The Arab-Muslim population of former European colonies, especially the Maghreb, was for the most part driven by economic and ideological forces to immigrate to countries like France and Holland. These forces can be summed up in the financial promises of Europe's open labor markets and the partial success of colonial educational and cultural inculcation of the colonized population without ever allowing them full Europeanization. Add to this, Muslim Arabs are not Europe's sole "immigrants." Take for example the intra-European refugees in the aftermath of World War II or the West-bound migrations that resulted from Communist dictatorships in Eastern Europe. Consider also the mass employments of Western European industrial powers and the crucial need for labor importation from countries like Yugoslavia, Italy, Greece and Turkey.

Clearly, the idea of a culturally established and homogeneous Europe no longer has the colonial glamour it once had. But in a postnationalist world of complex mobilities and internet capital transfers, the same could be said of many parts of the world, including the United States, Canada, and Australia. Anthony Giddens and his student David Held describe these global demographic transitions as a natural outcome of the problematic of "time-space compression."[44] Yet if these multi-ethnic global transformations are now thought to have undermined long-established ethno-national models in Europe and are so agitating that they drive some writers to highlight the threat of Muslims' transnational transgressions of European culture, then one has to view the turn to Islamophobic narratives in literary and cultural studies as well as in history and anthropology as among the unfortunate consequences of globalization and, worse still, as a eulogy to colonialism. As I have tried to show in this book, colonialism is not the opposite of an emancipated postcolonial era. Colonialism is not only the consequence of racist and biased European industrial modernity. Colonialism is also the constitutive condition and the diabolic prehistory to contemporary structures of trans-nationalism, globalism, multi-culturalism, and cosmopolitanism.[45]

Nonetheless, Caldwell's argument remains timely and fits right into the larger ongoing argument about globalization that overshadows the more specific histories of violence in Europe and the USA by which the rise of Islamic terrorism has commonly been defined. So far, much of the Islam/globalization debate has tended to be framed around questions of national security, citizenship, and immigration focused by the impact of "the war on terror," most evidently with respect to the events of September 11 and global aspirations for a terrorism-free world. But the turning away from public diplomacy to militarism has impeded the West's ability to discern the mechanics of terrorism or even confront the origins of "violence" in the last century. Therefore, if someone like Caldwell wants his argument to be taken seriously and not to be dismissed as a flagrant invocation of exclusionary Eurocentrism, he should not blame Muslim immigrants for causing all the violence in Europe, for this is a straw-man argument that has long been defeated.

Emphasis on Islam in the globalized world tends to be placed on counteracting terrorism, which inevitably works against *all* Muslims in Western Europe and America by continuing to mark them as 'Other.' While the focus in the war on terror and the fight for a homogeneous Europe tends to be on inciting aggressive cultural demarcation, closing borders, imposing tighter immigration laws, and intensifying investigations of Muslim citizens and visitors, the shameful history of profiling and stereotyping Muslims in the West tends not to be investigated. This ignorance creates the inevitable dilemma of guarding globalization against the Arab and Islamic worlds and the way this exclusion is guaranteed not only to destabilize the very meaning of globalization, but also to revive and reinforce old antagonistic perceptions of Islam as an incorrigible belief system that stands outside the 'global' attributes of the rest of the world.

Cosmopolitan Islam

Anthony Kwame Appiah's recent work *Cosmopolitanism* provides a simple yet noble philosophy for post-September 11 global coexistence. Written in part as a response to subsequent "cultural talk,"[46] especially the debates over the moral and cultural differences between "us" and "them," Appiah maintains that it is wrong to characterize conflicts in the world in terms of their moral values. Appiah attempts to offer a recipe for the present conflict-ridden human condition in the age of globalization, though 'globalization' is not a term Appiah would necessarily welcome. In fact, he believes that we do not live under the rubric of "globalization," a term originally used to describe "marketing strategy, and [that] then came to designate a macroeconomic thesis, and now can seem to encompass everything, and nothing."[47]

While Appiah admits he chose the term "cosmopolitanism" with "some ambivalence," he still believes that it can be "rescued" from its associations with "superiority towards the putative provincial." Appiah provides a very brief history of cosmopolitanism: how it originated with the Cynics of the fourth century BCE; how it was developed by Roman Stoics like Cicero, Seneca, and Epictetus; how it entered Christian diction during the Roman Empire; and how it assumed a philosophical status in the Enlightenment with European thinkers like Kant and Christopher Martin Wieland.[48]

Appiah's goal is to draw attention to the "interesting conceptual questions that lie beneath the facts of globalization."[49] Those questions include the validity of our value systems, the meaning of difference, questions of relativism, the clash between morals and manners, and, more importantly, the question of the place of strangers in a larger human context. Speaking from a crude philosophical viewpoint which he does not seek to hide, Appiah emphasizes the fated division of values between the local and the universal as a starting point to navigate all these questions. As he does in his work on *The Ethics of Identity*, Appiah offers an alternative framework of "liberal cosmopolitanism" in lieu of the hackneyed politics of cultural difference.

The real issue for Appiah is that it is futile to think that humans will ever agree on a hierarchy of values in our world, especially as the cosmos is getting more and more packed. In Appiah's opinion, dialogues between people from different cultures are unavoidable. Those dialogues or "conversations," Appiah maintains, must not be predicated on our particular religious identities; nor should they be based on our geopolitical differences; nor again should they be centered around our sexual orientations or our ethno-cultural and racial differences. While all those forms of human diversity exist, and while the recognition of every individual or group's uniqueness is an essential component of liberal democracy, we must find the essential sources central to the ways in which we understand, fashion, and reflect on our human existence as a whole.

These sought-after sources of cosmopolitanism push Appiah's thesis more towards an ethics or ethos of humanistic coexistence than political maneuvering. This is why someone like Sir Richard Francis Burton is important for Appiah's thesis. Burton's "citizenship of the world" serves as a model for 'cosmopolitanism' and as an approach to life that involves both a core set of commitments to one's individual background as well as a recognition and appreciation of cultural differences wherever and whenever one encounters them. To Appiah, Burton was able to see the essence of humanity underneath the veneers of cultures and religions. Burton exercised cosmopolitanism as a project for life:

> Burton's voracious assimilation of religions, literatures, and customs from around the world marks him as someone who was fascinated by the range of human invention, the variety of our ways of life and thought. And though he never pretended to anything like dispassion,

> that knowledge brought him a point where he could see the world from perspectives remote from the outlook in which he had been brought up. A cosmopolitan openness to the world is perfectly consistent with picking and choosing among the options you find in your search. Burton's English contemporaries sometimes thought he displayed more respect for Islam than for the Christianity in which was raised: though his wife was convinced that he had converted to Catholicism. I think it will be truer to say that he was, as W.H. Wilkins wrote in the *Romance of Isabel Lady Burton*, 'a Mohammedan among Mohammedans, a Mormon among Mormons, a Sufi among the Shazlis, and a Catholic among the Catholics.'[50]

But this does not mean that the world should be populated by cosmopolitans like Burton. Appiah admits that Burton was "an odd sort of mélange of cosmopolitan and misanthrope,"[51] who bought slaves, hated the Irish, looked down at French-Canadians, Pawnee Indians, Africans, and despised Americans. While Appiah admires Burton for wearing so many hats, he sees his "cosmopolitanism" as imperfect and faulty and regards his multilingualism and versatility as strong evidence that racism is not the child of ignorance. Still, what makes Burton useful for Appiah's project is precisely the understanding that despite his hatred and cynicism of others, he knew perfectly well that the worst mistake any human being could commit against humanity "is to think that your little shard of mirror can reflect the whole."[52]

If Burton's example is to teach us anything, it is that a cosmopolitanization of Islam is not just an appeal to all Muslims, especially the radical ones, to learn to live in and accept a world of difference, but also a call to all humans to recognize that others have different values and to learn to accept them as well. Acceptance does not mean compliance or conversion, but mainly recognition of one's responsibility to all human beings. Appiah thus ventures to introduce an overarching ideal that balances the diverse values of humanity and transcends cultural and religious affiliations. Appiah's 'cosmopolitanism' is thus a coexistential approach that appreciates human diversity and the importance of different customs, traditions, and religions, while transcending them all in order to find a détente, so to speak, or a working tool in an increasingly shrinking world where "hiv[ing] off from one another seems no longer a serious option."[53]

This philosophy which seeks to safeguard the psychological well-being of the globe is a very reasonable, indeed very sensible and perceptive one. Cosmopolitanism will ideally allow us to abandon a view of the world tainted with capitalistic ambitions, historical biases, and geopolitical prejudices. But what if cosmopolitanism is itself a product of geopolitics or a different strategy of assuming supremacy? After all, the history of cosmopolitanism Appiah cites is solely European, not to mention all the references that constitute the intellectual framework of his work. If cosmopolitanism is to be a global solution for our conflicting values, where is the globality in that very solution?

On one hand, Appiah's discussion of cosmopolitanism gives the impression of a balanced appreciation of the forces of religion embedded in all traditions; on the other hand, he pursues his ethics of cosmopolitanism, which is also the ethics of liberalism and of modernity, with a Europeanism hard to ignore. It is not wrong to base one's thesis on those principles, but if the goal is to reach a rapprochement between various traditions (though mainly Islam and the West are at the center of his book), then it behoves us to adopt a pluralistic and inclusive mode of thought. This well-meaning reliance on the Western tradition alone makes it look as though the world can be saved by a rationality that can only emanate from Western Europe. It would seem that Appiah is offering to resolve or challenge the problem of fanaticism and fundamentalism in the world through a dialectical 'advancement' of European thought. Is not cosmopolitanism, after all, a human heritage, intricate and interdisciplinary in nature, one that, as Said unfailingly reminds us, is not a matter of ownership, "but rather of appropriations, common experiences, and interdependencies of all kinds among different cultures"?[54]

To Appiah's credit, reference to Islam is for the most part benign and nostalgic, brought about by general knowledge, but mostly by scattered childhood memories of himself as a Christian child in multi-religious Ghana. In many respects, Appiah's book underscores the fruitful potential of cosmopolitanism as a teleological ideal, and this is what makes it more enjoyable, especially when he advances his case through the aesthetic and confessional mode of narrative and story-telling rather than traditional argument.

This remains a relatively small matter and in some way exemplifies Appiah's own cosmopolitanism. Nonetheless, it seems that in a candid attempt to approximate religio-cultural values between Islam and the West, Appiah does so in a Eurocentric manner (except perhaps for sporadic reference to anti-cosmopolitan figures like Bin Ladin and his band). What tends to slip out of view in Appiah's work is precisely the historical and global dimensions of cosmopolitanism: Appiah finds supreme examples in Horace, Homer, Sophocles, Richard Burton, Walter Benjamin, Edmund Burke, Kant, Hegel, Napoleon, Shakespeare, David Hume, Thomas Carlyle, T.S. Eliot, Charles Darwin, Adam Smith, George Eliot, Galileo, Bill Gates, and Michael Jackson. Why no *Gilgamesh*, *Sunjata*, *El-Cid*, or *Arabian Nights*; no Muhiyy al-Dīn Ibn 'Arabī, or al-Ḥallāj; no Muḥammad 'Abduh or Umm Kulthūm; no Naguib Mahfouz or Mohammed Arkoun? One can see that he does not wish to exclude famous advocates of cosmopolitanism,[55] and reasonably so, but he shies away from engaging with traditions of other parts of the world, not for lack of familiarity, but perhaps because he is for some reason less likely to imagine that they, too, hold views on cosmopolitanism and narratives that are fruitful and worthy of consideration.[56]

The most fitting reply I can envisage to this Eurocentric 'idea' of the cosmopolitan and the global is the one that Antonio Negri and Michael Hardt provide:

> Here is a non-Eurocentric view of the global multitude: an open network of singularities that links together on the basis of the common they share and the common they produce. It is not easy for any of us to stop measuring the world against the standard of Europe, but the concept of the multitude requires it of us. It is a challenge. Embrace it.[57]

In Appiah's case it appears that "the concept of the multitude" is tied more to a linguistic than a material reality, and this is precisely where his project of cosmopolitanism fails. If the ideal of cosmopolitanism, not the etymology of it, is solely Eurocentric, then there is a dangerous ideology at work, one that results from, as Paul de Man cleverly puts it, "the confusion of linguistic with natural reality, of reference with phenomenalism."[58] There will be in Eurocentric cosmopolitanism something very threatening, against which the non-Europeans who have a stake in joining the happy camp of cosmopolitans, would want to put themselves on their guard for fear it might just be yet another variation on the theme of Eurocentrism.

Giving Violence a New Name

When drawing attention to false continuums (like treating all Muslims as if they were threats to national security), I recall a mural in the Library of Congress that fascinated me when I saw it for the first time upon coming to the United States in 1993. This mural, which was designed by the American artist Edwin Howland Blashfield (1848–1936), decorates the dome of the main reading room in the Jefferson Building. On the ceiling of the lantern, the dome's highest point, is an exquisite image of a woman lifting a veil from her face with two cupid-like boys on each side of her. One is looking at a book (arguably the book of wisdom and knowledge) and the other is casting a downward look, perhaps towards the earth. The mural symbolizes human understanding, intellectual progress, and global solidarity and is itself the center of a larger circle consisting of twelve seated and winged figures. Those figures represent important cultural contributions to global history. Judea: Religion; Greece: Philosophy; Rome: Administration; The Middle Ages: Modern Languages; Italy: Fine Arts; Spain: Discovery; Germany: Painting; France: Emancipation; England: Literature; Egypt: Written Records. America: Science; and Islam: Physics.

I do not take this picture to be ideal or representative of global achievements, as it almost exclusively (except perhaps for four figures that are also connected to Europe) attributes the advancement of civilization to the West. The mural also confers on America a rather ambitious role in global progress, more nationalistically inspired than historically informed, while ignoring important contributors to human civilization of a wide range of other cultures and peoples. Still, there is an uncanny resemblance between Islam and America in this clock-like painting. Not only do both have the closest connection among the other figures in terms of global contribution, but they also share common features: they are both seated in a pensive philosopher-like pose while curiously pondering a problem of physics or science, working at the moment of their glorification in this global hall of fame. Despite their different appearances (Islam is a bare-chested bearded man with a turban and a medieval lab apparatus underneath his foot, and America is a young muscular man in work clothes attending to a machine of sorts), Islam and America are tied together in the sacred task of improving the human condition.

I have discussed Islam's contribution to human sciences elsewhere,[59] but to view a work of art in the middle of America's capital that brings Islam

Figure 6.1 The Library of Congress mural

and America together as tireless angels working for the benefit of mankind is as surrealistic as it is painfully ironic in today's world. When the construction of the Jefferson Building was completed by the end of the nineteenth century, the United States' ascendancy must have viewed Islam differently from the way it views it today.

Many scholars have done tremendous work on the history of Islam and America and the history of Islam *in* America.[60] It is crucial to remind ourselves now that a century before this mural was created in the Library of Congress, the mission and definition of America in the global world, especially in relation to Islam, had been the subject of heated debates. William Lancaster, an eighteenth-century anti-Federalist delegate of North Carolina, draws attention to a fearful prospect of a Muslim becoming president of the

United States. In the American Constitution Debate of 1788, Lancaster issues the following warning: "But let us remember that we form a government for millions not yet in existence. I have not the art of divination. In the course of four or five hundred years, I do not know how it will work. This is most certain, that Papists may occupy that chair, and Mahometans may take it."[61]

In opposing the separation between the church and the state, Lancaster used Islam as a hypothetical reference to underline the dreadful prospects if the second clause of Article 6, Chapter 3 of the Constitution were to be ratified. At that time, Islam in America was practiced mostly by African slaves. The clause stated: "The Senators and Representatives before mentioned, and the Members of the several State Legislatures, and all executive and judicial Officers, both of the United States and of the several States, shall be bound by Oath or Affirmation, to support this Constitution; but no religious Test shall ever be required as a Qualification to any Office or Public Trust under the United States."[62] There is no doubt that the mandate of religious freedom that America's Founding Fathers drafted and insisted on has put the American nation into challenging tests over the past two centuries. There is also no doubt that Lancaster's fear of a future where a 'Mahometan' and a 'slave' might be president, much like Anthony Burgess's and Christopher Caldwell's fearful admonitions that Islam may take over Europe, reflects deep-rooted Islamophobia and racism that have persisted for centuries and have come to haunt us today in the shadow of September 11.

The goal, as mentioned earlier, is not so much to dissolve our differences in a 'cosmopolitan' pot of coexistence as it is to challenge the notion that our cultural and national differences must necessarily inspire animosity or fuel hatred. These basic differences in no way constitute even the contours of a thorough study of the precise dynamics at work in the relationship between Islam and the West. Those who promote enmity and convey information based on the knowledge that we inhabit a world of rivalry only reveal severe ignorance when it comes to the divergences and continuities between Islamic and Western civilizations. We need to interrogate the terms of the differences promoted by those ideologies so that a more productive dialogue may take place. Despite the colonial encounters (and, ironically, because of them), the Arab-Muslim world is 'culturally' more contiguous with the West than it was a century ago.

Clearly, a great deal of historical research still needs to be done in order to expose interest-based conclusions masquerading as 'scientifically' verifiable historical knowledge, and usually coming to us from the other 'global' side of the world. Only a small plot of the soil of Islam with its vast areas has so far been sifted (mostly in studies on early conquests and classical Islam), despite the intensity of historical scholarship on Islam in Europe and North America. In all this turmoil, one fact remains clear: no religion, especially one with the magnitudes and multitudes of Islam, deserves to be reduced to a fossilized residual category, left behind while the premises of 'globalization' are being launched by a 'universal' West. Any serious historical research on Islam and its societies outside of Europe will have to adopt more accurate critically and linguistically informed methods predicated on respect for differences. Those who believe that they think in terms of free, detached, disinterested historicization when it comes to Islam, especially the kind of history that ascribes terrorism and violence to one religion at the expense of others, are unable to grasp the enormity of the experience of xenophobia that annuls their very thinking. As the desire to rid the world of terror has turned insidiously against itself, the inevitable task is to allow neither the power of the Empire nor our own powerlessness to confuse us. Our freedom from "terror" in all its manifestations would be gained not by choosing between Muslims and non-Muslims but by dismissing such a rigid way of thinking altogether. If history is what stays when we depart, then EuroAmerica has indeed entered a new era with an outworn historical epistemology, one that continues to abandon responsibility and self-critique while living narcissistically on the uses and abuses of the past.

NOTES

Prologue

1 Theodor Adorno, "Refuge for the Homeless," Selections from *Minima Moralia*, in *Theodor Adorno: Can One Live After Auschwitz? A Philosophical Reader*, ed. Rolf Tiedemann, trans. Livingstone and others (Stanford: Stanford UP, 2003), p. 41.

2 Matthew Arnold, "The Scholar Gypsy," *Poems* (New York: Macmillan and Co., 1884), p. 291.

3 Walter Benjamin, Thesis IX, "Theses on the Philosophy of History," in *Illuminations*, trans. Harry Zohan (London: Fontana, 1973), p. 257.

4 In Greek mythology, Laocoön is a Trojan priest who offended Apollo by breaking his oath of celibacy, mating with his wife in Apollo's sanctuary, and begetting children. As a result, Laocoön and his twin sons were squeezed to death by two great serpents sent by Apollo. The myth of Laocoön is represented in the works of many poets and artists, including Vergil's *Aeneid* (ii, 109 *et seq.*), and the Laocoön statue (currently located in the Vatican Museum) attributed to the three Rhodian sculptors, Agesander, Polydorus, and Athenodorus. The silent cry of pain captured in the sculptural piece inspired many writers, such as Johann Winckelmann and Ephraim Lessing, to reflect on the aesthetic experience of art.

5 Anderson Cooper interview with Tea Party leader Mark Williams, "Rising Anger: President Obama Protests: Crossing the Line?" (CNN: 360), 15 September 2009.

6 Frantz Fanon, *The Wretched of the Earth* (New York: Grove Press, 1968), p. 36.

7 Edward Said, *Culture and Imperialism* (New York: Pantheon Books, 1994), p. 35.

8 Albert Hourani, *Islam in European Thought* (Cambridge: Cambridge UP, 1991), p. 100.

9 Walter Benjamin, "Theses on the Philosophy of History," pp. 249, 255.

10 Lewis and Huntington are examples of Western scholars who believe that Islam is behind the rise of fundamentalism as well as the subsequent violence that drives the cultures and politics of the Islamic world. The risk inherent in this attitude – blaming a so-called adversary culture for violence – is that it creates a self-serving essentialist mode of thinking geared towards freeing one's own culture from any guilt or responsibility.

11 Kwame Anthony Appiah, *Cosmopolitanism: Ethics in a World of Strangers* (Norton, 2006); Thomas W. Simons, Jr., *Islam in a Globalizing World* (Stanford: Stanford UP, 2003).

12 Olivier Roy, *Globalized Islam* (New York: Columbia UP, 2004).

13 Gilles Kepel, *The War of Muslim Minds: Islam and the West* (Belknap Press of Harvard UP, 2004).

14 Saba Mahmood, *The Politics of Piety: The Islamic Revival and the Feminist Subject* (Princeton, N.J.: Princeton UP, 2005), p. 189.

15 Albert Hourani, "Islam and the Philosophers of History," *Middle Eastern Studies*, vol. 3, no. 3 (April, 1967), pp. 206–268.

16 Albert Hourani, "How Should we Write the History of the Middle East?" *International Journal of Middle Eastern Studies*. vol. 23, no. 2 (May, 1991), pp. 125–36, p. 128.

17 Daniel Pipes, "Battle of the super-systems," *Jerusalem Post* (January, 2003), p. 9.

18 The use of the terms 'Muslim' and 'Islamic' in this book follows the norm where the word 'Islamic' is often used to refer the civilization of Islam as well as to a context in which Islam is institutionalized. For example, Iran can be seen as an Islamic country as its laws are mainly derived from Islamic religious texts, whereas Egypt – with its family law derived from religious texts but its other laws being secular in nature – would be more appropriately described as a Muslim country, i.e., one with a Muslim majority and rampant elements of culture associated with its people and their history. My great indebtedness on this point goes to Ghada Osman, who brought to my attention this subtle English distinction of the terms as they are used within the field of Islamic Studies.

19 For Egypt, see Afaf Lutfi al-Sayyid Marsot, *Egypt and Cromer: A Study in Anglo-Egyptian Relations* (London, John Murray, 1968). For Algeria, see Azzedine Haddour, *Colonial Myths: History and Narrative* (Manchester: Manchester UP, 2000). For the Sudan, see Eve Troutt Powell, *A Different Shade of Colonialism: Egypt, Great Britain, and the Mastery of the Sudan* (Berkeley: University of California Press, 2003).

20 See J.A. Hobson, *Imperialism: A Study* (London, 1902); Jacques Berque, *Egypt: Imperialism and Revolution*, trans. Jean Stewart (Faber and Faber, 1972). Roger Owen, *Cotton and the Egyptian Economy, 1820–1914: A Study of Trade and Development* (Oxford: Oxford UP, 1969); Timothy Mitchel, *Colonising Egypt* (Cambridge: Cambridge UP, 1988). See also Talal Asad, "Refigurations of Law and Ethics in Colonial Egypt," in *Formations of the Secular: Christianity, Islam, Modernity* (Stanford: Stanford UP, 2003).

21 Yūsuf Khulayf, *Dirasāt fī al-Shi'r al-Jāhilī* [Studies in Pre-Islamic Poetry] (Cairo: Maktabat Gharīb, 1981).

22 See Munajjid Salāḥ al-Dīn, *Dirāsāt fī tārīkh al-Khaṭṭ al-'Arabī, mundhu bidāyātihi ilā nihāyāt al-'aṣr al-Umawī* (Bayrūt: Dār al-Kitāb al-Jadīd, 1972).

23 Many translate '*sharī'a*' as 'Islamic law,' but this is not entirely correct. For Muslims, *sharī'a* is God's Law, which one can only guess at (through practicing jurisprudence or *fiqh*). Seen through Muslim eyes, *sharī'a* is not just Islamic law but the Divine law that ideally everyone should follow.

24 This number includes Arab League countries like Djibouti and Somalia which have proclaimed Arabic as an official language in addition to their national languages.

25 See "Population and Development Report" (New York: United Nations Publications, E/ESCWA/SDD/2003/12, 2003). According to population prospects, the Arab world population is expected to grow up to 315million people by 2015. See United Nations, *World Population Prospects: The 1998 Review: Volume 1, Comprehensive Tables.*

26 Many people in Israel speak Arabic as a native language; Arabic is a first language of Arab Israelis (Jewish, Christian, and Muslim). Arabic is also the mother tongue of many Palestinians who live in Israel as well as thousands of Arab Jews who left their home countries and settled in Israel in the past six decades. Arabic is also a second language to many non-Arab Israelis.

27 See the definition of "عرب" in Ibn Manẓūr, *Lisān al-'Arab* (al-Qāhira: Dar al-Ma'ārif, n.d.). See also al-Zamakhsharī, *Asās al-Balāgha.*

28 See *al-Mughrib fī Tartīb al-Mu'rib*, anon. (al-Maktaba al-Islāmiyya): <http://www.al-eman.com/IslamLib/viewchp.asp?BID=390&CID=7#s15>.

29 Arab nationalism has not been completely Islamic in character. One of the points of focusing on Arab identity was that it avoided making Islam the automatic factor uniting the Arab world. That is why the Christians were so adamant to push the cause of Arab nationalism – so that they weren't left out, as they would be if Islamic nationalism became the principle uniting cause.

30 For various treatments of the relationship between colonialism, nationalism, and the rise of Islamic fundamentalism see the following: S. Al-Ḥuṣrī, *Al-Bilād al-'Arabiyya wa al-Dawla al-'Uthmāniyya* [Arab Countries under Ottoman Rule] (Beirut: n.p., 1966); C. Ernest Dawn, *From Ottomanism to Arabism: Essays on the Origin of Arab Nationalism* (Urbana: University of Illinois Press, 1973); Arthur Goldsmith, Jr., *A Concise History of the Middle East (*Boulder, Colo.: Westview Press, 1979); John Waterbury, John. *The Egypt of Nasser and Sadat: The Political Economy of Two Regimes* (Princeton, N.J.: Princeton UP, 1983); Tareq Y. Ismael, *International Relations of the Contemporary Middle East* (Syracuse, N.Y.: Syracuse UP, 1986); Georges Corm, *Fragmentation of the Middle East: The Last Thirty Years* (London: Hutchinson Education, 1988); Adeed Dawisha and I. William Zartman, eds, *Beyond Coercion: The Durability of the Arab State* (London: Croom Helm, 1988); M.E. Yapp, *The Near East Since the First World War* (London: Longman, 1991); Albert Hourani, *A History of the Arab People* (New York: Warner Books, 1991); Roger Owen, *State, Power and Politics in the Making of the Modern Middle East* (London: Routledge, 1992); Mohammad Salama, "Arabs, Islam, and the Arab World," in *Encyclopedia of the Modern World*, ed. Peter N. Stearns (Oxford: Oxford UP, 2008).

31 While modernity is often referred to as the era that started with the Renaissance and continued through rationalist philosophy, and the Enlightenment, many still use the two terms, modernism and modernity, interchangeably.

32 According to Rosalind Krauss, sculptural modernism took place late in the 19th century when the logic of the monument began to fade away, notably in Rodin's "Gates of Hell" and his statue of Balzac:

> With these two sculptural projects, I would say, one crosses the threshold of the logic of the monument, entering the space of what could be called its negative condition – a kind of sitelessness, or homelessness, an absolute loss of space. Which is to say one enters modernism, since it is the modernist period of sculptural production that operates in relation to this loss of site,

producing the monument as abstraction, the monument as pure marker or base, functionally placeless and largely self-referential.

Rosalind Krauss, "Sculpture in the Expanded Field," *The Anti-Aesthetic: Essays on Postmodern Culture* (Seattle: Bay Press, 1983), p. 35.

33 See Tzvetan Todorov, *Hope and Memory: Lessons from the Twentieth Century*, trans. David Bellos (Princeton, N.J.: Princeton UP, 2003).

34 Raymond Williams, *Keywords: A Vocabulary of Culture and Society* (New York, Oxford UP, 1976), p. 333.

35 Ibid., p. 333.

36 I use the term 'pan-Islamic nationalism' to refer to movements like Egypt's *Nahḍa* and pan-Arabism, which are covert pan-Islamic movements that arose in response to the Arab-Muslim world's encounter with European colonialism. Although *Nahḍa* includes broader and more diverse aspects of the Arabic tradition, including the humanities and social sciences, it is still anchored in a sense of restorative Islamic heroism, hence the Arabic naming 'Nahḍa' (uprising, awakening). While many important *nahḍa* literary voices were Christian, coming out of missionary schools in the Levant, pan-Arabism, especially in its early phases, was constructed so that Arab identity, not Islamic, would prevail and so as not to exclude Christian Arabs.

37 Partha Chatterjee *Nationalist Thought and the Colonial World: A Derivative Discourse* (Minneapolis: University of Minnesota Press, 1986), p. 51.

38 Arif Dirlik, "Is there a History after Eurocentrism?: Globalism, Postcolonialism, and the Disavowal of History," *Cultural Critique*, no. 42 (Spring, 1999), p. 17.

39 Michael Hardt and Antonio Negri, *Multitude: War and Democracy in the Age of Empire* (Penguin Books, 2004), p. 33–35.

40 Paul Gilroy, *Postcolonial Melancholia* (New York: Columbia UP, 2005), pp. 22, 23, 142.

41 See Judith Butler, *The Power of Mourning and Violence* (London: Verso, 2004) and Paul Gilroy, *Postcolonial Melancholia*.

42 Mahmood Mamdani, *Good Muslim, Bad Muslim: America, The Cold War, and the Roots of Terror* (New York: Pantheon Books, 2004).

43 Samuel Huntington, *The Clash of Civilizations and the Remaking of World Order* (New York: Simon and Schuster, 1997), p. 318.

44 Nasserism, for example, was viewed as a pan-Arabist anti-Western modernity, but one that had its own limitations. The Egyptian sociologist Anouar Abdel-Malek argued in the 1960s, that is, at the height of pan-Arabism, that the Arab-Muslim world had fallen prey to the economic and political practices of the West and that it was in grave jeopardy of losing its cultural identity to European imperialism. To Abdel Malek, the obvious sign of this danger was the creation of obstacles to prevent direct and unmediated economic relations between Asia and Africa. Abdel Malek cautioned that unless Arab cultures manage to promote all their resources and impose their specificity in their own market, it is likely that those cultures will disappear. See Anwar Abdel Malek, *Dirāsāt fī al-Thaqāfa al-Waṭaniyya* [Studies in National Culture] (n.p., 1963); see also Abdel Malek, *Nahḍat Miṣr* [Egypt's Renaissance] (n.p. 1983) and *Modern Arab Political Thought*, ed. Charles Issawi, trans. Ihsān 'Abbās (Princeton, N.J.: The Kingston Press, 1983).

45 Edouard Glissant, *Poetics of Relation*, trans. Betsy Wing (Ann Arbor: University of Michigan Press, 1997), p. 191.

46 Carlos J. Alonso, *The Burden of Modernity: The Rhetoric of Cultural Discourse in Spanish America* (New York, Oxford: Oxford UP, 1998), p. 28. I am grateful to Luis Madureira for bringing this passage to my attention.

47 Many prominent scholars have debunked the alleged presence of the wholly secular. See Mircea Eliade, *The Sacred and the Profane: The Nature of Religion* (Boston, Mass.: Houghton Mifflin Harcourt, 2001); see also Talal Asad, *Formations of the Secular: Christianity, Islam, Modernity* (Stanford, Cal.: Stanford UP, 2003). In this important work, Asad addresses Arab concerns over modernity and shows how secularism is just as prone to fabrication as 'religion' is. Asad interrogates the binary opposition between "traditionalism" and modernity in addressing Islam and the West. One among many salient points that Asad raises in his book is that "all Muslims today inhabit a different world from the one their medieval forebears lived in, so it cannot be said of any of them that they hold the classical theological view... . Both Arab nationalism and Islamism share a concern with the modernizing state that was put in place by Westernizing power:" *Formations of the Secular,* p. 198. In other words, "Islamism" is a different form of "nationalism" in the Arab-Islamic world. For more on Asad's views on modernity, see "Talal Asad, Modern Power and the Reconfiguration of Religious Traditions," interview by Saba Mahmood, *Stanford Humanities Review*, vol. 5, num. 1: <http://www.stanford.edu/group/SHR/5–1/text/asad.html>.

48 See Sir Robert Ensor, *The Oxford History of England: England 1870–1917* (London: Oxford UP, 1936), pp. 240–45.

49 Said, *Orientalism,* p. 60.

50 Ibid., p. 3.

51 Ibid., p. 333.

52 See Johannes Fabian, *Time and Other: How Anthropology Makes its Object* (New York: Columbia UP, 1982).

53 See Kanan Makiya (Samīr al-Khalīl), *Cruelty and Silence: War, Tyranny, Uprising in the Arab World* (New York: W.W. Norton, 1993), p. 357.

54 For instance, in a recent study of Islam in history, the Egyptian Muslim scholar Yūsuf al-Qaraḍāwī argues that despite the blunders and flaws that do not distinguish Islam from any other human history, the history of Islam has been misunderstood and curtailed by three types of scholars both in the Arab world and the West: historians lacking objectivity in their accounts of Islamic history; fiction writers who choose entertainment over facts; and modernists who reduce Islamic achievements to the Caliphate era. In al-Qaraḍāwī's defense of Islam, however, one-dimensionality also appears as he lists six achievements of Islam throughout history: profundity of divinity; transparency of human values; resolute morality; ability to transcend world crises; peaceful spread around the world; tolerance of other religions and beliefs. Those achievements could also be said of any other religion, not necessarily Islam, but al-Qaraḍāwī refuses to see it that way. See Yusūf al-Qaraḍāwī, *Tārīkhunā al-Muftarā 'Alayih* [Our tyrannized history] (Cairo: Al-Shurūq, 2005).

55 This list includes Iraqi writers like 'Abd al-Wahhāb al-Bayyātī and Badr Shakir al-Sayyāb, Gulf writers like 'Abd al-Rahmān Munīf, and Egyptian writers like

Yūsuf Idrīs, Ṣun'-Allah Ibrāhīm, and Nawāl al-Sa'dāwī, in addition to a significant number of writers in exile.

56 "I regret to say that the Arabic perception of *Orientalism*, despite Kamal Abu Deeb's remarkable translation, still managed to ignore that aspect of my book which diminished the nationalist fervor that some implied from my critique of Orientalism, which I associated with those drives to domination and control also to be found in imperialism... . Yet the sense of fraught confrontation between an often emotionally defined Arab world and even more emotionally experienced Western world drowned out the fact that *Orientalism* was meant to be a study in critique, not an affirmation of warring and hopelessly antithetical identities." Said, *Orientalism*, p. 338.

57 See for instance the latest discussion on the topic in "Orientalism Wake: The Ongoing Politics of a Polemic," in *Middle East Institute Viewpoints* (Washington D.C., September 2009).

58 See Gilles Kepel, *Le prophète et le pharaon: Les mouvements islamistes dans l'Egypte contemporaine* (Paris: La Découverte, 1984); see also Emanuel Sivan, *Radical Islam, Medieval Theology, and Modern Politics* (New Haven, Conn.: Yale UP, 1985), and Bruno Etienne, *L'Islamisme radical* (Paris: Hachette, 1987).

Chapter 1 Fact or Fiction?

1 Jacques Derrida, *The Gift of Death*, trans. David Wills (Chicago: University of Chicago Press, 1995), p. 4

2 Derrida's critique of Europe's failure to understand its own history is informed by his reading of the notion of "secrecy" in Jan Patouka's essay, "La civilisation technique est-elle une civilisation de décline, et pourquoi?" [Is technological civilization a civilization of decline, and why?), in *Essais hérétiques sur la philosophie de l'histoire* [Heretical essays on the philosophy of history], trans. Erika Abrams (Lagrasse: Verdier, 1981). See Derrida, *The Gift of Death*, pp. 1–34.

3 Timothy Mitchell, ed., *Questions of Modernity* (Minneapolis: University of Minnesota Press, 2000), p. 23.

4 See how Edward Said casts a suspicious look on Orientalist travelogues in the Arab-Muslim world: *Orientalism* (London: Routledge & Kegan Paul, 1978), pp. 49–72, 149–65.

5 See for example: Karl Popper, *The Poverty of Historicism* (Boston: Beacon Press, 1957); Jürgen Habermas, "Positivism, Pragmatism, Historicism," in *Knowledge and Human Interests*, trans. Jeremy J. Shapiro (Boston: Beacon Press, 1968), pp. 65–186.; Anthony Giddens, *Positivism and Sociology* (London: Heinemann, 1974); Catherine LeGouis, *Positivism and Imagination: Scientism and Its Limits in Emile Hennequin, Wilhelm Scherer and Dmitril Pisarev* (London: Bucknell UP, 1997).

6 Hayden White, "The Fictions of Factual Representation," *The Literature of Fact: Selected Papers from the English Institute*, ed. Angus Fletcher (New York, Columbia UP, 1976), p. 22.

7 Raymond Williams, *Marxism and Literature* (Oxford: Oxford UP, 1977), p. 45.

8 Raymond Williams, *Keywords: A Vocabulary of Culture and Society* (New York: Oxford UP, 1976), pp. 186–9.

9 White, "The Historical Text as a Literary Artifact," *The Writing of History*, ed. Robert H. Kamry and Henry Kozicki (Madison: University of Wisconsin Press, 1978), p. 46.

10 Ibid., p. 42.

11 Claude Lévi-Strauss, *The Raw and the Cooked*, trans. John and Doreen Weightman (New York: Harper and Row, 1969), p. 13.

12 See Lionel Gossman, 'History and Literature: Reproduction or Signification,' in *The Writing of History: Literary Form and Historical Understanding*, ed. Robert Canary and Henry Kozicki (Madison: University of Wisconsin Press, 1978).

13 This is the case without mentioning other external factors at work in the production of historical narratives: the position the historian adopts, political, social, idealistic, etc.; the decision the historian makes about sources and documents, omissions, selection, etc.; the target audience of the historian (the present), the nature of the historian's inferences, how the historian constructs an argument, the logic of relating events; the manner in which the historian constructs a narrative; the language s/he uses – declarative, suppositional, confessional, concessional, rhetorical; the theories invoked to address past happenings. All this, in addition to technical and publishing constraints of the time, for instance factors such as censorship, length, decorum, etc.

14 Paul Ricoeur, *Time and Narrative*, vol. 3 (Chicago: Chicago UP, 1983), p. 14.

15 Aristotle, *Poetics*, trans. Richard Janko (Indianapolis: Hackett, 1987), p. 12.

16 The notion of mimesis belongs to a long traditional chain that goes back to Plato and Aristotle. The use of language for purposes other than communicating literal truth was bound to be deprecated in dealing with moral ideas. That is why to Plato, literature is denigrated, not only as merely mimetic, but as more harmful than useful, more inclined to mislead the public and dissuade people's attention from pursuing the truth. Plato was the first to remark that in analyzing language we are analyzing social facts, dealing with the social use of material objects. Important here are the distinctions that have been endowed with meaning in relation to a higher cause: truth. Plato's *The Phaedrus* embraces such a doctrine through its distinction between good and bad uses of words:

> Socrates: when a speaker who does not know the difference between good and evil tries to convince a people as ignorant as himself – by representing evil as in fact good, and by a careful study of popular notions – succeeds in persuading them to do evil instead of good, what kind of harvest do you think his rhetoric will reap from the seed he has sown?"
>
> (*The Phaedrus*, p. 72.)

Here, Plato's concept of language is primarily an eclectic one, seeing language as a critical tool for reaching as well as teaching the social value of 'truth.' Literature to Plato is mimesis, a copying of reality, but different from Aristotle's concept of mimesis, in which literature is a representation of reality. Reality to Plato lies outside the domain of language and language is reduced to a mere construction in which man imitates the real. This makes one wonder what words refer to in the first place. Words in Plato are used exclusively to address external objects. There is a play between the internal and the external in Plato as far as language is concerned; that is, the external is not really external, or is at least only apparently so. Language as expressive of external objects is used as a means to reflect the internal truth of the soul.

17 The reference here is to Ferdinand de Saussure and his theory of "difference and similarity," a theory that gave birth to linguistic structuralism.

18 I am indebted to Fred Donner on this point and in particular to a reading of his unpublished paper, "The Historian, the Believer, and the Qur'ān," and our related correspondences. See also Fred Donner's *Narratives of Islamic Origins: The Beginnings of Islamic Historical Writing* (Princeton, N.J.: The Darwin Press, 1998). In this book, Donner focuses on the question of the "authenticity"/ historicity of the Muslim origin narratives and how those narratives developed. One of the book's main points is that such narratives – and maybe most historical narrations – are mere tools in a process of legitimation, be it political, religious, or cultural. While Donner does not say that those narratives are false or "untrue," he argues that their very verifications are intricately tied to the historical periods that produced them.

19 See Raymond Williams, *Keywords*.

20 'Abd al-Qādir al-Rāzī, *Mukhtār al-Ṣiḥāḥ* (al-Qāhira: Wazārat al-Ma'ārif al-'Umūmiyya, 1904), p. 13.

21 Immanuel Kant, "An Answer to the Question: 'What is Enlightenment?'," in *Kant's Political Writings*, ed. Hans Reiss, trans. B. Nisbet (Cambridge: Cambridge UP, 1970), p. 58.

22 Kant, "An Answer to the Question: 'What is Enlightenment?'," p. 58.

23 See Paul Gilroy, *The Black Atlantic* (Cambridge: Harvard UP, 1993).

24 See for instance Dilip Parameshwar Gaonkar, ed. *Alternative Modernities*, (Durham, N.C.: Duke UP, 2001).

25 See for instance Henri-Irénée Marrou, *De la connaissance historique* (Paris: Éditions du Seuil, 1954); Claude Lévi-Strauss, *Race et histoire* (Paris: UNESCO, 1952) and *Tristes tropiques* (Paris: Plon, 1955); see also Paul Veyne, *Comment on écrit l'histoire: Essai d'épistémologie* (Paris: Éditions du Seuil, 1971).

26 Marshall G.S. Hodgson, *The Venture of Islam: Conscience and History in a World Civilization*. vol. 1: *The Classical Age of Islam* (Chicago: University of Chicago Press, 1974), p. 208.

27 See 'Abd al-Raḥmān ibn Khaldūn, *Al-Muqaddima* (al-Qāhira: Būlāq, 1857), p. 383.

28 For more on the rationale of early Islamic expansion, see Fred Donner, *Early Islamic Conquests* (Princeton, N.J.: Princeton UP, 1981).

29 Leonard Binder, *Islamic Liberalism: A Critique of Development Theory* (Chicago: University of Chicago Press, 1988), p. 293.

30 Albert Hourani, *Islam in the Liberal Age* (Oxford: Oxford UP, 1969).

31 See p. J. Vatikiotis, *Egypt from Muḥammad Ali to Sadat* (Baltimore: The Johns Hopkins UP, 1980).

32 By "Azhari Islam," I mean the traditional scholastic Sunni Islam taught and practiced by al-Azhar mosque in Egypt. Founded in 970, al-Azhar is known to be the chief center of Hadīth and Qur'ān studies and is the oldest university known to the Islamic world. Today, al-Azhar Mosque maintains a prestigious status in the Islamic world where the '*ulamā'* (Muslim scholars) serve as authorities in such matters as *fatwa (*edicts) and *ijtihād* (interpretive reasoning).

33 See 'Abd al-'Azīz Dūrī, *The Historical Formation of the Arab Nation*, trans. Lawrence I. Conrad (Croom Helm: Centre for Arab Unity Studies, 1987), pp. 134–53; see also Israel Gershoni and James. p. Jankowski, *Egypt, Islam, and the Arabs: The Search for Egyptian Nationhood, 1900–1939* (Oxford: Oxford UP, 1986); Israel Gershon, Hakan Erdem, Ursula Woköck, eds, *Histories of the*

Modern Middle East: New Directions (Boulder, Col.: Lynne Rienner Publishers, 2002).

34 Traditionalist Salafī, or *al-Salafiyya*, is an Islamic Sunni movement that takes its names from *salaf* (predecessors). This movement calls for the return to and emulation of the early generation of Islam, particularly the age of *al-Khulafā' al-Rāshidūn* (the Pious Caliphs) who succeeded Muḥammad, namely, Abu Bakr, 'Umar, 'Uthmān, and 'Alī.

35 Ḥasan Ḥanafī, *Muqaddima fī 'Ilm al-Istighrāb* [Introduction to Occidentalism] (Beirut: al-Mu'assasa al-Jāmi'iyya lil-Dirāsāt wa al-Nashr wa al-Tawzī', 2000), p. 5. For more works by Ḥanafī that discuss the topic of Occidentalism, see *Les méthodes d'exégèse, essai sur la science des fondements de la compréhension, ilm Usul al-Fiqh* (Le Caire: Le conseil supérieur des arts, des lettres et des sciences sociales, 1965) ; see also *L'exégèse de la phénoménologie, l'état actuel de la méthode phénoménologique et son application au phénomène religieux* (Paris, 1966).

36 Emmanuel Kant, *Critique of Judgment*, trans. J.H. Bernard (New York: Hafner Press, 1951), § 26, p. 90.

37 See Michel Foucault, *The Order Of Things: An Archaeology of the Human Sciences* (New York: Pantheon Books, 1973), p. 17.

38 The historiography of the Renaissance, especially its relation to the new world and the question of the "other," has recently been subject to a sharp criticism by a number of the ablest critics. Tzvetan Todorov's *The Conquest of America* (New York: Harper and Row, 1984), Michel de Certeau's *The Writing of History* (New York: Columbia UP, 1988), and Stephen Greenblatt's *Marvelous Possessions: The Wonders of the New World* (Chicago: University of Chicago Press, 1991) are examples of this trend. Greenblatt summarizes Europe's encounter with the New World as follows:

> We are dealing not with the history of a great culture's salvation but with the chronicle of a great culture's destruction, a chronicle written for the most part by cruel and intolerant victors, often quite ignorant of the people they have conquered. Most Europeans turned upon the natives of America the indifferent gaze of men who do not care whether the beings before them live or die. Not only do the Renaissance's chronicles lack the intelligence and range of Herodotus's Histoire, but there is something inherently debased about their accounts of glorious conquests.
>
> Stephen Greenblatt, *Marvelous Possessions*, p. 128.

39 Samir Amin, *Eurocentrism* (New York: Monthly Review Press, 1988), p. 35.

40 St. Augustine pronouncedly refers to God as an explanatory principle underlying the whole of history. Ibn Khaldūn, on the other hand, avoids direct reference to divinity and chooses to refer to abstract mechanisms which he contends lie in the nature of things. See Theodore Mommsen, "St. Augustine and the Christian Idea of Progress," *Journal of the History of Ideas*, XII (1951), pp. 346–74.

41 See Michael Nerlich, *Ideology of Adventure: Studies in Modern Consciousness 1100–1750*, 2 vols. (Minneapolis: University of Minnesota Press, 1987).

42 Although the Enlightenment, as Williams suggests, was supposed to defend the language of history against the language of literature, the assumption of continuity (with its logic of narrativity) made the connection between the two disciplines even closer. According to White, two forms of explanation in historiography that arose in the first half of the nineteenth century need to

be distinguished: the direction that the analytical process is presumed to take (towards dispersion or integration), and the paradigm of the general aspect that the given set of phenomena will assume at the end of this process. According to White, the first came from the Romantic tradition and German idealist perspectives, which he calls "ideography," and defines as a scientific "desire to render the objects of perception clearer to the eye." The second, 'contextualization,' or 'colligation,' is a movement towards integrating historical events by relating them to a given context that gives the effect of completion. In White's opinion, both kinds "tend to conceive the explanation given by the historian to be virtually indistinguishable from the 'story' told in the course of narration." See Hayden White, "Interpretation in History," in *The Tropics of Discourse: Essays in Cultural Criticism* (Baltimore: The Johns Hopkins UP, 1978), pp. 64–65.

43 Peter Gay, *Style in History* (London: Jonathan Cape, 1974), p. 210.

44 Perry Anderson, *Lineages of the Absolutist State* (London: NLB, 1974), p. 8.

45 R.G. Collingwood, "Spengler's Theory of Historical Cycles," *Ideas of History*, vol. 1, ed. Roland N. Nash (New York: Dutton, 1969), p. 173. The idea that no form of history could ever be a simple reporting of what happened in the interim between two events has also been criticized later by Hayden White, who contends that any view of history as scientific is nothing but "a progressive redescription of sets of events in such a way as to dismantle a structure encoded in one verbal mode in the beginning so as to justify a recording of it in another mode in the end." Hayden White, *The Tropics of Discourse*, p. 98.

46 Kant, *The Idea of History with a Cosmopolitan Intent*, trans. Lewis White Beck, Robert E. Anchor, and Emil L. Fackenheim, ed. Lewis White Beck (New York: Macmillan Publishing Co., 1963), p. 29. It is important to clarify that Kant's concern here is not *Historie*, or what he calls "the task of mere empirical composition," but the formulation of an *a priori* concept of history, as *Geschichte*. The universal natural laws which govern what he calls the "regular progression of history in the phenomenal world" are not laws prescribed by man to nature (this is where the seeming fictivity lies) but rather vice versa. To Kant, it is to nature that we should ascribe all intentionality and "cosmopolitan intent":

> If one may nonetheless assume that nature does not proceed without a plan and final objective, even in the play of human freedom, this idea can still be useful; and while we are still too shortsighted to penetrate to the hidden mechanism of her workings, this idea may still serve as a guiding thread for presenting another planless aggregate of human actions as a system, at least in the large. This idea is only a reflection of what a philosophical mind (which must above all be well versed in history) could attempt to do from another perspective. Besides the otherwise laudable detail with which men now record the history of their times naturally causes everyone concern as to how after several centuries our distant descendants will come to grips of the burden of history that we shall leave to them. Without doubt they will treasure the history of the most ancient times whose documents will have long since vanished, but they will treasure them only from the standpoint of what interests them, namely, what peoples and governments have done to contribute to or to impair the objective of cosmopolitanism (Kant, p. 29).

47 G.W.F. Hegel, *Reason in History: A General Introduction to the Philosophy of History*, trans. Robert S. Harman (Indianapolis: Bobbs-Merrill, 1953). For more elaboration on the various kinds of history writing, see Hegel, "Three Methods of Writing History," in *Reason in History*, pp. 3–11.

48 This approach to history as emanating from self is set in sharp contrast with Herodotus' argument that in order for history to achieve proper epistemological principles, and in order for the historian to maintain historical authority, history has to be associated with mobility and must not "be bound within the walls of the city," as Stephen Greenblatt successfully summarizes the argument. Cognitive objectivity necessitates that in the writing of history, as Greenblatt argues, our knowledge must depend on "travel," on the "refusal to respect boundaries" and the "restless drive towards the margins." Stephen Greenblatt, *Marvelous Possessions*, p. 127. It is important to note that by mobility Herodotus meant the discursive sense of it, the sense that does not exclude or erase or even contain the other, but that which acknowledges and respects the other as cultural diversity, which later came to be known as anthropology. See François Hartog, *The Mirror of Herodotus: The Representation of the Other in the Writing of History*, trans. Janet Lloyd (Berkeley: University of California Press, 1988).

49 See Hegel's "Preface," in *The Phenomenology of the Spirit* (1807), trans. A.V. Miller (Oxford: Clarendon Press, 1977); see also pp. 395–486, 488, 492, 493.

50 "Latter to J. Bloch, Sept. 21–2, 1890," in *Marx and Engels: Selected Correspondence* (Moscow: Foreign Languages Publishing Hougse, 1953).

51 Foucault, *The Order of Things*, p. 262.

52 Robert Young, *White Mythologies: Writing History and the West* (London: Routledge, 1990), p. 3.

53 Tsenay Serequeberhan, "The critique of Eurocentrism and the practice of African philosophy," *Postcolonial African Philosophy: A Critical Reader*, ed. E.C. Eze (Cambridge: Blackwell, 1997), p. 143.

54 Pierre Bourdieu, "The Logic of Classes," *Practical Reason: On the Theory of Action* (Stanford: Stanford UP, 1998), pp. 10–13.

55 For more on the relation between science and history, see Paul Veyne, "Causality and 'Retrodiction'," *Writing History: Essay on Epistemology*, trans. Mina Moore-Rinvolucri (Middletown, Conn.: Wesleyan UP, 1984), pp. 144–72.

56 Hayden White, *The Tropics of Discourse*, p. 49.

57 Ibn Khaldūn's approach assumes craftiness at work in the writing of history. Absent from Franz Rosenthal's translation, which White relies on (perhaps on the assumption of redundancy, irrelevancy, or superfluous Arabic rhetoric), is the fact that Ibn Khaldūn refers to historiography as 'art'. This is actually the first sentence of the *Muqaddima*: "The *art of* history acquaints us with the conditions of past nations; it acquaints us with the biographies of the prophets and with the dynasties and policies of rulers." Ibn Khaldūn, Al-*Muqaddima*, p. 15 (my translation. my italics). Ibn Khaldūn's definition of history as art brings to mind Paul Veyne's theory that "history is a work of art because, while it is objective, it has no method and is not scientific. Similarly, if one tries to specify where the value of a history book lies, one will find oneself using words that would be applied to a work of art." Paul Veyne, "How History Is a Work of Art," in *Writing History*, p. 230.

58 See Hayden White, "The Poetic of History," *Metahistory* (Baltimore: The Johns Hopkins UP, 1973), pp. 1–42.

59 In his study of the nineteenth century, White also finds that the central problem of referent in modern historiography lies in realism, a thesis which he elaborates in later works such as *The Content of the Form* (Baltimore: The Johns Hopkins UP, 1987) and *Figural Realism* (Baltimore: The Johns Hopkins UP, 1999).

60 White, *Metahistory*, p. 2.

61 Ibid., p. xi.

62 Pierre Nora, "Nation," in *A Critical Dictionary of the French Revolution*, ed. François Furet and Mona Ozouf, trans. Arthur Goldhammer (Cambridge: Harvard UP, 1989), p. 749.

63 Nora, *Realms of Memory: The Construction of the French Past*, trans. Arthur Goldhammer (New York: Columbia UP, 1996), p. 3.

64 Michel de Certeau, *The Writing of History*, trans. Tom Conley (New York: Columbia UP, 1988), p. 5.

65 Jacques Derrida, *Of Grammatology*, trans. Gayatri Chakravorty Spivak (Baltimore: The Johns Hopkins UP, 1998).

66 De Certeau, *The Writing of History*, p. 232.

67 In his book *Heterologies*, de Certeau goes even further and describes writing as a devouring discourse, indeed a 'cannibalistic' one in the sense that it devours both place and speech:

> Historically, writing is excluded from that which it discusses and nevertheless it is a 'cannibalistic discourse.' It takes place of the history lost to it. For Freud, the writing process combines 'biblical fiction,' which establishes at the beginning of writing the separation of exile, and Greco-Roman 'fiction.' All proceeds as if writing has taken from time the double characteristic of loss of place (the exile) and of devouring life (cannibalism).
>
> De Certeau, *Heterologies: Discourse on the Other*, trans. Brian Massumi (Minneapolis: University of Minnesota Press, 1995), p. 29.

68 De Certeau, *The Writing of History*, p. 3.

69 Ibid., p. 3.

70 Ibid., p. 6.

71 Ibid., p. 44.

72 Ibid., p. 43.

73 Ibid., p. 232.

74 Reasons of space prevent me from providing an elaborate account of Jean de Léry's *Histoire*. Jean de Léry (1534–1613) was a Calvinist who had departed on a Protestant mission to Brazil. After conflicts developed with the commander of the settlement, de Léry withdrew from his mission and spent three months on the Brazilian coast with the Tupinambou people before finally returning home. To de Certeau, de Léry's *Histoire*, with its 22 chapters, is a journey that never actually left Europe, or one that left Europe physically but not ideologically. De Certeau contends that despite the so-called religious motivations of de Léry's *Histoire*, the work is only an act of appropriating instead of understanding the Other. The point is that writing could neither fully capture nor accurately represent the reality of the Tupinambou society. In the end, de Léry returns to his native country after a journey in which, to quote de Certeau, the "savage is invented."

75 De Certeau, *The Writing of History*, p. 209.

76 Ibid., p. 233.
77 Ibid., p. 215.
78 Ibid., p. 2.
79 Ibid., p. 216.
80 Ibid., p. 212. (my italics)
81 Ibid., p. 219.
82 Ibid., p. 216.
83 White, *Metahistory*, p. 152.
84 It is hard to situate Foucault in terms of a methodological or a philosophical stance. Some critics believe he is a Marxist despite his critique of Marxism, others regard him as a structuralist, a third group traces him back to Auguste Comte, and yet other critics think of him as counter-Freudian. His political tone is also brought into consideration, particularly his encouragement of various forms of resistance to power. In fact, Foucault is all these together. The impact of Nietzsche is also almost unavoidable and cannot be incidental. Nietzsche's concept of power-relation is always there in Foucault. The death of man and of God and the collapse of metaphysics inform the concept of history as a discontinuous series rather than a uniform unfolding of predetermined essence.
85 Foucault, *The Archaeology of Knowledge and The Discourse on Language*, trans. Sheridan Smith (New York: Pantheon Books, 1972), p. 203. In his 1969 essay, "What is an Author," Foucault also explains how and when the human subject took itself as a possible object of human epistemology. He makes it clear that we must get rid of our habit of looking for an author's authority, for he himself is nothing but an "ideological product," although Foucault uses the term "ideological" advisedly. Foucault shows instead that the power of discourse contains both the author and his utterances.
86 I focus more here on tracing Foucault's theory of history in his two works *The Order of Things* and *The Archaeology of Knowledge* without highlighting the major differences between the two studies, which are worthy of a more elaborate study. As he states in the introduction to *The Archaeology of Knowledge and The Discourse on Language*, Foucault writes in order to disambiguate, clarify, and add to some of the notions he already discussed in *The Order of Things*. In *The Archaeology of Knowledge* Foucault admits that his attempt in *The Order of Things* among other books was "an imperfect sketch," written in a "rather disordered way, with an articulation that was never clearly defined." See Foucault, *The Archaeology of Knowledge*, pp. 3–17.
87 Foucault, *The Order of Things*, p. 14.
88 Ibid., p. xxii.
89 Ibid., p. xxi.
90 Ibid., p. xiv.
91 Ibid., p. 17.
92 Ibid., p. 70.
93 Ibid., p. 23.
94 Foucault, "Nietzsche, Genealogy, History," *The Foucault Reader*, trans. Donald F. Bouchard and Sherry Simon, ed. Paul Rabinow (New York: Pantheon Books, 1984), p. 142.
95 At least in this particular context, the Nietzschean in Foucault surfaces, especially in his rejection of the axiom that history is the creation of individual

ideas, but is rather based on discursive structures beyond the transcendental supremacy of the subject.

96 Roland Barthes, "The Discourse of History," trans. Stephen Bann, *Comparative Criticism*, vol. 3, ed. E.S. Shaffer (Cambridge: Cambridge UP, 1981), p. 9.

97 Mohammed Arkoun, *Rethinking Islam: Common Questions, Uncommon Answers*, trans. Robert D. Lee (Boulder, Col.: Westview Press, 1994).

Chapter 2 Postcolonial Battles over Ibn Khaldūn

1 Róbert Simon, *Ibn Khaldūn: History as Science and the Patrimonial Empire* (Budapest: Akademiai Kiado, 2002), p. 11.

2 See Johann Fück's *Die arabischen Studien in Europa bis den Anfang des 20. Jahrhundert* (Leipzig: Otto Harrassowitz, 1955); Norman Daniel, *Islam and the West: The Making of an Image* (Oxford: Oneworld Publications, 1960) and *The Arabs and Medieval Europe* (London: Longman, 1975); see B.Z. Kedar, *Crusade and Mission: European Approaches towards the Muslims* (Princeton, N.J.: Princeton UP, 1989); see Maxime Rodinson, *Le fascination de l'Islam* (Paris: F. Maspero, 1980), translated as *Europe and the Mystique of Islam* (London: I.B.Tauris, 1987). In this study, Rodinson attempts to diffuse the discourse of violence around Islam and offers a theoretical breakdown of the transformations of Europe's image of Islam; see also Albert Hourani, *Islam in European Thought* (Cambridge: Cambridge UP, 1991).

3 My particular reference here is to Muḥammad Jābir al-Anṣārī's recent study, *Liqā' al-Tārīkh bil-'Aṣr: Da'wā li-Badhr al-Khuldūniyya fī Wa'y al-Sha'b Ta'sīsann li-Thaqāfat al-'Aql* [The encounter of history and the present: a call for planting Khaldūnism in national consciousness for the establishment of a culture of the mind] (Beirut: al-Mu'assasa al-'Arabiyya lil-Dirāsāt wa al-Nashr, 2006), pp. 15–23. In his book, al-Anṣārī invokes Ibn Khaldūn as an embodiment of sound intellectual thinking and as a thinker whose scholarly heritage is so much needed in the present time to steer the Arab-Muslim world away from the romance and poetic language that has contributed to its current relapse. Al-Anṣārī sees Ibn Khaldūn as a memory for the future of the Arab world.

4 Franz Rosenthal translates the word *'umrān* as 'civilization.' See Franz Rosenthal, *Ibn Khaldūn, The Muqaddimah: An Introduction to History*, vol. 1 (London: Routledge & Kegan Paul, 1958), p. lxxvi. The term "civilization" is one of many meanings of *'umrān*, which also denotes the movement from the desert life with its tents and minimal agricultural production to city life with its cultural growth and more structured architecture. Moreover, the word refers to sociological and geographical remappings, as well as sociogeographic relations, as in Ibn Khaldūn's section "The Influence of Almanac on People's Manners." There could also be a Qur'ānic influence at work. The verb *ya'muru* is used in the Qur'ān to mean 'establish,' 'visit,' and 'inhabit,' often associated with establishing prayers and continuously visiting *masājid* (the houses of God). See Sūrat al-Tawba (Penance Chapter): 18.

5 Franz Rosenthal and others use the transliteration '*Al-Muqaddimah*' with an aspirated 'h' at the end to refer to Ibn Khaldūn's work. Other scholars prefer English terms like 'Introduction' or 'Prolegomena' to refer to the same text. For the sake of clarity, I honor all variations on the title used by each scholar. As far as my own reference to the term is concerned, I use the transliteration

'Al-Muqaddima' without the final aspirated 'h' to remain faithful to the Arabic word "المقدمة" which ends in a *tā' marbūta* rather than an '*h*.'

6 Based on his review of Franz Rosenthal's translation of Ibn Khaldūn, White's early critique of Ibn Khaldūn raises interesting questions about Ibn Khaldūn's modern ideas of history, but does not address this particular issue of history as a rhetorical act which White dwells upon later, perhaps because the description of history as "art" in Ibn Khaldūn's original is missing from F. Rosenthal's translation which White relied solely upon. See Hayden White, "Ibn Khaldūn in World Philosophy of History," in *Comparative Studies in Societies and Histories,* vol. 2 (October, 1959), pp. 110–25.

7 Aristotle's philosophy was not accepted wholeheartedly by all Muslim philosophers. Some, notably al-Ghazālī, were very critical of Aristotelianism and all Greek philosophy. Some believe that it was Aristotle who nourished the metaphysical aspirations of medieval Islamic historical thinking through his theory on the existence of the first motionless mover. The purely spiritual and immaterial substance of the "first motionless mover" and the unity and creative nature of all things are said to have appealed to many Muslim philosophers. But for many of them, Aristotle still had to be studied and applied carefully and sometimes eclectically, especially after Averroës dug deeper into his philosophy and came up with points such as Aristotle's denial of the immortality of the individual soul. It is important to stress that the existence of Aristotelian thought among medieval Muslims does not necessarily establish a direct case of influence, but it suggests at least that they were aware of his ideas.

8 The word '*tārīkh*' is used by the Arabs to refer to their history writings. The term implies dating and taking exact notes of events as they happen. Arab scholars avoided using the word history, which they knew from the Greeks, to designate their *tārīkh* and used it instead to refer to legends (*hustara,* 'history'). There is strong evidence that Qur'ānic Arabic is responsible for this association. Note that Ibn Khaldūn avoids using the word '*tārīkh*' in his title, and prefers the word '*kitāb*' (book) and '*ayyām*' (days), presumably because he wanted to challenge the traditional method of writing history. For more on the etymology of the word '*tārīkh*,' see A. Laroui, *La Crise des Intellectuels Arabes* (Paris: Maspero, 1974), or its English translation, *The Crisis of Arab Intellectuals*, trans. Diarmid Cammell (Los Angeles: University of California press, 1976). See also H. Gibb, *Tārīkh: Studies on the Civilization of Islam* (Princeton, N.J.: Princeton UP, 1962), pp. 108–37.

9 Samir Amin, *Eurocentrism*, p. 50.

10 One way of translating the complete title of Ibn Khaldūn's work is as follows: "The book of exemplars and the divan of the subject and the predicate on the days of the Arabs and the Berbers and the great Sultans who lived among them". Ibn Khaldūn divides his book into three large parts under the following headings:

I Society and its inherent phenomena, such as sovereignty, authority, labor, trades, industries, and causes and effects pertaining to them. This book is also known as the Prolegomena.

II History of the Arabs, their generations and dynasties from the creation to the author's time, with the annals of some of the contemporary nations and great men and their dynasties, such as the Syrians, the Persians, the Jews, the Copts, the Greeks, the Romans, the Turks, and the Franks.

III History of the Berbers and the tribes associated with them, such as Zanāta, and the kingdoms and dynasties of North Africa.

11 Ibn Khaldūn, 'Abd al-Raḥmān, *Kitāb al-'Ibar, wa Dīwān al-Mubtada' wal-Khabar, fī Ayyām al-'Arab wal-'Ajam wal-Barbar, wa man 'Āsharahum min Dhawī al-Sulṭān al-Akbar,* vol. IV (Beirut: 1959), p. 206. See also in the same volume his account on the story of al-Kāhina, the North African woman who formed a resistance against the Muslim armies invading Algeria.

12 Ibn Khaldūn, *Al-Muqaddima,* vol. I, pp. 15–16.

13 Ibn Jarīr al-Ṭabarī, *Ta'rīkh al-Rusul wa-l-Mulūk,* quoted in 'Ābid al-Jabrī, *Bunyat al-'Aql al-'Arabī* [The structure of Arab reason], vol. 2 (Casablanca: al-Markaz al-Thaqāfī al-'Arabī, 1986), p. 563.

14 Ibn Khaldūn, *Al-Muqaddima,* vol. III, p. 6.

15 This relationship between myth and history has been a constant sort of anxiety to many modern and contemporary Western scholars. For instance, in his fourth chapter of *Myth and Meaning,* Claude Lévi-Strauss speaks about the possibility of "myth" becoming "history." The problem of "where does mythology end and where does history start" becomes to Lévi-Strauss one of archiving, and especially of orality versus writing. See Claude Lévi-Strauss, *Myth and Meaning: Cracking the Code of Culture* (New York: Schocken Books, 1995), p. 38. Michel de Certeau also dwells on the nexus between myth and history. See also Michel de Certeau, "Myth and History," *The Writing of History,* pp. 44–45.

16 Michel Foucault, *The Archaeology of Knowledge and The Discourse on Language,* trans. Sheridan Smith (New York: Pantheon Books, 1972), p. 80. I use the word 'discourse' here in the Foucauldian sense, as a practice composed of statements/events which function as a constellation of historical rules, limited to the time and place of their production. In a given period of time, 'discourse' serves to define the framework within which the statement/event takes place. See Foucault, "Defining the Statement," *The Archaeology of Knowledge,* pp. 79–87.

17 Ibn Khaldūn, *Al-Muqaddima,* vol. 1, pp. 55–6.

18 Ibid., pp. 287–80.

19 Ibid., p. 281.

20 Ahmed Abdesselem: *Ibn Khaldun et ses lecteurs : Essais et conférences, Collège de France* (Paris: Presses Universitaires de France, 1983). See B.B. Lawrence, ed., *Ibn Khaldūn and Islamic Ideology,* International Studies in Sociology and Social Anthropology, vol. XL (Leiden: E.J. Brill,, 1984).

21 See Aziz al-Azmeh, *Ibn Khaldūn in Modern Scholarship: A Study in Orientalism* (London: Third World Centre, 1981), pp. 68, 88–97, 100, 165.

22 Lawrence, *Ibn Khaldūn and Islamic Ideology,* p. 5.

23 Important seventeenth- and eighteenth-century Turkish historians like Muṣṭafā 'Alī (1541–1600), Katib Çelebi (1609–75), Muṣṭafā Na'īma (1653–1716), and Mehmed Sāhib Pirizade (1671–1749) wrote extensive commentary and translated most of Ibn Khaldūn's work, especially *al-Muqaddima.* For more on pre-colonial Arab scholarship on Ibn Khaldūn, see Sa'īd al Ghānimī, *al-'Aṣabiyya wa al-Ḥikma: Qirā'a fī Falsafat al-Tārīkh 'Inda Ibn Khaldūn* (Beirut: al-Mu'assasa al-'Arabiyya lil-Dirāsāt wa al-Nahr, 2006); see also Róbert Simon, *Ibn Khaldūn: History as Science and the Patrimonial Empire* (Budapest: Akademiai Kiado, 2002).

24 Lawrence, *Ibn Khaldūn and Islamic Ideology,* pp. 81–2

25 Tāhā Ḥusayn, *Falsafat Ibn Khaldūn al-Ijtimāʿiyya* (1925), trans. Muḥammad ʿInān (Beirut: Dār al-Kitāb al-Lubnānī, 1973), p. 25. The original French title of Husayn's thesis is *Etude analytique de la philosophie sociale d'Ibn Khaldoun.*, Thèse de doctorat d'Université (Paris, 1917).

26 Lawrence, *Ibn Khaldūn and Islamic Ideology*, p. 69.

27 Another example of this lack of specialization in Lawrence's volume is Miriam Cooke's article "Ibn Khaldūn and Language," in which she inexplicably conjectures that Ibn Khaldūn was a "closet poet," one who secretly composed his own poems and attributed them to other poets, a practice she claims was "a well-known literary phenomenon in Islamic writings." Lawrence, p. 36.

28 To support Franz Rosenthal's views, many scholars, including Yves Lacoste, for instance, consider Ibn Khaldūn the founder of "the science of history." See Lacoste, *Ibn Khaldoun, naissance de l'histoire, passé du tiers-monde* (Paris: Maspero, 1966). See also Svetlana Mihailovka Bacieva's *Isztoriko-szociologiceseszkij tratktat Ibn Halduna "Mukaddima"* (Moszkva: Izdatyelsztvo, 1965). Bacieva's book appeared in Arabic as *Al-ʿUmrān al-Basharī fī Muqadimmat Ibn Khaldun*, trans. Ridwān Ibrāhīm (Tunis, 1978). Focusing on social feudalism in Ibn Khaldūn's work, Bacieva adopts a Marxist approach in her study of landed aristocracy and property rights in thirteenth- and fourteenth-century North Africa; see also Heinrich Simon, *Ibn Khaldūns Wissenschaft von der menschlichen Kultur* (Leipzig, 1959). Simon's work, translated into English by Fuad Baali (Delhi, 1997), emphasizes the deterministic aspect of Ibn Khaldūn's cyclical theory of history and connects him to the tradition of (Muslim) Aristotelians.

29 It is unfortunate that al-Azmeh praises de Slane's French translation of Ibn Khaldūn's *Muqaddima* while unconvincingly dismissing Franz Rosenthal's as faulty. While there are some ellipses and infelicities here and there, Franz Rosenthal's work is perhaps the most impressive and daunting rendition of an Arabic text into English over the last century, an achievement to which many scholars have been and will continue to be indebted for generations to come.

30 H.A.R. Gibb, "The Islamic Background of Ibn Khaldūn's Political Theory" (1933), *Studies on the Civilization of Islam*, ed. Stanford J. Shaw and William R. Polk (London: Routledge & Kegan Paul, 1962), pp. 166–75.

31 Ernest Gellner, *Muslim Society* (Cambridge: Cambridge UP, 1981), pp. 88–9.

32 Muhsin Mahdi, *Ibn Khaldūn's Philosophy of History* (New York: Phoenix edn., 1964). See Aziz al-Azmeh, *Ibn Khaldūn in Modern Scholarship* and *Ibn Khaldūn: An Essay in Reinterpretation* (London: Frank Cass, 1982). See also Arkoun's review of al-Azmeh (in French) in *Arabica*, T. 32, Fasc. 2 (July, 1985), pp. 245–6.

33 See Raymond Schwab, *The Oriental Renaissance: Europe's Rediscovery of India and the East, 1680–1880*, trans. G. Patterson-Black and V. Reinking (New York: Columbia UP, 1984), pp. 295–8.

34 Rodinson, *Europe and the Mystique of Islam*, p. 70.

35 Said, *Orientalism* (London: Routledge and Kegan Paul, 1978), pp. 126–7.

36 See Philippe Lucas and Jean Claude Vatin, *L'Algerie des anthropologies* (Paris: Maspero, 1975), p. 16 ; see also Said, *Orientalism*, pp. 84–7.

37 Al-Azmeh's book is primarily on Ibn Khaldūn and is a published version of his dissertation submitted to the University of Oxford in 1977. The book is an important contribution to Middle Eastern studies and includes a useful and

detailed bibliography. As its title indicates, the book aims to study Western scholarship through a critical analysis of the way modern Orientalism interprets the writings of Ibn Khaldūn. This approach is promising and valuable in principle. Al-Azmeh's book, however, does not clearly emphasize the distinction between its main thesis and the actual content of the book. While a substantial part of al-Azmeh's work is effectively devoted to Ibn Khaldūn's writings, especially the *Muqaddima*, there is little to no discussion of the "Orientalism" thesis that al-Azmeh's title addresses. The complexity of the language employed, the intricacy of style, and the scholastic density with which al-Azmeh chooses to write might make it difficult for his message to get across. However, this does not lessen the book's value as a major contribution to this less widely studied historian of Islam. See Aziz Al-Azmeh's *Ibn Khaldun in Modern Scholarship: A Study in Orientalism* (London, Third World Center for Research, 1981).

38 A.J. Toynbee, *A Study of History*, vol. III (London: Oxford UP, 1935), p. 322.

39 Said, "Foucault and the Imagination of Power," *Reflections on Exile and Other Essays* (Cambridge, Mass.: Harvard UP, 2000), p. 240.

40 There are other editions published in Beirut and Egypt. For the purpose of this study, my main textual reference will be *Muqaddimat al-'Allama Ibn Khaldūn*, the vocalized Arabic edition published in Beirut in 1900.

41 See Franz Rosenthal, *Ibn Khaldun, The Muqaddimah: An Introduction to History*, p. lxviii.

42 Al-Azmeh, *Ibn Khaldūn in Modern Scholarship*, p. 126–7.

43 Ibid., p. 209. Al-Azmeh makes a strong point by arguing that a selective reading of Ibn Khaldūn was used by some Orientalists to justify the French colonial mission in the Maghreb: pp. 209–10.

44 Said, *Orientalism*, p. 97.

45 Hayden White, "Ibn Khaldūn in World Philosophy of History," *Comparative Studies in Society and History*, vol. 2, no. 1, (October, 1959), p. 110.

46 In this context, White also states that the "the original *is* impressive." White, p. 112 (White's italics). This comment begs the question of how White could possibly have the knowledge and authority to comment on the original (as opposed to Franz Rosenthal's translation).

47 White, "Ibn Khaldūn in World Philosophy of History," p. 114.

48 Ibid., p. 115 fn.

49 It is highly probable that White consulted Gaston Bouthoul's 1930 sociological study of Ibn Khaldūn. Relying on de Slane's translation, Bouthoul examined Ibn Khaldūn's work from an exclusively Eurocentric standpoint, compared him to Renaissance figures, and concluded that he does not believe in the importance of the individual. See Gaston Bouthoul, *Ibn Khaldūn: Sa philosophie sociale* (Paris, 1930), p. 81. White could have benefited from other studies that argued exactly the opposite and focused on humanistic or psychological aspects in Ibn Khaldūn. See H.A.N. Schmidt, *Ibn Khaldūn: The Historian, the Sociologist, and Philosopher* (New York: n.p., 1930, reprint 1967), pp. 34–46. See also Kāmil 'Ayyād, *Die Geschichts-und Gesellschaftslehre Ibn Khaldūns* (Stuttgart-Berlin J.D. Cotta'sche Buchhandlung Nachfolger, 1930).

50 Wlad Godzich, *The Culture of Literacy* (Cambridge: Harvard UP, 1994), p. 57.

51 Samir Amin, *Eurocentrism*, p. 90.

52 Stephen Frederic Dale, "Ibn Khaldūn: The Last Greek and the First *Annaliste*

Historian," *International Journal of Middle Eastern Studies*, vol. 38, no. 3 (August 2006), p. 431.

53 Al-Ghazālī's text has been famously translated as *The Incoherence* and *Self-Contradiction of the Philosophers*. While these translations clarify the content of the book, I choose to stay faithful to the original meaning of the title 'tahāfut' and thus retain the simile that compares philosophers to large edifices and establishments that collapse and fall. In addition, there is a strong analogy in the al-Ghazālī's title to the demolition of *aṣnām* (worshipped statues and relics) to give concretization to this task: "We did not intend this book to be an introduction," al-Ghazālī writes, "but a demolition of philosophy, and that's why we called it the collapse of the philosophers." Al-Ghazālī, *Tahāfut al-Falāsifa*: <http://www.ghazali.org>, p. 45.

54 Ibn Khaldūn, *al-Muqaddima*, p. 568

Chapter 3 How Did Islam Make It into Hegel's Philosophy of World History?

1 Some recent studies have traced elements of racism and bias in Hegelian philosophy as well as post-Hegelian thought. Susan Buck Morss, for instance, has convincingly debunked Hegel's position on slavery and exposed his racial bias, taking the philosopher down from the ivory tower of idealism to the realism of street talk, coffee shop gatherings, and morning newspaper culture. See Susan Buck-Morss, *Hegel, Haiti, and Universal History* (Pittsburgh, Penn.: University of Pittsburgh Press, 2009). See also "Hegel and Haiti," *Critical Inquiry*, vol. 26, no. 4 (Summer, 2000), pp. 821–65. Ian Almond has also dwelt on Hegel's philosophy and its persistent continuity in works of contemporary thinkers like Slavoj Žižek. See Ian Almond, "Iraq and the Hegelian Legacy of Žižek's Islam," *The New Orientalists: Postmodern Presentations of Islam from Foucault to Baudrillard* (London: I.B.Tauris, 2007), pp. 176–95. See also Frantz Fanon, *The Wretched of the Earth*, trans. Constance Farrington (New York: Grove Press, 1968). In his book, Fanon interrogates European philosophy to expose European (white) hegemony. He uses both Marx and Freud to re-interpret Hegel's master–slave dialectic in order to theorize the necessity of violent struggle by Third World nations. According to Fanon, who worked and lived in Algeria during the French occupation, colonized nations seek to overcome colonialism as well the duplicitous humanism of Western Europe, so that they could attain equal recognition in terms of their own cultural values.

2 G.W.F. Hegel, *Introduction to the Philosophy of History*, trans. Leo Rauch (Indianapolis: Hackett Publishing Company), p. 27.

3 For more on Hegel's influence on Marx's views on Islam, see Rosalind C. Morris, "Theses on the Questions of War: History Media, Terror," *Social Text*, vol. 20, no. 3 (2002), pp. 149–75.

4 Here we must clarify Hegel's reference to Christianity. For Hegel, Catholicism became a reactionary and conservative force that was chained by traditional and institutional "medievalism." If anything, Hegel was in favor of Lutheranism because it leaves room for academic contemplation and penetrative analysis of the universe. On Hegel's views on Christianity and Catholicism, see Lawrence S. Stepelevich, "Hegel and Roman Catholicism," *Journal of the American Academy of Religion*, vol. 60, no. 4 (Winter, 1992), pp. 673–91.

5 G.W.F. Hegel, *The Phenomenology of the Spirit*; see also Jürgen Habermas, *Knowledge and Human Interests,* trans. Jeremy Shapiro (Boston: Beacon Press, 1968), pp. 3–24, and George Mosse, *The Culture of Western Europe* (Boulder, Col.: Westview Press, 1988), pp. 148–58.

6 Perry Anderson, *Lineages of the Absolutist State* (London: NLB, 1974), p. 7.

7 Ibid., p. 11.

8 Ibid., p. 10.

9 Ibid., p. 11.

10 Ibid., p. 397.

11 Ibid., p. 397.

12 "The entire Turkish empire is ruled by one master, and all other men are his servants; he divided his kingdom into *sandjaks* and dispatched various administrators to govern them, whom he transfers and changes at his pleasure ... They are slaves, bounden by him." *Il Principe e Discorsi,* pp. 26–7. Quoted from Anderson, p. 397.

13 Ibid., p. 398.

14 Islam was no doubt a subject of heated historical debates among many intellectuals in the seventeenth and eighteenth centuries. On the one hand, Humphrey Prideaux's *The True Nature of Imposture Revealed in the Life of the Impostor Mohammad* (1697) is a remarkable example of this derisive historiographic polemic. On the other, a work like Henry Stubbe's *An Account of the Rise and Progress of Mahometanism with the Life of Mahomet and a Vindication of Him and His Religion from the Calumnies of Christians* (1676) expresses respect for Islam and favorably likens it to elements in Christianity. In his book, Stubbe described Muḥammad as a "political genius." The difference of course is in circulation. Whereas Prideaux's work circulated widely in Europe and North America, Stubbe's work remained unpublished. For more on the political turmoil and place of Islam in constitutional debates in eighteenth-century Europe and America, see Denise A. Spellberg, "Could a Muslim be President: An Eighteenth-Century Constitutional Debate," *Eighteenth-Century Studies* vol. 39, no. 4 (2006): 485–506; see also Albert Hourani, "Islam and the Philosophers of History," *Middle Eastern Studies*, vol. 3, no. 3 (April, 1967), pp. 206–68.

15 See Siep Stuurman, "François Bernier and the Invention of Racial Classification," *History Workshop Journal*, no. 50 (Oxford: Oxford UP, 2000), pp. 1–21.

16 Said, *Culture and Imperialism* (New York: Vintage Books, 1993), p. 240.

17 Montesquieu, quoted in Anderson, *Lineages of the Absolutist State,* p. 400.

18 Said, *Orientalism*, p. 119.

19 Theodor W. Adorno, *History and Freedom: Lectures 1964–1965,* ed. Rolf Tiedemann, trans. Rodney Livingston (Malden: Polity Press), p. 26.

20 Paul de Man, "Sign and Symbol in Hegel's Aesthetics" (1964), *Aesthetic Ideology* (Minneapolis: University of Minnesota Press, 1996), p. 92.

21 Adorno, *History and Freedom: Lectures 1964*–1965, p. 65.

22 Among strong advocates of Hegelian philosophy is the French theorist Maurice Blanchot who argues that in Hegel "philosophy comes together and accomplishes itself." Maurice Blanchot, *The Infinite Conversation*, trans. Susan Hanson (Minnesota: University of Minnesota Press, 1993), p. 4; see also Maurice Blanchot, *The Step Not Beyond*, trans. Lycette Nelson (New York: State University of New York Press, 1992).

23 Despite the claim of many writers like Adorno, de Man, and Maurice Blanchot that there is no outside Hegel, Marx attempts to position himself differently by critiquing Hegel for making the individual a property of the state. Moreover, according to Marx, Hegel turned man into an abstract category. Marx, who saw humans as concrete individuals forming social forces, believed that it was erroneous of Hegel to treat humans as if they were a categorical type. However, Marx's theory of 'capital' is impossible without the Hegelian dialectic. To bridge this divide, the term 'Hegelian Marxists' emerged to address critics who benefit from both streams, including Georg Lukács, Arthur Koestler, and Harold Laski. See Sidney Hook's *From Hegel to Marx: Studies in the Intellectual Development of Karl Marx* (New York: Columbia UP, 1994); Herbert Marcuse, *Hegel and the Rise of Social Theory* (Amherst, N.Y.: Humanity Books, 1999); Alexandre Kojève's *Introduction to the Reading of Hegel: Lectures on the Phenomenology of the Spirit* (Ithaca, N.Y.: Cornell UP, 1980).

24 I mean by this term a theory that, instead of discarding its Others, employs them in order to further distinguish itself (i.e. in opposition to them). Such theories thus work by utilizing their Others in the service of self-definition. A prominent example of this type of theory is Augustine of Hippo's explanation of why the Jews had become dispersed on the earth and yet still survived. He wrote that the presence of Jews should serve as a negative example to guide the Christians in their behavior: "it will be readily apparent to believing Christians from the survival of the Jews, how those who killed the Lord when proudly empowered have merited subjection." Augustine, *Contra Faustum,* 12.12, pp. 341–2. Cited in J. Cohen, *Living Letters of the Law* (Berkeley: University of California Press, 1999), p. 29. I am grateful to Rachel Friedman for bringing this reference to my attention.

25 G.W.F. Hegel, *Lectures on the Philosophy of Religion*, vol. 2, *Determinate Religion*, trans. R.F. Brown, p. C. Hodgson, and J.M. Stewart, ed. Peter C. Hodgson (Berkeley: University of California Press, 1987), p. 55. My italics.

26 Ibid., p. 158.

27 The German definition of *Fanatismus* reads: "Begeisterung für ein Abstraktes, für einen abstrakten Gedanken, der negierend sich zum Bestehenden verhält" (passion for an abstraction, for an abstract thought, which relates as negating force to the existing object/thought). I am indebted to my colleague Volker Langbehn for providing me with this translation.

28 Ibid., p. 50.

29 See *sūrat al-Baqara* [The cow]: 256.

30 See Martin Goodman, *Mission and Conversion: Proselytizing in the Religious History of the Roman Empire* (Oxford: Oxford UP, 1994) and Shaye Cohen, *The Beginnings of Jewishness* (Berkeley: University of California Press, 2001).

31 Hegel, *Lectures on the Philosophy of Religion,* p. 156.

32 G.W.F. Hegel, *Introduction to the Philosophy of History*, trans. Leo Rauch (Indianapolis: Hackett Publishing Company, 1988), p. 22.

33 G.W.F. Hegel, *Lectures on the History of Philosophy*, trans. E.S. Haldane and Frances H. Simon, vol. I (London: Routledge & Kegan Paul, 1892), pp. 118–19.

34 Jean-Luc Nancy, *The Experience of Freedom*, trans. Bridget McDonald (Stanford, Cal.: Stanford UP, 1994), p. 20.

35 Ibid., p. 20.
36 See Adorno, *History and Freedom: Lectures 1964–1965*, pp. 5–9.
37 Hegel, *Lectures on the History of Philosophy*, p. 34.
38 See Tsenay Serequeberhan, "The Idea of Colonialism in Hegel's Philosophy of Right," *International Philosophical Quarterly*, vol. 39 (1989), pp. 301–18.
39 Hourani, "Islam and the Philosophers of History," *Middle Eastern Studies*, vol. 3, no. 3 (April, 1967), p. 246.
40 I borrow the term "continuist" from Gayatri Spivak, who employs it to critique Goux's isomorphic analogy of Freud, Lacan, and Marx in connection to the development of money-form and the psychological account of the emergence of genital sexuality in his work *Numismatiques*. See Gayatri Spivak, "Scattered Speculations on the Question of Value," *Diacritics*, vol. 15, no. 4, *Marx after Derrida* (Winter, 1985), pp. 73–93.
41 Jean-Joseph Goux, "Untimely Islam: September 11th and the Philosophies of History," *SubStance*, issue 115, vol. 37, no. 1 (2008), pp. 52–71.
42 Ibid., p. 56.
43 Ibid., p. 55.
44 Ibid., pp. 57–8.
45 Ibid., p. 58.
46 Hegel, *Introduction to the Philosophy of History*, p. 98.
47 Ibid., p. 98.
48 Ibid., p. 97.
49 Ibid., p. 98.
50 Ibid., p. 98.
51 Note that Hegel did the same thing with Christianity – dissociating it from the Crusades.
52 Goux, "Untimely Islam: September 11th and the Philosophies of History," pp. 55–6.

Chapter 4 The Emergence of Islam as a Historical Category in Early British Colonial Thought

1 Albert Hourani, *A Vision of History: Near Eastern and Other Essays* (Beirut: Khayats, 1961), p. 50.
2 Ibid., pp. 54–8.
3 James Joyce, "Daniel Defoe," (1911), trans. and ed. Joseph Prescott, *Buffalo Studies*, vol. 1, no. 1 (1964): 24–5.
4 Edward Said, *Culture and Imperialism* (New York: Vintage Books, 1993), p. 64.
5 Peter Hume, *Colonial Encounters: Europe and the New Caribbean: 1492–1797* (London, 1986).
6 Derek Walcott, *Remembrance and Pantomime: Two Plays* (1978) (New York: Farrar, Straus & Giroux, 1980).
7 My reference to Robinson Crusoe as the first English novel is informed by Ian Watt's work *The Rise of the Novel.* Controversial in many respects, Watt's work connects the emergence of individualism and the rise of the economic man, or *homo economicus*, to the birth of the English novel. According to Watt's argument, all of Defoe's heroes are after money and book-keeping. He sees Western civilization as based on individual contractual relationships. Watt uses the famous line from Moll Flanders, "With money in the pocket one is at home anywhere,"

to support his claim. See Ian Watt, *The Rise of the Novel* (Berkeley: University of California Press, 1964). Watt sees this theme as characteristic of all Defoe's heroes who either have no family, like Colonel Jacque, and Captain Singleton, or leave it at an early age never to return or return late, like Roxana and Robinson Crusoe. However, if this is an expected trend in adventure stories, the absence or death of conventional family ties, especially of the father, still exemplifies the project of a modernity that glorifies the subject and shuns its connection with the past.

8 Michel de Certeau, *The Writing of History*, trans. Tom Conley (New York: Columbia UP, 1988), p. 232.

9 Daniel Defoe, *Robinson Crusoe* (New York: Random House Modern Library Classics, 2001), p. 83.

10 Ibid., p. 2

11 Ibid., p. 101.

12 Ibid., p. 112.

13 Peter Hume, *Colonial Encounters*, p. 176.

14 Karl Marx, *Capital: A Critique of Political Economy* (New York: The Modern Library, 1906), p. 88.

15 In *Modern Egypt*, Lord Cromer justifies the British mission in Egypt by emphasizing the inadequacy of Islam as a social system and dismisses the possibility of Egyptians' ability to exercise self-rule and have their own independent government. See the Earl of Cromer (Evelyn Baring), *Modern Egypt*, 2 vols. (New York: McMillan, 1908).

16 Cromer, *Modern Egypt*, vol. II., p. 145–50.

17 Ibid., pp. 127–8. See also Wilfrid Scawen Blunt, *Secret History of the English Occupation of Egypt. Being a Personal Narrative of Events* (1907) (New York: Alfred. K. Knopf, 1922).

18 See Cromer, "The Government of Subject Races," *Edinburgh Review*, 207 (January, 1908), pp. 1–27.

19 Cromer, *Modern Egypt*, p. 134.

20 Cromer, *Political and Literary Essays (1908–1913)* (London: Macmillan, 1913), p. 28.

21 See Robert L. Tignor, "Lord Cromer: Practitioner and Philosopher of Imperialism," *Journal of British Studies*, vol. 2, no. 2 (May, 1963), pp. 142–59.

22 Defoe, *Robinson Crusoe*, p. 144.

23 Ibid., p. 121.

24 Samuel Johnson, *The History of Rasselas, Prince of Abissinia* (Oxford: Oxford UP, 1999), p. 28.

25 Ibid., pp. 28–9.

26 Sir Robert Walker, *An Inquiry into the Smallpox, Medical and Political. Wherein A Successful Method of Treating That Disease Is Proposed, the Cause of Pits Explained, and the Method of Their Prevention Pointed Out* (London, 1790), pp. 17–18.

27 Felicity A. Nussbaum, *The Limits of the Human: Fictions of Anomaly, Race, and Gender in the Long Eighteenth Century* (Cambridge: Cambridge UP, 2003), p. 114.

28 Ibid., p. 115.

29 James Plumptre, *The Plague Stayed: A Scriptural View of Pestilence, Particularly of That Dreadful Pestilence the Small-Pox, With Consideration on the Cow-Pock; in Two Sermons* (London, 1805), p. 12.

30 In *Culture and Imperialism*, Said makes the passing comment that "in the writings of British residents abroad, from Lady Wortley Montagu to the Webbs, one finds a language of casual observation [of the East, India, and Africa]." If by "casual," Said refers to a 'conversational' or 'informal' style of writing, what we see in Lady Montagu's account instead is nothing less than an investment which, while not innocent of expected fascination with a different culture, cannot be reduced to exoticism or dismissed as part of the laid-back culture of British tourism. Said makes the argument that even "casual conversations" are part of the power of an "imperial society." There is truth to this statement, but if there is nothing "casual" about Lady Montagu's observations other than its form and style, her writings, particularly the *Turkish Embassy Letters*, would unquestionably fall *outside* the imperial discourse of power Said delineates. See Said, *Culture and Imperialism*, p. 99.

31 Lady Mary Wortley Montagu, *Selected Letters* (London: Penguin, 1997), p. 169.

32 Ibid., pp. 160–1.

33 Lady Montagu, "Plain Account of the Innoculating [sic] of the Small Pox by a Turkey Merchant," in *Essays and Poems and "Simplicity, A Comedy,"* ed. Robert Halsband and Isobel Grundy (Oxford: Clarendon Press, 1977), p. 96.

34 John Richardson, "Dissertation on the languages, literatures, and manners of eastern nations," in *Dictionary, Arabic, Persian, and English* (1777), p. ix.

35 In eighteenth-century England, "Sinbad, "Aladdin," and "Ali Baba" were published in chapbook editions; plots from these stories also became stock elements in English pantomime. By the middle of the century, most English children were fairly familiar with these particular tales. See Felicity Nussbaum and Saree Makdisi, eds, *The Arabian Nights in Historical Conquest: Between East and West* (Oxford: Oxford UP, 2008).

36 See for instance, Benedict Anderson, *Imagined Communities: Reflections on the Origins and Spread of Nationalism* (London: Verso, 1991); see also George Mosse, *Nationalism and Sexuality: Middle-Class Morality and Sexual Norms in Modern Europe* (Madison: University of Wisconsin Press, 1988).

37 Edward William Lane, *An Account of the Manners and Customs of Modern Egyptians* (London: n.p., 1836).

38 I particularly refer here to work like John Adams' *The Flowers of Modern History* (1795) and John Antes' *Observations on the Manners of the Egyptians* (London, 1800).

39 H.S Deighton, "The Impact of Egypt on Britain: A Study of Public Opinion," in *Political and Social Change in Modern Egypt*, ed. P. M. Holt (London: Oxford UP, 1968) 236.

40 Said, *Orientalism*, p. 157. According to Said, the second category of residing Orientalists includes a kind of writer who intends to benefit from his residence in the Orient in order to enrich the European scientific discourse of Orientalism without sacrificing "the eccentricity and style of his individual consciousness to impersonal Orientalist definitions"; the third and final category is more personal and involves a "writer for whom a real or metaphorical trip is the fulfillment of some deeply felt and urgent project." To the second category belong such works like Burton's *Pilgrimage to al-Madinah and Meccah;* to the third, Nerval's *Voyage en Orient*. Said, *Orientalism*, p. 158.

41 Ibid., p. 160.
42 Records show that there was massive demand for Lane's book in England. The first printing sold out in a couple of weeks; the subsequent cheaper printing also sold out before the end of the year. See Deighton, "The Impact of Egypt on Britain: A Study of Public Opinion," p. 236.
43 Lane, *An Account of the Manners and Customs of Modern Egyptians*, p. 27.
44 Ibid., p. 201.
45 James Augustus St. John's *Egypt and Mohammed Ali; Or Travels in the Valley of the Nile* (1834).
46 P.R.O., F.O. 27. To Cowley (in Paris) no. 761, July 18, 1855.
47 P.R.O., F.O. 189/27. Volume of Confidential Print, December 19, 1865. *Correspondences Relating to the Suez Canal: 1859–1865*. Colquhoun's no. 146 of April 1, 1862.
48 P.R.O., F.O.189/27. Russell to Bulwer, no. 8, Feb. 11, 1863.
49 Ibid., 189/27.
50 Townsend, *The Spectator*, June 9, 1866. The reference is to Samuel W. Baker's famous travelogue, *Albert N'yanza, Great Basin of the Nile* (London, 1866).
51 See, for example, Sir Robert Ensor, *The Oxford History of England: England 1870–1917*, pp. 77–86.
52 In 1862 Lady Lucie Duff Gordon travelled to Egypt after having been diagnosed with tuberculosis. Her letters were first published in England in 1865 and the second edition appeared in 1875. Her letters had the appeal of the memoirs of a dying woman triggered both by the tragedy of her impending death and the great consideration she showed for Egyptian peasants. Her background as a Unitarian and as daughter of the famous Benthamite intellectual John Austin had also played a role in the massive circulation of her letters. See Gordon Waterfield, *Lucie Duff Gordon in England, South Africa and Egypt* (New York, 1917), p. 205.
53 Meredith Townsend, *The Spectator*, February 3, 1876. Quoted from Deighton, "The Impact of Egypt on Britain: A Study of Public Opinion," pp. 239–40. Townsend was the editor of *The Spectator* at the time and is said to have been a fervent supporter of British intervention in and control over the Orient, and especially a strong advocate for what came to be known as Britain's "guardianship" of Egypt. In the same article cited above, he writes: "If anything is clear it is that Englishmen have a talent for governing Oriental peoples ... without pressing too severely upon their social freedom."
54 One of Lady Duff Gordon's most condemning letters elaborates on the Mahdi rebellion in Upper Egypt as a reaction to Ismail's harsh economic policy and usurpation of *fallāḥīn* land. See Lady Duff Gordon, "Letter to Mrs. Austin, May 21, 1863," in *Letters from Egypt: 1862–1869*, ed. Gordon Waterfield (London: Routledge & Kegan Paul, 1969).
55 Ibid., p. 201.
56 Ibid., p. 300.
57 Ibid., p. 319.
58 Ibid., p. 300.
59 Ibid., p. 245.
60 "Publisher's Note," in J.C. McCoan, *Egypt As It Is* (New York: Peter Fenelon Collier, 1882), pp. vii–viii.

61 German idealism and its major figures like Kant and Hegel looked back to Greece as ideal, and Husserl did the same in *The Origin of Geometry*. This scholastically informed exclusivity is problematic enough to allow for a serious reconsideration of the role of the peripheries in the staging of this modernity.

62 *Frankenstein* is famous as a novel of monstrosity. It tells the story of a mad scientist who, enraged by the death of his own mother, tries to put an end to death and its subsequent sufferings by creating a man in his laboratory. When he eventually succeeds in his endeavor, the "thing" he created ends up turning against his creator. Contrary to the Halloweenish Hollywood image of him in American popular culture, Frankenstein, who carries the name of his creator (itself an ironical gesture), is actually not a brainless zombie, but a creature capable of thinking, of passing reflective judgment, and of revolting against his creator.

63 The story of Safie has triggered a number of postcolonial and feminist critiques. Gayatri Spivak, for instance, sees Safie's education as a mutation into 'a domesticated Other that consolidates the Imperial self.' Spivak, *A Critique of Postcolonial Reason: Towards a History of the Vanishing Present* (Cambridge, Mass.: Harvard UP, 1999), p. 253; Mohja Kahf brilliantly unveils the imperial gender-dimension of Safie's exotic background, in addition to the subtle implications of her conversion and re-haremization. See Kahf, *Western Representations of the Muslim Woman: From Termagant to Odalisque* (Austin: University of Texas Press, 1999), pp. 165–8.

64 Mary Shelley, *Frankenstein* (Oxford: Oxford UP, 1969), pp. 123–4.

65 A famous academic discipline involved in that particular field of colonial cultural production is anthropology, which was perhaps the most productive rubric under which the native "Other" was imported and exported from Europe. From the real differences of non-European peoples, nineteenth-century anthropologists constructed another being of a different nature; differential cultural and physical traits were constructed as the essence of the African, the Arab, the Aboriginal, and so forth. When colonial expansion was at its peak while European powers were engaged in the scramble for Africa, anthropology and the study of non-European peoples became not only a scholarly endeavor but also a broad field of public instruction. The so-called Other was imported to Europe – in natural history museums, public exhibitions of primitive peoples, in sociological and archeological research – and thus made increasingly available for the popular imaginary. Nineteenth-century anthropology presented the Islamic world, as well as many non-European peoples and cultures, as underdeveloped versions of Europeans and their civilizations, namely, as signs of primitiveness that represented stages on a very long road of European civilizations. The anthropological presentation of non-European others within the evolutionary theory of civilizations served to confirm and validate the eminent position of Europeans and thereby legitimate the colonialist project as a whole. See Gérard Leclerc, *Anthropologie et colonialisme: essai sur l'histoire de l'africanisme* (Paris: Fayard, 1972). See also Talal Asad, ed., *Anthropology and the Colonial Encounter* (London: Ithaca Press, 1973); Nicholaus Thomas, *Colonialism's Culture: Anthropology, Travel, and Government* (Princeton, N.J.: Princeton UP, 1994); Michel de Certeau, *The Writing of History*; and Michael Hardt and Antonio Negri, *Empire* (Cambridge, Mass.: Harvard UP, 2000).

66 Frantz Fanon, *The Wretched of the Earth*, trans. Constance Farrington (New York: Grove Press, 1963), p. 38.
67 Fanon, *The Wretched of the Earth*, p. 42.
68 Said, *Orientalism*, pp. 4–5, 104.

Chapter 5 Colonizing Islam: Egypt, a Case Study

1 See Gayatri Spivak, "Can the Subaltern Speak?" *The Postcolonial Critic; Outside in the Teaching Machine* (London: Routledge, 1993); Ranajit Guha, "On Some Aspects of the Historiography of Colonial India," *Subaltern Studies: Writings on South Asian History and Society* (Oxford: Oxford UP, 1982); and Homi Bhabha, "Difference, Discrimination, and the Discourse of Colonialism," *The Politics of Theory*, ed. Francis Barker, Peter Hulme, Margret Iversen, and Diana Loxley (Colchester: University of Essex, 1983).
2 Edward Said, *Orientalism* (London: Routledge & Kegan Paul, 1978), p. 60.
3 M. Lavisse, *Vue générale sur l'histoire politique de l'Europe* (Paris, 1890), p. 181.
4 J.M. Coetzee, *Stranger Shores: Literary Essays: 1986–1999* (New York: Viking, 2001), p. 191.
5 For further elaboration on the debate on Islam and modernity during the French Campaign, see Afaf Lutfi al-Sayyid, 'L'expédition d'Egypte et le débat sur la modernité,' *Egypte/Monde Arabe,* 1 (1999), pp. 47–54. See also *Gender and Citizenship in the Middle East*, ed. Suad Joseph (Syracuse, N.Y.: Syracuse UP, 2000), p. xv. The volume offers a genealogy of gendered citizenship in the Middle East. Although the volume does not offer a direct historical treatment of European colonialism and its influence on gender relations in the Middle East, it poses crucial questions on how some of the Middle East's current institutional and bureaucratic hierarchies may have been shaped by Western liberal notion of citizenship that likely began with the French occupation of Egypt.
6 The first direct "colonial" contact between France and the Arab world began with the occupation of Algeria in 1830, lasting more than a hundred years, until it ended in 1962. But *l' Expédition Bonaparte* (the Napoleonic Campaign) is said to have created a different kind of influence on Arab-European relations in general. Although there were Egypto-European relations prior to that time, dating back to the Fatimid and Ayyubid dynasties, they were mostly commercial in nature. During the Crusades, France entertained the idea of colonizing Egypt, which ended in the Seventh Crusade Attempt by Saint-Louis (Louis IX), King of France, and his subsequent defeat and capture in al-Mansūra in 1249. The battle also signals the fall of the Ayyubid dynasty and the beginning of Mameluke rule in Egypt. For more on the literary and cultural conditions of Egypt prior to and during the French Campaign, see Kawsar Abdel Salam El-Beheiry, 'L'Égypte avant l'Expédition Bonaparte' and 'L'Égypte pendent l'Expédition,' in *L'Influence de la Littérature Francaise sur le Roman Arabe* (Québec: Éditions Naaman de Sherbrooke, 1980), pp. 14–47. El-Beheiry's work is an engaging effort to map French thought and its accompanying impact on Arabic literature and culture. The book also provides a scholarly and detailed analysis of the influence of major French authors on Arab writers and novelists from al-Ṭahṭāwī to Naguib Mahfouz.
7 See Muḥammad Muṣṭafā Ziyāda, *Nihāyāt al-Ṣalāṭīn al-Mamālīk fī Miṣr* (al-Qāhira: Mijālat al-Jam'iyya al-Miṣrīyya lil-Dirāsāt al-Tārīkhiyya, 1951). For

more recent studies on Mameluke history see Sa'īd 'Ashūr, *al-'Aṣr al-Mamālīkī fī Miṣr wa al-Shām* (al-Qāhira: al-Nahḍa al-'Arabiyya, 1965) and Muḥammad Suhayl Takkūsh, *Tārīkh al-Mamālīk fī Miṣr wa Bilād al-Shām: 1250–1517* (Beirut: Dar al-Nafā'is, 1997).

8 J. Christopher Herold, *Bonaparte in Egypt* (New York: Harper and Row, Publishers, 1962), p. 12.

9 See George A. Haddad, "A Project for the Independence of Egypt, 1801," *Journal of the American Oriental Society*, vol. 90, no. 2. (April–June, 1970), pp. 169–83.

10 See Christopher Lloyd, *The Nile Campaign: Nelson and Napoleon in Egypt* (New York: Barnes and Noble Books, 1973).

11 After withdrawing from Egypt, France maintained its interest in the country throughout the nineteenth century, yet focused its main colonial attention on North Africa, which culminated in the occupation of Algeria in 1830, Tunisia in 1881, and Morocco in 1911.

12 Said, "Afterword," *Orientalism*, p. 334.

13 See al-Rāghib al-Aṣfahānī, *Mufradāt Alfāẓ al-Qur'ān al-Karīm* [The vocabulary of the Holy Qur'ān], 4th edn (Beirut : al-Dār al-Shāmīyah, 2009).

14 'Abd al-Raḥmān al-Jabartī, *'Ajā'ib al-Āthār fī al-Tarājim wa al-Akbār*, 4 vols. (al-Qāhira: Būlāq, 1879), vol. 2. pp. 20–1. All English translations from al-Jabartī's text are my own. For available translations of some of al-Jabartī's work in English, see Shmuel Moreh, *Chronicle of the First Seven Months of the French Occupation of Egypt* (Leiden: E.J. Brill, 1975) and *Napoleon in Egypt: Al-Jabartī's Chronicle of the French Occupation 1798* (Princeton, N.J.: Markus Wiener Publishers, 1993).

15 Arnold J. Toynbee, "Preface," in Shafik Ghorbal, *The Beginning of the Egyptian Question and the Rise of Mehmet Ali: A Study in the Diplomacy of the Napoleonic Era Based on Researches in the British and French Archives* (London: George Routledge & Sons, 1928), pp. x–xi.

16 André Raymond, *Egyptiens et Français au Caire 1798–1801* (Cairo: Institut Francais d'Archeologie Orientale (IFAO), 1998).

17 Galland's translation is a 12-volume work that includes in addition to the frame story of Shahryar and Scheherazade such stories as *Miṣbāḥ 'Alā' al-Dīn* [The lamp of Aladdin] and *'Alī Bāba wa al-Arba'ūn Ḥarāmī* (Ali Baba and the forty thieves).

18 Raymond, *Egyptiens et Français au Caire 1798–1801*, pp. 212–13. In addition to al-Jabartī, Raymond refers to the Levantine Christian scholar Nīqūlā al-Turk (1763–1828), who shares in his memoirs al-Jabartī's contempt for the French regarding their immoral attitudes towards Egyptian women and the looseness of their own women. "It is worth mentioning that Al-Jabartī and Nicolas Turk, a Muslim and a Christian, responded in the same manner." Raymond, p. 301. For accounts on the interpersonal and social relations between the French and Egyptians during the French occupation of Egypt, see 'Umar 'Abd al-'Azīz 'Umar, *'Abd al-Raḥmān al-Jabartī wa Niqūlā al-Turk: Dirāsa Muqārana* (Beirut: Jam'iyyat Beirut al-'Arabiyya, 1978). See also Jean-Joël Brégeon, *L'Egypte de Bonaparte* (Paris: Perrin, 1991); Patrice Bret, *L'Egypte au temps de l'expédition de Bonaparte, 1798–1801* (Paris: Hachette, 1998), and de Constant, *Memoires intimes de Napoléon, par Constant, son valet de chambre* (Paris: Société des Publications Littéraires Illustrées Paris, n.d.).

19 Al-Jabartī, *'Ajā'ib al-Āthār*, vol 2., p. 12.

20 Ibid., pp. 161–2.

21 Raymond, *Egyptiens et Français au Caire 1798–1801*, p. 318.

22 Al-Jabartī's later writings reflect the fact that the chaos in Egyptian society is due primarily to misguided religious practices, relinquishment of the true spirit of Islam, and lapse into pre-Islamic superstitious practices.

23 Although not clear in al-Jabartī's context, "al-Qarabāna" may refer to a long, loud, high-pitched wail declaring the death of someone. In the Coptic Orthodox tradition, "al-Qarabana" is a round piece of bread with God's name written on it given to a dying person as a token of absolution.

24 Al-Jabartī, *'Ajā'ib al-Āthār*, vol. 3, pp. 35–6. For more on al-Jabartī's chronicles and their relationship to Egyptian historiography in the eighteenth century, see Maḥmūd al-Sharqāwī, *Dirasāt fī Tārīkh al-Jabartī: Miṣr fī al-Qarn al-Thāmin 'Ashar* [Studies in al-Jabartī's History: Egypt in the eighteenth century] (al-Qāhira: n.p., 1955). On al-Jabartī's life, see Jamāl al-Dīn al-Shayyāl's study, *al-Tarīkh wa al-Mu'arrikhūn fī Miṣr fī al-Qarn al-Tāsi' 'Ashar* (Cairo: n.p., 1958), pp. 10–27.

25 Al-Jabartī, *'Ajā'ib al-Āthār*, vol. 3., p. 33.

26 Said, *Orientalism*, p. 82.

27 Al-Jabartī, *'Ajā'ib al-Āthār*, vol. 2., p. 182.

28 Said, *Orientalism*, p. 82.

29 See Muḥammad Murū, *Tārīkh Miṣr al-Ḥadīth: Min al-Ḥamla al-Faransiyya ilā Ḥamlat Frīzar: al-Juz' al-Awwal* [A history of modern Egypt: from the French occupation to Fraser's campaign: Part 1] (Cairo, 2005).

30 'Abd al-Muḥsin Ṭāhā Badr, *Taṭawwur al-Riwāya al-'Arabiyya al-Ḥadītha fī Miṣr: 1870–1938* [The development of the modern Arabic novel in Egypt: 1870–1938] (al-Qāhira: Dār al-Ma'ārif, 1968), p. 16. Badr's critique is primarily a sociohistorical one. He structures the development of the Egyptian novel in relation to five major themes: Didactic; Pleasure; Artistic (a.k.a. Novelistic); Analytical; and Autobiographical.

31 The lives of early nineteenth-century Egyptian peasants were horrendous. They were mostly treated as the mob, the unwashed, the unknown, and the crowd. They were not much different from their succeeding generations throughout the Ali dynasty. They lived in severe circumstances, surrounded by dirty water and poor health conditions; they raised cattle and lived on their produce; they only had primitive methods of cleaning water for irrigation by an earth bucket known as "al-shadūf"; and many had to take long walks from their homes to the fields and back, afflicted with bilharziasis (schistosomiasis), a disease so rampant among the *fallāḥīn* that members of the French Campaign thought Egyptian men, like their women, had monthly menstruations. Not only was the peasant community of Egypt broken by squalor, disease, and hunger, but education was non-existent except for some gathering for Qur'ānic recitation and memorization known as *al-Kuttāb*. See *Aḥwāl al-fallāḥīn fī Rīf Miṣr* (Human Rights Open Library, 2001); see also Israel Gershoni and James P. Jankowski, "The Egyptian People and the Egyptian Peasantry," in *Egypt, Islam, and the Arabs* (Oxford: Oxford UP, 1986), pp. 205–8.

32 S. Mureh, *Chronicle of the First Seven Months of the French Occupation of Egypt*, p. 23. In his intensive and detailed introduction of al-Jabartī's oeuvre, Mureh points to the change in al-Jabartī's later writings in connection to the latter's

attitude towards the French: "For this reason, comparing *Mazhar and Mudda* on the one hand, and *'Ajā'ib al-āthār* on the other is of great importance. For in these different sets al-Jabartī represents two conflicting attitudes towards Western culture, i.e. the former that of a zealous Muslim, highly subjective in his attitude, the latter that of an enlightened scholar who observes events in as objective a manner as his background allows him." S. Mureh, 23–4.

33 Other authors and other texts might well have found a place here, and my choices, while not arbitrary and indeed dictated by the logic of thematic and referential necessity, are also shaped by personal engagement and investment. Consideration of space has led to the exclusion of such writers as J.M. Robertson, Wilfrid Blunt, and Khedive 'Abbās II, but their work is equally central to this study. I have quite often drawn on their work for inspiration, clarification, and conceptualization. Oral tradition on Denshawai is also unexplored in this study. For more on Denshawai's oral narratives, see Pierre Cachia, *Popular Narrative Ballads of Modern Egypt* (Oxford: Clarendon Press, 1989), 274–58. For other works inspired by the Denshawai event, see Muḥammad Hāmid Sharīf, *Hādithat Dinshawāy wa-Ṣadāhā fī al-Adab al-'Arabī al-Ḥadīth wal-Ṣaḥāfa al-'Arabiyya* [The Denshawai incident and its repercussions in modern Arabic literature and the Arab press] (Cairo: al-Ḥay'a al-Arabiyya al-'Āma lil-Kitāb, 1997).

34 For an elaborate discussion of various versions of the Denshawai event, see Muḥammad Ali Al-Masaddī, *Denshawai* (Cairo: al-Hay'a al-Miṣryyia al-'Āmma lil-Kitāb, 1974). Another version is given by Jacques Berque in *Egypt: Imperialism and Revolution*, trans. Jean Stewart (London: Faber and Faber, 1972). Berque's version reads:

> Some officers out pigeon-shooting set fire to a threshing-floor. In the ensuing affray, one of them was killed. The facts are uncertain, the incident itself not of the first importance. But Cromer exaggerated it. 'He seems', wrote one diplomat, 'to have been influenced by those who demand excessive reprisals.' He wanted to make an example. An extraordinary tribunal was immediately convened at Shbin al-Kumm. The sentence was carried out under conditions that combined the cruelty of Eastern justice and the unpleasantness of colonial justice; the condemned men were flogged and hanged in their own village, while their families, gathered in the terraces, looked on. The chairman of the court was Butrus Ghāli; Fathi Zaghlūl, speaking for the prosecution, praised the magnanimity of these officers, 'famed for their heroism, who might well have shot down their aggressors instead of pigeons!' The incident aroused terrible emotions. The poets of the time, led by Shawqī, poured forth odes of vengeance. The peasants became martyrs. A violent controversy broke out between liberal and governmental newspapers. The Mu'aiyad passionately challenged the Egyptian Gazette, which described the fellahs as 'African savages'. Jāwīsh, in *al-Liwā'*, attacked the Egyptian magistrates: they had contributed to the judgment which 'tore these innocent souls from their bodies, as threads of silk are torn off a thorn bush.
>
> Jacque Berque, *Egypt: Imperialism and Revolution*, pp. 237–8.

35 Hannah Arendt, *The Origins of Totalitarianism* (New York: Harcourt Brace, 1975), p. 207.

36 Earl of Cromer, *Modern Egypt* vol. 2 (London: The Macmillan Co., 1908), pp. 567–85. Cromer's book sold 9,000 copies in hard cover in the USA alone in

its first two years of publication before it was published in cheaper editions. See The Marquess of Zetland, *Lord Cromer, Being the Authorized Life of Evelyn Baring, First Earl of Cromer* (London, 1932), pp. 305–6. For more on Cromer's life and rule in Egypt, see Afaf Lutfi al-Sayyid, *Egypt and Cromer: A Study in Anglo-Egyptian Relations* (London: John Murray, 1968).

37 Earl Cromer, "Report for 1906" (Cd. 3394; Egypt no. 1, 1907), p. 7.

38 *Al-Liwā'*, April 12, 1907, p. 7.

39 Cromer, *Modern Egypt*, vol. II, pp. 556–7.

40 Cromer's work teems with examples of that sort. See for instance Chapter XXXIX, "The Machinery of Government," Chapter XL, "The British Officials," Chapter XLI, "The International Administrations," Chapter XLLII, "The Judicial System," Chapter LI, "Corruption," Chapter LIII, "Finance," Chapter LIV, "Irrigation," Chapter LVIII, "Justice," Chapter LIX, "Education," and Chapter LXII, "The Future of Egypt," *Modern Egypt*, vol. II.

41 During those early years of British intervention, Egypt gained the same international status of any major European country. Moberley Bell, the manager of *The Times* in the early 1910s, worked as a news reporter in Egypt in the 1880s. See Coles Pasha, *Recollections and Reflections* (London: Saint Catherine Press, 1918), pp. 24–5. The political weight of the events there could be reflected in an ongoing media war between the French press and its British counterpart. France was alleged to have been the patron of several Arabic newspapers. The patronage stopped or declined with the signing of the *Entente Cordiale* between England and France in 1904.

42 See al-Masaddī, "The Conditions of the Egyptian Society before Denshawai," *Denshawai*, pp. 39–65.

43 See *al-Mū'ayyad*, Nov. 13, 14, 1893; Nov. 28, Dec. 23, 1894; Jan 14; Feb. 17–19, March 17, 18, June 25, 1895; Jan. 20, March 13, Oct. 28, 1900; Feb. 3, June 16, 1901; March 4, Oct. 8, 1902; see also *al-Liwā'*: Jan. 30, Feb. 11, 23, June 28, 1901; Oct. 18, 19, Nov. 7, 1904.

44 For more details on these events, see Al-Masaddī, "The Fallāḥīn and Metropolitan Revolutions during the British Occupation," *Denshawai*, pp. 14–36.

45 Muṣṭafā Kāmil and his supporters were not the only nationalist group in Egypt at the time. Early twentieth-century nationalism in Egypt could roughly be divided into three groups: the extremists, represented by Muṣṭafā Kāmil, who were openly opposed to British rule and denouncing Cromer's policy in Egypt; the "Khedivials," represented by Shaikh 'Alī Yūsuf, who saw that cooperation with the occupier was the only alternative left for them if Egypt was ever to achieve autonomous rule; and finally the moderates, of whom the most remarkable figure, al-Imam Muḥammad 'Abduh, sided with the occupation only to weaken the authority of the Khedive. The voice of Muṣṭafá Kāmil and his newspaper, *Al-Liwā'* (The Banner), was not the only call raised against Britain during the occupation, but perhaps the loudest. 'Alī Yūsif's *Al-Mū'ayyad* and another paper, *Al-Manār*, were also critical of the British policy of education and especially of their practices in Sudan.

46 Edward Said, "Orientalism Reconsidered," *Europe and its Others*, ed. Francis Barker et al,. vol. 1. (Colchester: University of Essex, 1985), p. 17.

47 See Fredric Jameson, "Third World Literature in the Era of Multinational Capitalism," *Social Text*, 15 (Fall, 1986), pp. 65–88. Jameson's article was the

subject of many debates. With a situational consciousness of his own position, Aijaz Ahmad responded with a sustained critique of Jameson's claim, accusing Jameson's ideology of "dividing the world between those who make history and those who are mere objects of it." See Aijaz Ahmad, "Jameson's Rhetoric of Otherness and the National Allegory," *Social Text*, 17 (Fall, 1987), p. 7.

48 For more on the connection between poetry and nationalism in modern Egypt see Mounah A. Khouri, *Poetry and the Making of Modern Egypt (1882–1922)* (Leiden: E.J. Brill, 1971).

49 This interventionist role of modern Egyptian literature was not just born with Denshawai. In the early 1900s, poetic nationalism appeared in Egypt first as a cultural movement, directed not just against the British, but also against the depredations and abuses of Khedives. Socially, Egypt was split between a feudal aristocracy and a rural proletariat. Nationalism already fed the dream of social equity and hope of many nineteenth-century poets and scholars like Mahmūd Sāmī al-Barūdī and al-Imām Muḥammad 'Abduh. With the advent of the British occupation, poetic nationalism shifted from a romantic dream of a republican utopia to a rhetorical call against colonialism. See Salma Khadra Jayyusi, ed., *Modern Arabic Literature: An Anthology* (New York: Columbia UP, 1987), p. 10. See also *Tradition and Modernity in Arabic Literature*, ed. Issa J. Boullata and Terri DeYoung (Fayetteville: University of Arkansas Press, 1997), p. 8.

50 One among many famous attempts to marginalize British literature is by Shawqī, who in his re-writing of the story of Cleopatra in *Maṣra' Klībātrā* [*The death of Cleopatra*]_(al-Qāhira, 1928) opposes Shakespeare's version *Antony and Cleopatra*. In Shawqī's play we are not offered a shallow promotion of the native culture of Egypt, but rather a vigilant scrutiny geared at revealing the internal silences within the history of the colonizer. Those silences, gaps, or misconstructions of colonial history become fuel for the Egyptian historical narrative. Thus, a theatrical rewriting of history becomes a way of subverting imperial constructs. It has enormous restorative values that help break through the yoke of imperial domination and allow room for national transformation.

51 See for instance Shawqī's poem *Fī Maṣra' Butrus Ghālī* [On the death of Butrus Ghālī], written in 1910, which stresses the unity between Egyptian Muslims and Christians after the assassination of Butrus Ghālī due to his collaboration with Britain in the Denshawai trial. See also Jābir Qumayḥa, *Ṣawṭ al-Islām fī Shi'r Ḥāfiẓ Ibrāhīm* [The voice of Islam in Hāfiẓ Ibrāhīm's poetry] (Cairo, 1990). It is important to emphasize that none of these writers was a nationalist in the contemporary sense of the word. They did not demand the creation of a nation-state or the unification of Arab nations. To them nationalism was not a political or a racial concept but essentially a spiritual and a moral one. Politically, they remained active and revolutionary, which resulted in their temporary banishment (al-Bārūdi was banished to Serendip, present-day Sri Lanka; Shawqī was exiled to Spain). They realized that national awakening demanded the active participation of the people. But the challenge was greater. Whereas English nationalism was in its origin connected with the concept of individual liberty as foreshadowed by John Stuart Mill, Egyptian nationalism, still in its infancy and not yet firmly rooted in socioreligious or political reality, lacked a philosophical grounding. When Shawqī and Ibrāhīm wrote poems in defiance of Britain with its cruel militarism and rational political ends, they did

not succeed in galvanizing Egyptian opposition to British colonial rule. In fact, during those early years, Egyptian nationalism appeared more complicated than British nationalism and the quest for its meaning and its "mission," as the Denshawai poems of Ibrāhīm and Shawqī imply, remained yet obscure.

52 "Yā layta shi'rī" is a poetic interjection that has been used in Arabic poetry since the pre-Islamic times. The phrase has become genre-specific, like the traditional opening of fairy tales, "Once upon a time."

53 Aḥmad Shawqī, *Dīwān Shawqī*, vol. II (al-Qāhira: Dār Nahḍat Miṣr Lil-Ṭibā'a wa al-Nashr, 1980), p. 545.

54 Ḥāfiẓ Ibrāhīm here is playing on the expression "dhāta al-ṭawq," an idiomatic reference to ring-nicked pigeons.

55 Shawqī's and Ibrāhīm's repeated reference to the Roman Empire and the reign of Nero echoes the defeat of the Ptolemaic kings. Ḥāfiẓ Ibrāhīm, *Dīwān Ḥāfiẓ Ibrāhīm* (Beirut: Mu'assasa al-'Ālamiyya Lil-Maṭbū'āt, 1971), pp. 134–5.

56 In Islamic tradition, there are greetings for the dead as well as the living. The famous greeting *al-salāmu 'alaykum* commonly used among Muslims to greet each other, is inverted to *'alayka/'alayki al-salām* when someone visits a graveyard and greets a dead person. Shawqī uses a metonymic benediction in *yā Denshawai 'alā rubākī salām* to refer to the village's dead victims.

57 Pierre Macherey, *A Theory of Literary Production*, trans. Geoffrey Wall (London: Routledge & Kegan Paul, 1978), p. 87.

58 "Kināna" is another name for Egypt, literally meaning "a quiver of arrows," metaphorically, "the protected land." Prophet Muḥammad is reported to have foretold the might of Egyptian soldier and that "Egypt is the Kināna of God on His Earth." The term could also refer to the Kināna tribe, allegedly thought to have originated in Egypt.

59 Ibrāhīm, *Dīwān Ḥāfiẓ Ibrāhīm*, p. 135.

60 Maḥmūd Ṭāhir Ḥaqqī, *'Adhrā' Denshawai* (n.p., 1909), p. 1.

61 Ḥaqqī, "Muqaddima" [Introduction], *Adhrā' Denshawai*, p. 1.

62 Georg Lukács, *The Historical Novel*, trans. H. and S. Mitchell (Nebraska: Nebraska UP, 1983), p. 76.

63 Ḥaqqī, *'Adhrā' Denshawai*, p. 41.

64 Hayden White, *Tropics of Discourse: Essays in Cultural Criticism* (Baltimore: The Johns Hopkins UP, 1978), p. 61.

65 Hayden White, "The Historical Text as Literary Artifact," *The Writing of History: Literary Form and Historical Understanding*, ed. Robert H. Canary and Henry Kozicki (Madison: University of Wisconsin Press, 1978), p. 15. See also Hayden White, "The Question of Narrative in Contemporary Historical Theory," *The Content of the Form* (Baltimore: The Johns Hopkins UP, 1987), and "Interpretation of History," *Tropics of Discourse*.

66 Cromer, Parliamentary Papers: Accounts and Papers: vol. CXXXVII, (Egypt. no. 4, Session: February, 1906–21 December, 1906), p. 8.

67 Fredric Jameson, *Marxism and Form: Twentieth-Century Dialectical Theories of Literature* (Princeton, N.J.; Princeton UP, 1971), p. 47.

68 G.B. Shaw, "Preface for Politicians" (To the First Edition of 1906), *John Bull's Other Island* (1907). Bernard Shaw, *Complete Plays with Prefaces*, vol. II (New York: Dodd, Mead & Company, 1963), p. 495.

69 Paul Ricoeur, *Time and Narrative*, vol. III, p. 99.

70 Shaw, "Preface," pp. 492, 493.
71 Ibid., pp. 485–6.
72 Ibid., p. 492.
73 The subsequent rhetoric of nationalism used by bourgeois leaders like Muṣṭafá Kāmil, and later Sa'ad Zaghlūl, would only create for the *fallāḥīn* a substitute body; it will replace their direct language and efface their community by imposing a rhetorical discourse that does not necessarily address their cause. This movement of the Denshawai event from the social to the political inadvertently inflicts more violence on the body of *fallāḥīn* by reducing it to mere rhetorical statements voiced here and there in international arenas like England and France, so that the *fallāḥīn* themselves become grist for the mill of the political campaigns of bourgeois nationalists.
74 Ahdaf Soueif, *The Map of Love* (New York: Anchor Books, 1999), pp. 427–8.
75 The *salamlek* is one of the three major compounds in a seventeenth century mansion built on the Ottoman architectural style. The *salamlek* is the guesthouse which usually consists of the reception area, living room, and dining halls. The remaining two components are *haremlek*, the upstairs quarters for women's and the house servants; and the *khazeen*, the storehouse where the provisions of the house are kept.
76 See for instance Ian Almond, "Nietzsche's Peace with Islam: My Enemy's Enemy is My Friend," *German Life and Letters*, vol. 56, no. 1 (2003), pp. 43–55. See also Roy Jackson, *Nietzsche and Islam* (London: Routledge, 2007).
77 Some of the material in this chapter appeared in an article entitled "The Ruses of Denshawai: History, Event, Fiction," published in *The Journal of Middle Eastern and North African Intellectual and Cultural Studies* (Spring, 2006). I am particularly thankful to R. Kevin Lacey, Professor of Arabic Studies and Director of the Arabic Studies Program at Binghamton University, and to Ralph M. Coury, Professor of History and Cultural Studies, Fairfield University, for the impressive and thorough editorial suggestions they provided for that article.

Epilogue

1 See Michael Hardt and Antonio Negri, *Empire*, (Cambridge, Mass.: Harvard UP, 2000), pp. 240–1.
2 Ironically, US military officials used the newly digitalized version of Gillo Pontecorvo's Fanon-inspired film *La Battaglia di Algeri* (1966) [The battle of Algiers] as an instructional visual for their planned strategic occupation of Iraq. Pontecorvo's film includes numerous torture scenes and opens with a stark shot of an old Algerian man physically exposed and brutally tortured by the French Occupation Army. The film was considered a manual for revolutionary success against superior force, for in the end Algiers would prove to be France's most humiliating loss in the same manner that Vietnam was destined to become America's most embarrassing defeat. See Maria Esposito's interview with Gillo Pontercorvo, "Stay Close to Reality," *World Socialist Website* (June 9, 2004): <http://www.wsws.org/articles/2004/jun2004/pont-j09.shtml>.
3 See Aijaz Ahmad, "Islam, Islamism, and the West," in *Social Register* (London: Merlin, 2008), p. 25.
4 See Edward Said, *Covering Islam: How the Media and the Experts Determine How We See the Rest of the World* (Vintage, 1997).

5 See Hardt and Negri, *Empire.*
6 Arif Dirlik, "Is There History after Eurocentrism?: Globalism, Postcolonialism, and the Disavowal of History," *Cultural Critique*, no. 42 (Spring, 1999), pp. 1–34.
7 See Jytte Klausen, *The Islamic Challenge: Politics and Religion in Western Europe* (New York: Oxford University Press, 2005).
8 See Jocelyne Césari, *When Islam and Democracy Meet: Muslims in Europe and in the United States* (New York, N.Y.: Palgrave, 2006).
9 There is also a third camp that does not directly endorse or oppose globalization, but still uses the term in reference to a set of recent historical circumstances from which political thinking of and action towards the Muslim world now take place. Qualified critics of globalization and advocates of Muslim human rights in international relations include Rashid Khalidi and Mahmood Monshipour. See Rashid Khalidi, *Sowing Crisis: The Cold War and American Dominance in the Middle East* (Boston: Beacon Press, 2009); Mahmood Monshipouri, *Muslims in Global Politics: Identities, Entities, and Human Rights* (Philadelphia: University of Pennsylvania Press, 2009).
10 Said, "Afterword," in *Orientalism*, pp. 329–52; Harry Magdoff, "Globalisation – To What End?" *Socialist Register 1992: New World Order*, ed. Ralph Miliband and Leo Panitch (New York: Monthly Review Press, 1992), pp. 1–32.; Masao Miyoshi, "A Borderless World? From Colonialism to Trans-nationalism and the Decline of the Nation State," *Critical Inquiry*, vol. 19, no. 4 (Summer, 1993), pp. 328–56.; Arif Dirlik, "The Postcolonial Aura: Third World Criticism in the Age of Global Capitalism," *Critical Inquiry*, vol. 20, no. 2 (Winter, 1994), pp. 328–56.
11 Said, *Orientalism*, p. 349.
12 Olivier Roy, *Globalized Islam: The Search for a New Ummah* (New York: Columbia UP, 2004), p. ix.
13 Ibid., p. 24.
14 Ibid., p. 24.
15 Ibid., p. 25.
16 Ibid., p. 25
17 Ibid., p. 22.
18 Ibid., p. 248.
19 Ibid., p. 234.
20 In the catchy chapter subheading, "Is *jihad* closer to Marx than to the Koran," Roy dwells on the roots of Al-Qaeda's violence and argues that it has more to do with "a Western tradition of individual and pessimistic revolt for an elusive ideal world than with the Koranic conception of martyrdom." Ibid., p. 43.
21 See "Jihad Defined and Redefined," *Islam in Transition: Muslim Perspectives*, ed. John J. Donohue and John L. Esposito (Oxford: Oxford UP, 2007), pp. 393–472.
22 Roy, *Globalized Islam*, p. 340. My italics.
23 Ibid., p. 339–40.
24 Sigmund Freud, "Lecture XXXII: Anxiety and Instinctual Life," *The Freud Reader*, ed. Peter Gay (New York: Norton & Co., 1989), pp. 774–5.
25 Ibid., p. 775.

26 Confirmed in personal correspondence, January 23, 2011.

27 William Gibson, "Panther Modern's Eyes," (October 31, 2004), <http://www.williamgibsonbooks.com/blog/2004_10_01_archive.asp>.

28 Anthony Burgess, *1985* (London: Arrow Books, 1980), p. 105.

29 Ibid., pp. 120–1.

30 Ibid., p. 184.

31 Ibid., p. 121.

32 Ibid., pp. 124–5.

33 Christopher Caldwell, *Reflections on the Revolution in Europe: Immigration, Islam, and the West* (London: Doubleday, 2009).

34 Ibid., pp. 24, 162, 168.

35 Ibid., pp. 24–7.

36 Ibid., p. 26.

37 Ibid., p. 349.

38 Ibid., pp. 217–20.

39 Claude Langlois, "Catholics and Seculars," *Realms of Memory: The Construction of the French Past*, vol. 1: *Conflicts and Divisions,* ed. Pierre Nora, trans. Arthur Goldhammer (New York: Columbia UP, 1996), p. 116.

40 Ibid., p. 116.

41 Ibid., p. 115. Quoted in Marcel Launay, *L'Église et l'école en France, XIXe–XXe siècle* (Paris: Desclée, 1988), p. 156.

42 Adolf Muschg, "'Core Europe': Thoughts about the European Identity," in Daniel Levy, Max Pensky, and John Torpey, eds, *Old Europe, New Europe, Core Europe, Transatlantic Relations after the Iraq War* (London: Verso, 2005), p. 26.

43 See Jonathan Xavier Inda, Renato Rosaldo, eds, *The Anthropology of Globalization: A Reader* (Oxford: Blackwell, 2002).

44 See David Held and Anthony McGrew, "The Great Globalization Debate: an Introduction," in David Held and Anthony McGrew, eds, *The Global Transformations Reader: An Introduction to the Globalization Debate* (Cambridge: Polity, 2000), pp. 3–4.

45 See Tony Judt, *Postwar: A History of Europe since 1945* (New York: Penguin, 2005); see also Kristin Ross, *Fast Cars, Clean Bodies: Decolonization and the Reordering of French Culture* (Cambridge, Mass.: MIT Press, 1996).

46 This phrase is coined by Mahmood Mamdani. See "Culture Talk; Or, How Not to Talk about Islam and Politics," *Good Muslim, Bad Muslim: America, the Cold War, and the Roots of Muslim Terror* (New York: Pantheon, 2004), pp. 17–62.

47 Anthony Kwame Appiah, *Cosmopolitanism: Ethics in a World of Strangers* (New York: Norton, 2006), p. xiii.

48 Ibid., p. xx.

49 Ibid., p. xx.

50 Ibid., pp. 5–6.

51 Ibid., p. 7.

52 Ibid., p. 8.

53 Ibid., p. xx.

54 Said, *Culture and Imperialism* (New York: Vintage Books, 1994), p. 217.

55 Appiah, *Cosmopolitanism*, p. 49.

56 For a more inclusive treatment of 'cosmopolitanism', see Guy Ankerl, *Global Communication Without Universal Civilization*, vol. 1, *Coexisting Contemporary Civilizations: Arabo-Muslim, Bharati, Chinese, and Western* (Geneva: INU Societal Research, 2000).

57 Michael Hardt and Antonio Negri, *Multitude: War and Democracy in the Age of Empire* (London: Penguin Books, 2004), p. 129.

58 Paul de Man, *The Resistance to Theory* (Minneapolis: University of Minnesota Press, 1986), p. 11.

59 See Mohammad Salama, "Science in Islam," *Encyclopedia of the Islamic World*, ed. John L. Esposito (Oxford: Oxford UP, 2009).

60 See for example the following: Kathleen Moore, *Al-Mughtaribun: American Law and the Transformation of Muslim Life in the United States* (Albany: State University of New York Press, 1995); Isaac Kramnick and R. Laurence Moore, *The Godless Constitution: The Case Against Religious Correctness* (New York: Norton and Co., 1996); Thomas J. Kidd, "'Is it Worse to Follow Mahomet than the Devil?': Early American Uses of Islam," *The American Society of Church History*, 72 (December, 2003), pp. 767–89; Denise A. Spellberg, "Could a Muslim Be President? An Eighteenth-Century Constitutional Debate," *Eighteenth-Century Studies*, vol. 39, no. 4 (2006), pp. 485–506.

61 Mr. William Lancaster, Delegate to the North Carolina Constitutional Convention, July 30, 1788; Jonathan Elliot, ed., *The Debates in the Several State Conventions on the Adoption of the Federal Constitution, as Recommended by the General Convention at Philadelphia, in 1787*, 5 vols. (Philadelphia: J.B. Lippincott Company, 1888), vol. 4, p. 215.

62 The United States Constitution, Article VI, Section 3.

BIBLIOGRAPHY

'Abd al-'Azīz Dūrī. *The Historical Formation of the Arab Nation*, trans. Lawrence I. Conrad (London: Croom Helm, Centre for Arab Unity Studies, 1987).

'Abd al-Qādir al-Rāzī. *Mukhtār al-Ṣiḥāḥ*. (al-Qāhira: Wazārat al-Ma'ārif al-'Umūmiyya, 1904).

'Ashur, Sa'īd. *al-'Aṣr al-Mamālīkī fī Miṣr wa al-Shām* (al-Qāhira: al-Nahḍa al-'Arabiyya, 1965).

'Ayyād, Kāmil. *Die Geschichts und Gesellschaftslehre Ibn Khaldūns* (Stuttgart, Berlin: J.D. Cotta'sche Buchhandlung Nachfolger, 1930).

Abdesselem, Ahmed. *Ibn Khaldun et ses lecteurs: essais et conférences, Collège de France* (Paris: Presses Universitaires de France, 1983).

Adams, John. *The Flowers of Modern History* (London, 1795).

Adorno, Theodor W. *History and Freedom: Lectures 1964–1965*, ed. Rolf Tiedemann, trans. Rodney Livingston (Malden: Polity Press, 2008).

—— "Refuge for the Homeless," Selections from *Minima Moralia*, in *Theodor Adorno: Can One Live After Auschwitz? A Philosophical Reader*, ed. Rolf Tiedemann, trans. Livingstone and others (Stanford, Cal.: Stanford UP, 2003).

Ahmad, Aijaz. "Islam, Islamism, and the West," *Social Register* (London: Merlin, 2008).

—— "Jameson's Rhetoric of Otherness and the National Allegory," *Social Text*, 17 (Fall, 1987), pp. 3–25.

al-Ṭabarī, Ibn Jarīr. *Tārīkh al-Rusul wa al-Mulūk*, quoted in 'Ābid al-Jabrī, *Bunyat al-'Aql al-'Arabī* [The structure of Arab reason: a critical analysis of epistemology in Arab culture], vol. 2 (Casablanca: al-Markaz al-Thaqāfī al-'Arabī, 1986).

al-Anṣārī, Muḥammad Jābir. *Liqā' al-Tārīkh bil-'Asr: Da'wā li-Badr al-Khuldūniyya fī Wa'iyy al-Sha'b Ta'sīsann li-Thaqāfat al-'Aql* [The encounter of history and the present: a call for planting Khaldūnism with its present dimensions in national consciousness for the establishment of a culture of the mind] (Beirut: al-Mu'assasa al-'Arabiyya lil-Dirāsāt wa al-Nashr, 2006).

al-Azmeh, Aziz. *Ibn Khaldūn: An Essay in Reinterpretation* (London: Frank Cass, 1982).

—— *Ibn Khaldūn in Modern Scholarship: A Study in Orientalism* (London: Third World Centre, 1981).

al-Ghānimī, Sa'īd. *al-'Asabiyya wa al-Ḥikma: Qirā'a fī Falsafat al-Tārīkh 'Ind Ibn Khaldūn* (Beirut: al-Mu'ssasa al-'Arabiyya lil-Dirāsāt wa al-Nashr, 2006).

al-Ghazālī, *Tahāfut al-Falāsifa*: <http://www.ghazali.org>.

al-Jabartī, 'Abd al-Raḥmān. *Napoleon in Egypt: Al-Jabartī's Chronicle of the French Occupation 1798*, trans. Shmuel Moreh (Princeton, N.J.: Markus Wiener Publishers, 1993).

—— *Chronicle of the First Seven Months of the French Occupation of Egypt*, trans. Shmuel Moreh (Leiden: E.J. Brill, 1975).

—— *'Ajā'ib al-Āthār fī al-Tarājim wa al-Akbār*, 4 vols. (al-Qāhira: Būlāq, 1879).

al-Masaddī, Muḥammad 'Alī. *Denshawai* (Cairo: al-Hay'a al-Miṣryyia al-'Āmma lil-Kitāb, 1974).

Almond, Ian. *The New Orientalists: Postmodern Presentations of Islam from Foucault to Baudrillard* (London: I.B.Tauris, 2007).

—— "Nietzsche's Peace with Islam: My Enemy's Enemy is My Friend," *German Life and Letters*, vol. 56, no. 1 (2003), pp. 43–55.

Alonso, Carlos J. *The Burden of Modernity: The Rhetoric of Cultural Discourse in Spanish America* (Oxford: Oxford UP, 1998).

al-Sayyid, Afaf Lutfi. "L'expédition d'Egypte et le débat sur la modernité," *Egypte/Monde Arabe* 1 (1999), pp. 47–54.»

—— *Egypt and Cromer: A Study in Anglo-Egyptian Relations* (London: John Murray, 1968).

al-Sharqāwī, Maḥmūd. *Dirasāt fī Tārīkh al-Jabartī: Miṣr fī al-Qarn al-Thāmin 'Ashar* [Studies in al-Jabartī's History: Egypt in the eighteenth century] (al-Qāhira: n.p., 1955).

al-Shayyāl, Jamāl al-Dīn. *al-Tarīkh wa al-Mu'rrikhūn fī miṣr fī al-Qarn al-Tāsi' 'Ashar* (Cairo: n.p., 1958).

Amin, Samir. *Eurocentrism* (New York: Monthly Review Press, 1988).

Anderson, Benedict. *Imagined Communities: Reflections on the Origins and Spread of Nationalism* (London: Verso, 1991).

Anderson, Perry. *Lineages of the Absolutist State* (London: NLB, 1974).

Ankerl, Guy. *Global Communication without Universal Civilization*, vol. 1, *Coexisting Contemporary Civilizations: Arabo-Muslim, Bharati, Chinese, and Western* (Geneva: INU Societal Research, 2000).

Anon. *al-Mughrib fī Tartīb al-Mu'rib (al-Maktaba al-Islāmiyya)*: <http://www.al-eman.com/IslamLib/viewchp.asp?BID=390&CID=7#s15>.

Antes, John. *Observations on the Manners of the Egyptians* (London, 1800).

Appiah, Anthony Kwame. *Cosmopolitanism: Ethics in a World of Strangers* (New York: Norton, 2006).

Arendt, Hannah. *The Origins of Totalitarianism* (New York: Harcourt Brace, 1975).

Aristotle. *Poetics*, trans. Richard Janko (Indianapolis, Ind.: Hackett, 1987).

Arkoun, Mohammed. *Rethinking Islam: Common Questions, Uncommon Answers*, trans. Robert D. Lee (Boulder, Col.: Westview Press, 1994).

—— "Review of al-Azmeh's '*Ibn Khaldūn: An Essay in Reinterpretation*'," *Arabica*, T. 32, Fasc. 2 (July, 1985).

Arnold, Matthew. "The Scholar Gypsy," *Poems* (New York: Macmillan & Co., 1884), pp. 291–9.

Asad, Talal. *Formations of the Secular: Christianity, Islam, Modernity* (Stanford: Stanford UP, 2003).

—— ed. *Anthropology and the Colonial Encounter* (London: Ithaca Press, 1973).

Bacieva, Svetlana Mihailovka. *Isztoriko-szociologiceseszkij tratktat Ibn Halduna "Mukaddima"* (Moszkva: Izdatyelsztvo, 1965).

Badr, 'Abd al-Muḥsin Ṭāhā. *Taṭawwur al-Riwāya al-'Arabiyya al-Ḥaditha fi Miṣr: 1870–1938* [The development of the modern Arabic novel in Egypt: 1870–1938] (al-Qāhira: Dār al-Ma'ārif, 1968).
Baker, Samuel W. *Albert N'yanza, Great Basin of the Nile* (London, 1866).
Barthes, Roland. "The Discourse of History," trans. Stephen Bann, *Comparative Criticism*, vol. 3, ed. E.S. Shaffer (Cambridge: Cambridge UP, 1981).
Benjamin, Walter. *Illuminations*, trans. Harry Zohn (London: Fontana, 1973).
Brégeon, Jean-Joël. *L'Egypte de Bonaparte* (Paris: Perrin, 1991).
Bret, Patrice. *L'Egypte au Temps de l'Expédition de Bonaparte, 1798–1801* (Paris: Hachette, 1998).
Berque, Jacques. *Egypt: Imperialism and Revolution*, trans. Jean Stewart (London: Faber and Faber, 1972).
Bhabha, Homi. "Difference, Discrimination, and the Discourse of Colonialism," *The Politics of Theory*, ed. Francis Barker, Peter Hulme, Margret Iversen, and Diana Loxley (Colchester: University of Essex, 1983).
Binder, Leonard. *Islamic Liberalism: A Critique of Development Theory* (Chicago: University of Chicago Press, 1988).
Blanchot, Maurice. *The Infinite Conversation*, trans. Susan Hanson (Minneapolis: University of Minnesota Press, 1993).
—— *The Step Not Beyond*, trans. Lycette Nelson (New York: State University of New York Press, 1992).
Bloch, J. 1890 (*Marx and Engels: Selected Correspondence* (New York, 1935).
Blunt, Wilfrid Scawen. *Secret History of the English Occupation of Egypt, Being a Personal Narrative of Events (1907)* (New York: Alfred. K. Knopf, 1922).
Boullata, Issa J. and Terri DeYoung, eds. *Tradition and Modernity in Arabic Literature*. (Fayetteville: University of Arkansas Press, 1997).
Bourdieu, Pierre. "The Logic of Classes," *Practical Reason: On the Theory of Action* (Stanford, Cal.: Stanford UP, 1998).
Bouthoul, Gaston. *Ibn Khaldūn: Sa philosophie sociale* (Paris, 1930).
Brégeon, Jean-Joel. *L'Egypte de Bonaparte* (Paris: Perrin, 1991).
Bret, Patrice. *L'Egypte au temps de l'expédition de Bonaparte, 1798–1801*, (Paris: Hachette, 1998).
Buck-Morss, Susan. "Hegel and Haiti," *Critical Inquiry*, vol. 26, no. 4 (Summer, 2000), pp. 821–65.
—— *Hegel, Haiti, and Universal History* (Pittsburgh, Penn.: University of Pittsburgh Press, 2009).
Burgess, Anthony. *1985* (London: Arrow Books, 1980).
Butler, Judith. *The Power of Mourning and Violence* (London: Verso, 2004).
Cachia, Pierre. *Popular Narrative Ballads of Modern Egypt* (Oxford: Clarendon Press, 1989), pp. 274:58.
Caldwell, Christopher. *Reflections on the Revolution in Europe: Immigration, Islam, and the West* (London: Doubleday, 2009).
Césari, Jocelyne. *When Islam and Democracy Meet: Muslims in Europe and in the United States* (New York: Palgrave, 2006).
Chatterjee, Partha. *Nationalist Thought and the Colonial World: A Derivative Discourse* (Minneapolis: University of Minnesota Press, 1986).
Coetzee, J.M. *Stranger Shores: Literary Essays: 1986–1999* (New York: Viking, 2001).
Cohen, J. *Living Letters of the Law* (Berkeley: University of California Press, 1999).

Cohen, Shaye. *The Beginnings of Jewishness* (Berkeley: University of California Press, 2001).
Collingwood, R.G. "Spengler's Theory of Historical Cycles," *Ideas of History*, vol. 1, ed. Roland N. Nash (New York: Dutton, 1969).
Cromer, the Earl of (Evelyn Baring). 'Report for 1906' (Cd.3394; Egypt no. 1, 1907).
—— "The Government of Subject Races," *Political and Literary Essays* (London: Macmillan, 1913).
—— *Modern Egypt*, 2 vols. (New York: Macmillan, 1908).
—— Parliamentary Papers: Accounts and Papers: vol. CXXXVII (Egypt. no. 4, Session: February, 1906–21 December 1906).
Dale, Stephen Frederic. "Ibn Khaldūn: The Last Greek and the First *Annaliste* Historian," *International Journal of Middle Eastern Studies*, vol 38, no. 3 (August 2006).
Daniel, Norman. *Islam and the West: The Making of an Image* (Oxford: Oneworld Publications, 1960).
—— *The Arabs and Medieval Europe* (London: Longman, 1975).
De Certeau, Michel. *Heterologies: Discourse on the Other*, trans. Brian Massumi (Minneapolis: University of Minnesota Press, 1995).
—— *The Writing of History*, trans. Tom Conley (New York: Columbia UP, 1988).
De Constant, *Memoires intimes de Napoléon, par Constant, son valet de chambre* (Paris: Société des Publications Littéraires Illustrées Paris, n.d.).
De Man, Paul. "Sign and Symbol in Hegel's Aesthetics" (1964), *Aesthetic Ideology* (Minneapolis: University of Minnesota Press, 1996).
Defoe, Daniel. *Robinson Crusoe* (New York: Random House Modern Library Classics, 2001), p. 83.
Deighton, H.S. "The Impact of Egypt on Britain: A Study of Public Opinion," in *Political and Social Change in Modern Egypt*, ed. P.M. Holt (London: Oxford UP, 1968).
Derrida, Jacques. *Of Grammatology*, trans. Gayatri Chakravorty Spivak (Baltimore: The Johns Hopkins UP, 1998).
—— *The Gift of Death*, trans. David Wills (Chicago: University of Chicago Press, 1995).
Dirlik, Arif. "Is There History after Eurocentrism?: Globalism, Postcolonialism, and the Disavowal of History," *Cultural Critique*, no. 42 (Spring, 1999), pp. 1–34.
—— "The Postcolonial Aura: Third World Criticism in the Age of Global Capitalism," *Critical Inquiry*, vol. 20, no. 2 (Winter, 1994), pp. 328–56.
Donner, Fred. *Narratives of Islamic Origins: The Beginnings of Islamic Historical Writing* (Princeton, N.J.: The Darwin Press, 1998).
—— *The Early Islamic Conquest* (Princeton, N.J.: Princeton UP, 1981).
Donohue, John J. and John L. Esposito. "Jihad Defined and Redefined," in John J. Donohue and John L. Esposito, eds, *Islam in Transition: Muslim Perspectives*, (Oxford: Oxford UP, 2007), pp. 393–472.
El-Beheiry, Kawsar Abdel Salam. 'L'Égypte avant l'expédition Bonaparte' and 'L'Égypte pendent l'expédition,' in *L'Influence de la littérature Francaise sur le Roman Arabe* (Québec: Éditions Naaman de Sherbrooke, 1980), pp. 14–47.
Eliade, Mircea. *The Sacred and the Profane: The Nature of Religion* (New York: Houghton Mifflin Harcourt, 2001).

Elliot, Jonathan, ed. *The Debates in the Several State Conventions on the Adoption of the Federal Constitution, as Recommended by the General Convention at Philadelphia, in 1787,* 5 vols. (Philadelphia: J.B. Lippincott Company, 1888), vol. 4, p.215.

Engels, Friedrich. "Latter to J. Bloch, Sept. 21–2, 1890", in *Marx and Engels: Selected Correspondence* (Moscow: Foreign Languages Publishing Houose, 1953)

Ensor, Sir Robert. *The Oxford History of England: England 1870–1917* (London: Oxford UP, 1936).

Esposito, Maria. "Stay Close to Reality," *World Socialist Website* (9 June, 2004): <http://www.wsws.org/articles/2004/jun2004/pont-j09.shtml>.

Etienne, Bruno, *L'Islamisme radical* (Paris: Hachette, 1987).

Fabian, Johannes. *Time and Other: How Anthropology Makes its Object* (New York: Columbia UP, 1982).

Fanon, Frantz. *The Wretched of the Earth*, trans. Constance Farrington (New York: Grove Press, 1963).

Foucault, Michel. "Nietzsche, Genealogy, History," *The Foucault Reader*, trans. Donald F. Bouchard and Sherry Simon, ed. Paul Rabinow (New York: Pantheon Books, 1984).

—— *The Order of Things: An Archaeology of the Human Sciences* (New York: Pantheon Books, 1973).

—— *The Archaeology of Knowledge and The Discourse on Language*, trans. Sheridan Smith (New York: Pantheon Books, 1972).

Freud, Sigmund. "Lecture XXXII: Anxiety and Instinctual Life," *The Freud Reader*, ed. Peter Gay (New York: Norton & Co., 1989).

Fück Johann. *Die arabischen Studien in Europa bis den Anfang des 20. Jahrhundert* (Leipzig: Otto Harrassowitz, 1955).

Gaonkar, Dilip Parameshwar, ed. *Alternative Modernities* (Durham, N.C.: Duke UP, 2001).

Gay, Peter. *Style in History* (London: Jonathan Cape, 1974).

Gellner, Ernest. *Muslim Society* (Cambridge: Cambridge UP,1981).

Gershoni, Israel and James. P. Jankowski. *Egypt, Islam, and the Arabs: The Search for Egyptian Nationhood, 1900–1939* (Oxford: Oxford UP, 1986).

Gibb, H.A.R. *Studies on the Civilization of Islam*, ed. Stanford J. Shaw and William R. Polk (London : Routledge & Kegan Paul, 1962).

Gibson, William. "Panther Modern's Eyes" (October 31, 2004): <http://www.williamgibsonbooks.com/blog/2004_10_01_archive.asp>.

Giddens, Anthony. *Positivism and Sociology* (London: Heinemann, 1974).

Gilroy, Paul. *Postcolonial Melancholia* (New York: Columbia UP, 2005).

—— *The Black Atlantic* (Cambridge: Harvard UP, 1993).

Glissant, Edouard. *Poetics of Relation*, trans. Betsy Wing (Ann Arbor: University of Michigan Press, 1997).

Godzich, Wlad. *The Culture of Literacy* (Cambridge, Mass.: Harvard UP, 1994).

Goodman, Martin. *Mission and Conversion: Proselytizing in the Religious History of the Roman Empire* (Oxford: Oxford UP, 1994).

Gordon, Lady Lucie Duff. *Letters from Egypt: 1862–1869*, ed. Gordon Waterfield (London: Routledge & Kegan Paul, 1969).

Gossman, Lionel. "History and Literature: Reproduction or Signification," in Robert Canary and Henry Kozicki, eds, *The Writing of History: Literary Form and Historical Understanding* (Madison: University of Wisconsin Press, 1978).

Goux, Jean-Joseph. "Untimely Islam: September 11th and the Philosophies of History," *SubStance*, issue 115, vol. 37, no. 1 (2008), pp. 52–71.
Greenblatt, Stephen. *Marvelous Possessions: The Wonders of the New World* (Chicago: University of Chicago Press, 1991).
Guha, Ranajit. "On Some Aspects of the Historiography of Colonial India," *Subaltern Studies: Writings on South Asian History and Society* (Oxford: OUP, 1982).
Habermas, Jürgen. *Knowledge and Human Interests*, trans. Jeremy Shapiro (Boston: Beacon Press, 1968).
Haddad, George A. "A Project for the Independence of Egypt, 1801," *Journal of the American Oriental Society*, vol. 90, no. 2. (April–June, 1970), pp. 169–83.
Ḥanafī, Ḥasan. *L'exégèse de la phénoménologie, l'état actuel de la méthode phénoménologique et son application au phénomène religieux* (Paris, 1966).
—— *Les méthodes d'exégèse, essai sur la science des fondements de la compréhension, ilm Usul al-Fiqh* (Le Caire: Le conseil supérieur des arts, des lettres et des sciences sociales, 1965).
—— *Muqaddima fī 'Ilm al-Istighrāb* [Introduction to Occidentalism] (Beirut: al-Mu'assasa al-Jāmi'iyya lil-Dirāsāt wa al-Nashr wa al-Tawzī', 2000).
Ḥaqqī, Maḥmūd Ṭāhir. *'Adhrā' Denshawai* (n.p., 1909).
Hardt, Michael and Antonio Negri. *Multitude: War and Democracy in the Age of Empire* (Penguin Books, 2004).
—— *Empire* (Cambridge, Mass.: Harvard UP, 2000).
Hegel, G.W.F. *Introduction to the Philosophy of History*, trans. Leo Rauch (Indianapolis: Hackett Publishing Company, 1988).
—— *Lectures on the Philosophy of Religion*, vol. 2, *Determinate Religion*, trans. R. F. Brown, P. C. Hodgson, and J. M. Stewart, ed. Peter C. Hodgson (Berkeley: University of California Press, 1987).
—— *The Phenomenology of the Spirit* (1807), trans. A.V. Miller (Oxford: Clarendon Press, 1977).
—— *Reason in History: A General Introduction to the Philosophy of History*, trans. Robert S. Harman. (Indianapolis: Bobbs-Merrill, 1953).
—— *Lectures on the History of Philosophy*, trans. E.S. Haldane and Frances H. Simon vol. I (London: Routledge and Kegan Paul, 1892).
Held, David and Anthony McGrew, "The Great Globalization Debate: an Introduction," in David Held and Anthony McGrew, eds, *The Global Transformations Reader: An Introduction to the Globalization Debate* (Cambridge: Polity, 2000).
Herold, J. Christopher. *Bonaparte in Egypt* (New York: Harper & Row, Publishers, 1962).
Hobson, J.A. *Imperialism: A Study* (London, 1902).
Hodgson, Marshall G.S. *The Venture of Islam: Conscience and History in a World Civilization*, vol. 1, *The Classical Age of Islam* (Chicago: University of Chicago Press, 1974).
Hook, Sidney. *From Hegel to Marx: Studies in the Intellectual Development of Karl Marx* (New York: Columbia UP, 1994).
Hourani, Albert. "How Should We Write the History of the Middle East?" *International Journal of Middle Eastern Studies*. vol. 23, no. 2 (May, 1991), 125–36.
—— *A History of the Arab Peoples*. (New York: Warner Books, 1991).
—— *Islam in European Thought* (Cambridge: Cambridge UP, 1991).
—— *Islam in the Liberal Age* (Oxford: Oxford UP, 1969).

—— "Islam and the Philosophers of History," *Middle Eastern Studies,* vol. 3, no. 3 (April, 1967).
—— *A Vision of History: Near Eastern and Other Essays* (Beirut: Khayats, 1961).
Hume, Peter. *Colonial Encounters: Europe and the New Caribbean: 1492–1797* (London, 1986).
Huntington, Samuel. *The Clash of Civilizations and the Remaking of World Order* (New York: Simon and Schuster, 1997).
Ḥusayn, Ṭāhā. *Falsafat Ibn Khaldūn al-Ijtimā'iyya* (al-Qāhira, 1925).
Ibn Khaldūn, 'Abd al-Rahmān. *Kitāb al-'Ibar, wa dīwān al-Mubtada' wa al-Khabar, fī Ayyām al-cArab wa al-cAjam wa al-Barbar, wa man cĀsharahum min Dhawyy al-Ṣulṭān al-Akbar,* vol. IV (Beirut: 1959).
—— *The Muqaddimah: An Introduction to History*, trans. Franz Rosenthal, 3 vols. (London: Routledge & Kegan Paul, 1958).
—— *Al-Muqaddima* (al-Qāhira: Būlāq, 1857).
Ibn Manẓūr, *Lisān al-'Arab* (al-Qāhira: Dar al-Ma'ārif, n.d.).
Ibrāhīm, Ḥāfiz. *Dīwān ḥāfiz Ibrāhīm* (Beirut: Mu'assasa al-'Ālamīyya Lil-Maṭbu'āt, 1971).
Ibrāhīm, Riḍwān. *Al-'Umrān al-Basharī fī Muqadimmat Ibn Khaldūn* (Tunis, 1978).
Inda, Jonathan Xavier and Renato Rosaldo, eds. *The Anthropology of Globalization: A Reader* (Oxford: Blackwell, 2002).
Israel Gershon, Hakan Erdem, Ursula Woköck, eds. *Histories of the Modern Middle East: New Directions* (Boulder, Col.: Lynne Rienner Publishers, 2002).
Jameson, Fredric. "Third World Literature in the Era of Multinational Capitalism," *Social Text*, 15 (Fall, 1986), pp. 65–88.
—— *Marxism and Form: Twentieth-Century Dialectical Theories of Literature* (Princeton, N.J.: Princeton UP, 1971).
Jayyusi, Salma Khadra, ed. *Modern Arabic Literature: An Anthology* (New York: Columbia UP, 1987).
Johnson, Samuel. *The History of Rasselas Prince of Abissinia* (Oxford: Oxford UP, 1999).
Joseph, Suad, ed. *Gender and Citizenship in the Middle East* (Syracuse, N.Y.: Syracuse UP, 2000).
Joyce, James. "Daniel Defoe" (1911), trans. and ed. Joseph Prescott. *Buffalo Studies* vol. 1, no. 1 (1964).
Judt, Tony. *Postwar: A History of Europe since 1945* (New York: Penguin, 2005).
Kahf, Mohja. *Western Representations of the Muslim Woman: from Termagant to Odalisque* (Austin: University of Texas Press, 1999).
Kāmil, Muṣṭfā. *Al-Liwā'* (April 12, 1907).
Kant, Immanuel. "An Answer to the Question: 'What is Enlightenment?'," *Kant's Political Writings*, ed. Hans Reiss, trans. B. Nisbet (Cambridge: Cambridge UP, 1970).
—— *The Idea of History with a Cosmopolitan Intent*, trans. Lewis White Beck, Robert E. Anchor, and Emil L. Fackenheim, ed. Lewis White Beck (New York: Macmillan Publishing Co., 1963).
—— *Critique of Judgment,* trans. J.H. Bernard (New York: Hafner Press, 1951).
Kedar, B.Z. *Crusade and Mission: European Approaches towards the Muslims* (Princeton, N.J.: Princeton UP, 1989).
Kepel, Gilles, *Le prophète et le pharaon: Les mouvements islamistes dans l'Egypte contemporaine* (Paris, La Découverte, 1984).

Khalidi, Rashid. *Sowing Crisis: The Cold War and American Dominance in the Middle East* (Boston: Beacon Press, 2009).
—— *British Policy Towards Syria and Palestine 1906–1914* (London; Ithaca Press, 1980).
Khouri, Mounah A. *Poetry and the Making of Modern Egypt (1882–1922)* (Leiden: E.J. Brill, 1971).
Khulayf, Yūsuf. *Dirasāt fi al-Shi'r al-Jāhilī* [Studies in pre-Islamic poetry] (Cairo: Maktabat Gharīb, 1981).
Kidd, Thomas J. "'Is it Worse to Follow Mahomet than the Devil?': Early American Uses of Islam," *The American Society of Church History*, 72 (December 2003), pp. 767–89.
Klausen, Jytte. *The Islamic Challenge: Politics and Religion in Western Europe* (New York: Oxford UP, 2005).
Kojève, *Alexandre. Introduction to the Reading of Hegel: Lectures on the Phenomenology of the Spirit* (Ithaca, N.Y.: Cornell UP, 1980).
Kramnick, Isaac and R. Laurence Moore, *The Godless Constitution: The Case Against Religious Correctness* (New York: Norton & Co., 1996).
Krauss, Rosalind. *"Sculpture in the Expanded Field": The Anti-Aesthetic: Essays on Post-modern Culture* (Seattle: Bay Press, 1983).
Lacoste, Yves. *Ibn Khaldoun, naissance de l'histoire, passé du tiers-monde* (Paris: Maspero, 1966).
Lane, Edward W. *An Account of the Manners and Customs of Modern Egyptians* (London, 1836).
Langlois, Claude. "Catholics and Seculars," *Realms of Memory: The Construction of the French Past*, vol. 1, *Conflicts and Divisions*, trans. Arthur Goldhammer, ed. Pierre Nora (New York: Columbia UP, 1996).
Laroui, A. *La crise des intellectuels Arabes* (Paris: Maspero, 1974).
—— *The Crisis of Arab Intellectuals*, trans. Diarmid Cammell (Los Angeles: University of California Press, 1976).
Launay, Marcel. *L'Église et l'école en France, XIXe–XXe siècle* (Paris: Desclée, 1988).
Lavisse, M. *Vue générale sur l'histoire politique de l'Europe* (Paris, 1890).
Lawrence, B.B., ed. *Ibn Khaldūn and Islamic Ideology*. International Studies in Sociology and Social Anthropology, vol. XL (Leiden: E.J. Brill, 1984).
Leclerc, Gérard. *Anthropologie et colonialisme: essai sur l'histoire de l'africanisme* (Paris: Fayard, 1972).
LeGouis, Catherine. *Positivism and Imagination: Scientism and Its Limits in Emile Hennequin, Wilhelm Scherer and Dmitril Pisarev* (London: Bucknell UP., 1997)
Lévi-Strauss, Claude. *Myth and Meaning: Cracking the Code of Culture* (New York: Schocken Books, 1995).
—— *The Raw and the Cooked*, trans. John and Doreen Weightman (New York: Harper and Row, 1969).
—— *Tristes tropiques* (Paris: Plon, 1955).
—— *Race et histoire* (Paris: UNESCO, 1952).
Lloyd, Christopher. *The Nile Campaign: Nelson and Napoleon in Egypt* (New York: Barnes and Noble Books, 1973).
Lucas, Philippe and Jean Claude Vatin. *L'Algerie des anthropologies (*Paris: Maspero, 1975).
Lukács, Georg. *The Historical Novel*, trans. H. & S. Mitchell (Nebraska: Nebraska UP, 1983).

Macherey, Pierre. *A Theory of Literary Production*, trans. Geoffrey Wall (London: Routledge & Kegan Paul, 1978).

Magdoff, Harry. "Globalisation – To What End?" *Socialist Register 1992: New World Order*, ed. Ralph Miliband and Leo Panitch (New York: Monthly Review Press, 1992), pp. 1–32.

Mahdi, Muhsin. *Ibn Khaldūn's Philosophy of History* (New York: Phoenix edn., 1964).

Mahmood, Saba. *The Politics of Piety: The Islamic Revival and the Feminist Subject* (Princeton, N.J.: Princeton UP, 2005).

Mamdani, Mahmood. *Good Muslim, Bad Muslim: America, the Cold War, and the Roots of Terror* (New York: Pantheon Books, 2004).

Marcuse, Herbert. *Hegel and the Rise of Social Theory* (Amherst, N.Y.: Humanity Books, 1999).

Markaz al-Arḍ li-Ḥuqūq al-Insān. *Aḥwāl al-Fallāḥīn fī Rīf Miṣr* (Human Rights Open Library, 2001).

Marrou, Henri-Irénée. *De la connaissance historique* (Paris: Éditions du Seuil, 1954).

Marx, Karl. *Capital: A Critique of Political Economy* (New York: The Modern Library, 1906), p. 88.

McCoan, J. C. *Egypt As It Is* (New York: Peter Fenelon Collier, 1882).

MEI. "Orientalism Wake: The On Going Politics of a Polemic," *Viewpoints* (Washington D.C., September 2009).

Mitchell, Timothy, ed. *Questions of Modernity* (Minneapolis: University of Minnesota Press, 2000).

—— *Colonizing Egypt* (Cambridge: Cambridge UP, 1988).

Miyoshi, Masao. "A Borderless World? From Colonialism to Transnationalism and the Decline of the Nation State," *Critical Inquiry*, vol. 19, no. 4 (Summer, 1993), pp. 328–56.

Mommsen, Theodore. "St. Augustine and the Christian Idea of Progress," *Journal of the History of Ideas*, XII (1951).

Monshipouri, Mahmood. *Muslims in Global Politics: Identities, Entities, and Human Rights* (Philadelphia: University of Pennsylvania Press, 2009).

Montagu, Lady Mary Wortley. *Selected Letters* (Penguin, 1997).

—— "Plain Account of the Innoculating [sic] of the Small Pox by a Turkey Merchant," *Essays and Poems and "Simplicity, A Comedy,"* ed. Robert Halsband and Isobel Grundy (Oxford: Clarendon Press, 1977).

Moore, Kathleen. *Al-Mughtaribun: American Law and the Transformation of Muslim Life in the United States* (Albany: State University of New York Press, 1995).

Morris, Rosalind C. "Theses on the Questions of War: History Media, Terror," *Social Text*, vol. 20, no. 3 (2002), pp. 149–75.

Mosse, George. *Nationalism and Sexuality: Middle-Class Morality and Sexual Norms in Modern Europe* (Madison: University of Wisconsin Press, 1988).

—— *The Culture of Western Europe* (Boulder, Col.: Westview Press, 1988).

Murū, Muḥammad. *Tārīkh Misr al-Hadīth: Min al-Hamla al-Faransiyya ila Hamlat Frīzar: al-Juz' al-Awwal* [A history of modern Egypt: from the French occupation to Fraser's campaign: Part 1] (Cairo, 2005).

Muschg, Adolf. "'Core Europe': Thoughts about the European Identity," in Daniel Levy, Max Pensky, and John Torpey, eds, *Old Europe, New Europe, Core Europe, Transatlantic Relations after the Iraq War* (London: Verso, 2005).

Nancy, Jean-Luc. *The Experience of Freedom*, trans. Bridget McDonald (Stanford, Cal.: Stanford UP, 1994).

Nerlich, Michael. *Ideology of Adventure: Studies in Modern Consciousness 1100–1750*, 2 vols. (Minneapolis: University of Minnesota Press, 1987).

Nora, Pierre. *Realms of Memory: The Construction of the French Past*, trans. Arthur Goldhammer (New York: Columbia UP, 1996).

—— "Nation," in Francois Furet and Mona Ozouf, eds, *A Critical Dictionary of the French Revolution*, trans. Arthur Goldhammer (Cambridge: Harvard UP, 1989), p. 749.

Nussbaum, Felicity A. *The Limits of the Human: Fictions of Anomaly, Race, and Gender in the Long Eighteenth Century* (Cambridge: Cambridge UP, 2003).

Nussbaum, Felicity A. and Saree Makdisi, eds. *The Arabian Nights in Historical Conquest: Between East and West* (Oxford: Oxford UP, 2008).

Owen, Roger. *Cotton and the Egyptian Economy, 1820–1914: A Study of Trade and Development* (Oxford: Oxford UP, 1969).

Pasha, Coles. *Recollections and Reflections* (London: Saint Catherine Press, 1918).

Patouka, Jan. "La civilisation technique est-elle une civilisation de décline, et pourquoi?" [Is technological civilization a civilization of decline, and why?), *Essais hérétiques sur la philosophie de l'histoire* [Heretical essays on the philosophy of history], trans. Erika Abrams (Lagrasse: Verdier, 1981).

Pipes, Daniel. "Battle of the super-systems: Europe vs America," *Jerusalem Post* (January, 2003).

Plumptre, James. *The Plague Stayed: A Scriptural View of Pestilence, Particularly of That Dreadful Pestilence the Small-Pox, With Consideration on the Cow-Pock; in Two Sermons* (London, 1805).

Popper, Karl. *The Poverty of Historicism* (Boston: Beacon Press, 1957).

Prideaux, Humphrey. *The True Nature of Imposture Revealed in the Life of the Impostor Mohammad* (London, 1697).

Qumayḥa, Jābir. *Ṣawṭ al-Islām fī Shi'r Ḥāfiẓ Ibrahīm* [*The voice of Islam in Hafiz Ibrahim's poetry*] (al-Qāhira, 1990).

Raymond, André. *Egyptiens et Français au Caire 1798–1801* (Cairo: Institut Francais d'Archeologie Orientale (IFAO), 1998).

Richardson, John. "Dissertation on the Languages, Literatures, and Manners of Eastern Nations," *Dictionary, Arabic, Persian, and English* (1777).

Ricoeur, Paul. *Time and Narrative*, 4 vols (Chicago: Chicago UP, 1983).

Rodinson, Maxime. *Europe and the Mystique of Islam* (London: I.B.Tauris, 2006).

—— *Le fascination de l'Islam* (Paris: F. Maspero, 1980).

Ross, Kristin. *Fast Cars, Clean Bodies: Decolonization and the Reordering of French Culture* (Cambridge, Mass.: MIT Press, 1996).

Roy, Olivier. *Globalized Islam: The Search for a New Ummah* (New York: Columbia UP, 2004).

Said, Edward. "Foucault and the Imagination of Power," *Reflections on Exile and Other Essays* (Cambridge, Mass.: Harvard UP, 2000).

—— *Covering Islam: How the Media and the Experts Determine How We See the Rest of the World* (New Youk: Vintage, 1997).

—— *Culture and Imperialism* (New York: Vintage Books, 1993).

—— "Orientalism Reconsidered," *Europe and its Others*, vol. 1., ed. Francis Barker et al. (Colchester: University of Essex, 1985).

—— *Orientalism* (London: Routledge & Kegan Paul, 1978).
Ṣalāḥ al-Dīn, Munajjid. *Dirāsāt fī tārīkh al-Khaṭṭ al-'Arabī, mundhu bidāyātihi ilá nihāyāt al-aṣr al-Umawī* (Bayrūt: Dār al-Kitāb al-Jadīd,1972).
Schmidt, H.A.N. *Ibn Khaldūn: The Historian, the Sociologist, and Philosopher* (New York, 1930, reprint 1967).
Schwab, Raymond. *The Oriental Renaissance: Europe's Rediscovery of India and the East, 1680–1880*, trans. G. Patterson-Black and V. Reinking (New York: Columbia UP, 1984).
Serequeberhan, Tsenay. "The critique of Eurocentrism and the practice of African philosophy" in E. C. Eze, ed., *Postcolonial African Philosophy: A Critical Reader* (Cambridge: Blackwell, 1997).
—— "The Idea of Colonialism in Hegel's Philosophy of Right," *International Philosophical Quarterly*, vol. 39 (1989), pp. 301–18.
Sharīf, Muḥammad Hāmid. *Hādithat Dinshawāy wa-Ṣadāhā fī al-Adab al-'Arabī al-Ḥ adīth wal-Ṣaḥāfa al-'Arabiyya* [The Denshawai incident and its repercussions in modern Arabic literature and the Arab press] (Cairo: al-Ḥay'a al-Arabiyya al-'Āma lil-Kitāb, 1997).
Shaw, G.B. *Complete Plays with Prefaces*, vol. II (New York: Dodd, Mead & Company, 1963).
Shawqī, Aḥmad. *Dīwān Shawqī, Al-Majmū'a Al-Th* [The complete poems of Shawqī, vol. II] (al-Qāhira: Dār Nahđat Miṣr Lil-Ṭibā'a wa al-Nashr, 1980).
—— *Maṣra' Klībātrā* [*The death of Cleopatra*] (al-Qāhira, 1928).
—— *Qaṣīda Fī Maṣra' Butrus Ghālī* [A poem on the death of Butrus Ghālī] (al-Qāhira, 1910).
Shelley, Mary. *Frankenstein* (Oxford: Oxford UP, 1969).
Simon, Heinrich. *Ibn Khaldūns Wissenschaft von der menschlichen Kultur* (Leipzig, 1959), trans. into English by Fuad Baali (Delhi, 1997).
Simon, Róbert. *Ibn Khaldūn: History as Science and the Patrimonial Empire* (Budapest: Akademiai Kiado, 2002).
Sivan, Emanuel, *Radical Islam, Medieval Theology, and Modern Politics* (New Haven, Conn.: Yale UP, 1985).
Soueif, Ahdaf. *The Map of Love* (New York: Anchor Books, 1999).
Spellberg, Denise A. "Could a Muslim be President? An Eighteenth-Century Constitutional Debate," *Eighteenth-Century Studies* vol. 39, no. 4 (2006), pp. 485–506.
Spivak, Gayatri C. *Outside in the Teaching Machine* (New York: Routledge, 2008).
—— *A Critique of Postcolonial Reason: Towards a History of the Vanishing Present* (Cambridge: Harvard UP, 1999).
—— "Can the Subaltern Speak?" *The Postcolonial Critic: Interviews, Strategies, Dialogues* (New York: Routledge, 1993).
—— "Scattered Speculations on the Question of Value," *Diacritics*, vol. 15, no. 4, *Marx after Derrida* (Winter, 1985), pp. 73–93.
St. John, James Augustus. *Egypt and Mohammed Ali; Or Travels in the Valley of the Nile* (1834).
Stepelevich, Lawrence S. "Hegel and Roman Catholicism," *Journal of the American Academy of Religion*, vol. 60, no. 4 (Winter, 1992), pp. 673–91.
Stubbe, Henry. *An Account of the Rise and Progress of Mahometanism with the Life of Mahomet and a Vindication of Him and His Religion from the Calumnies of Christians* (1676).

Stuurman, Siep. "Francois Bernier and the Invention of Racial Classification," *History Workshop Journal*, no. 50 (Oxford UP, 2000), pp. 1–21.
Takush, Muḥammad Suhayl. *Tārīkh al-Mamālīk fī Miṣr wa Bilād al-Shām: 1250–1517* (Beirut: Dār al-Nafā'is, 1997).
Thomas, Nicholaus. *Colonialism's Culture: Anthropology, Travel, and Government* (Princeton, N.J.: Princeton UP, 1994).
Tignor, Robert L. "Lord Cromer: Practitioner and Philosopher of Imperialism," *Journal of British Studies*, vol. 2, no. 2 (May, 1963), pp. 142–59.
Todorov, Tzvetan. *Hope and Memory: Lessons from the Twentieth Century*, trans. David Bellos (Princeton, N.J.: Princeton UP, 2003).
—— *The Conquest of America: The Question of the Other*, trans. Richard Howard (New York: Harper and Row, 1984).
Tolufson, Harold. *Policing Islam: The British Occupation of Egypt and the Anglo-Egyptian Struggle Over Control of the Police, 1882–1914* (Westport, Conn.: Greenwood Press, 1999).
Toynbee, A.J. *A Study of History*, 3 vols. (London: Oxford UP, 1935).
—— "Preface" in Shafik Ghorbal, *The Beginning of the Egyptian Question and the Rise of Mehemet Ali: A Study in the Diplomacy of the Napoleonic Era Based on Researches in the British and French Archives* (London: George Routledge & Sons, 1928).
Vatikiotis, P.J. *Egypt from Muḥammad Ali to Sadat* (Baltimore: The Johns Hopkins UP, 1980).
Veyne, Paul. *Writing History: Essay on Epistemology*, trans. Mina Moore-Rinvolucri (Middletown, Conn.: Wesleyan UP, 1984).
—— *Comment on écrit l'histoire: Essai d'épistémologie* (Paris: Éditions du Seuil, 1971).
Walcott, Derek. *Remembrance and Pantomime: Two Plays* (1978) (New York: Farrar, Strauss & Giroux, 1980).
Walker, Sir Robert. *An Inquiry into the Smallpox, Medical and Political. Wherein a Successful Method of Treating That Disease is Proposed, the Cause of Pits Explained, and the Method of Their Prevention Pointed Out*, (London, 1790).
Waterfield, Gordon. *Lucie Duff Gordon in England, South Africa and Egypt* (New York, 1917).
Watt, Ian. *The Rise of the Novel* (Berkeley: University of California Press, 1964).
White, Hayden. *Figural Realism: Studies in the Mimesis Effect* (Baltimore: The Johns Hopkins UP, 1999).
—— *The Content of the Form: Narrative Discourse and Historical Representation* (Baltimore: The Johns Hopkins UP, 1987).
—— "Interpretation in History," in *Tropics of Discourse: Essays in Cultural Criticism* (Baltimore: The Johns Hopkins UP, 1978).
—— "The Historical Text as Literary Artifact," in Robert H. Canary and Henry Kozicki, eds, *The Writing of History: Literary Form and Historical Understanding* (Madison: University of Wisconsin Press, 1978).
—— "The Fictions of Factual Representation," in Angus Fletcher, ed., *The Literature of Fact: Selected Papers from the English Institute* (New York, Columbia UP, 1976).
—— *Metahistory* (Baltimore: The Johns Hopkins UP, 1973).
—— "Ibn Khaldūn in World Philosophy of History," *Comparative Studies in Society and History* (CSSH), vol 2, no. 1 (October, 1959).

Williams, Raymond. *Keywords: A Vocabulary of Culture and Society* (London: Fontana Paperbacks, 1983).
—— *Marxism and Literature* (Oxford: Oxford UP, 1977).
—— *Keywords: A Vocabulary of Culture and Society* (New York: Oxford UP, 1976).
Young, Robert. *White Mythologies: Writing History and the West* (London: Routledge, 1990).
Zetland, Marquess of. *Lord Cromer, Being the Authorized Life of Evelyn Baring, First Earl of Cromer* (London: Hodder & Stoughton, 1932).
Ziyāda, Muḥammad Muṣtafa. *Nihāyāt al-Ṣalāṭīn al-Mamālīk fī Miṣr* (al-Qāhira: Mijālat al-Jamʿiyya al-Miṣrīyya lil-Dirāsāt al-Tārīkhiyya, 1951).

INDEX